"Gene Veith is one of the most powerful thinkers and apologists in the Christian world today. In *Family Vocation*, Veith and Moerbe have really hit the mark—we must learn to think of marriage and families as vocations from God. Here is an ancient and sacred vision of marriage and family that we would do well to understand, promote, and most importantly live out."

Chuck Colson, Founder, Prison Fellowship and the Colson Center for Christian Worldview

"A great president once referred to the family as the 'unseen pillar of civilization.' He was right, and so is Gene Veith in this luminous book, which underscores the centrality of family, marriage, and parenting. Timely and absorbing, this book arrives on the scene at exactly the right time."

Tim Goeglein, Vice President, Focus on the Family

"*Family Vocation* is a thorough and thoughtful look at family as a calling from God. Using Martin Luther's teaching on family living as a starting point, Gene Veith and his daughter Mary Moerbe have produced a foundational book addressing all the callings of family life. In a marketplace in which so many family books only scratch the surface, *Family Vocation* digs down deep. The things I look for in a book on family are all here: a focus on nurture, the priority of internal change, and the power of grace and the gospel to enable. A worthy read!"

Tedd Tripp, pastor, author, conference speaker

"The phrase 'gospel-centered' has become almost a cliché when describing Christian writing. Every Christian author would desire such an epitaph for his or her work. However, in so many books, especially those dealing with family, gospel-centered deteriorates into 'be like Jesus.' *Family Vocation* is the epitome of what gospel-centered truly means. The authors introduce it plainly, 'The gospel—that is, the message of Christ crucified for sinners—relates to every moment of the believer's life.' Every chapter has its foundation, built not upon what we do in our various vocations, but upon what God has done in Christ. This approach to vocation is the means through which Christian families can truly be strengthened and restored, and then bring their influence to bear on our culture."

James I. Lamb, Executive Director, Lutherans for Life

"The ageless questions we've pondered about marriage, divorce, sexuality, and parenting are asked candidly and answered faithfully by Veith and Moerbe in this timely application of Luther's doctrine of vocation. The word family has been hijacked by our culture and Christians reel with each new and dysfunctional incarnation of the concept. What is family? What is marriage? What is God's call to be a husband, wife, parent, or child? The authors offer rich, biblical responses to these questions and bring clarity to our understanding about cross-bearing love and sacrifice. *Family Vocation* is sure to find a home on the desks of pastors, teachers, and counselors who seek an engaging resource for Bible classes, spiritual care conversations, and godly counsel. This book leads the way to abiding grace and hope in God's promises—a 'need-to-read' for Christian husbands, wives, mothers, fathers, daughters, and sons!"

Beverly K. Yahnke, Department Chair of Social Sciences, Concordia University Wisconsin

"Martin Luther identified marriage and family as one of three fundamental estates of human life instituted by God for the good of his creation. In this book, a father and daughter team up to bring Luther's rich insights into the twenty-first century in a way that challenges and encourages Christians to see the family as the arena for God's work. In an age when the fabric of the family is strained by cultural forces of self-interest and hedonism, this book suggests a way forward for Christian families to see life together as husband/wife, parent/child—encompassed in vocation lived out under the cross."

John T. Pless, Assistant Professor of Pastoral Ministry and Missions, Concordia Theological Seminary

"In the church today, there is no more significant issue than the family. This divine institution is in the crosshairs of every evil plan and purpose of the Devil himself. Take down the family, and with it go education, order, decency, law, church, and even faith. How my years in a struggling inner-city parish taught me that the gospel does not thrive in a community of chaos, dilapidation, crime, and disorder! The root cause of it, as I came to be convinced, is institutional and spiritual forces attacking the stability of God's best agent for good in both the kingdom of the civil realm and that of the church—the family. What was once more commonly an urban reality has become a rural and suburban way of life. As we all struggle in the families we have—often rag-tag rings of sinners, sometimes a patchwork quilt of multiple families and forces—we need Christ and the vocation to forgive."

Matthew Harrison, President, The Lutheran Church—Missouri Synod

FAMILY VOCATION

Other Crossway Books by Gene Edward Veith Jr.

God at Work: Your Christian Vocation in All of Life

*Postmodern Times: A Christian Guide to
Contemporary Thought and Culture*

*Loving God with All Your Mind: Thinking as a Christian
in the Postmodern World*

Reading between the Lines: A Christian Guide to Literature

State of the Arts: From Bezalel to Mapplethorpe

FAMILY VOCATION

God's Calling in Marriage, Parenting, and Childhood

GENE EDWARD VEITH JR. AND MARY J. MOERBE

CROSSWAY

WHEATON, ILLINOIS

Cover design: LeVan Fisher Design

Cover image: iStock and Shutterstock

First printing 2012

Printed in the United States of America

Scriptures marked Contemporary English Version are taken from the Contemporary English Version Copyright © 1995 by American Bible Society. Used by permission.

Unless otherwise indicated, Scripture quotations are from the ESV® Bible (*The Holy Bible, English Standard Version®*), copyright © 2001 by Crossway. Used by permission. All rights reserved.

Scripture quotations marked *The Holman Christian Standard Bible* are from *The Holman Christian Standard Bible®*. Copyright © 1999, 2000, 2002, 2003 by Holman Bible Publishers. Used by permission.

Scripture quotations marked King James Version are from the *King James Version* of the Bible.

Scripture quotations marked The Message are from *The Message*. Copyright © by Eugene H. Peterson 1993, 1994, 1995, 1996, 2000, 2001, 2002. Used by permission of NavPress Publishing Group.

Scripture references marked New Living Translation are from *The Holy Bible, New Living Translation*, copyright © 1996, 2004. Used by permission of Tyndale House Publishers, Inc., Wheaton, IL., 60189. All rights reserved.

Scripture marked New International Version (1984) are taken from the HOLY BIBLE, NEW INTERNATIONAL VERSION®. Copyright © 1973, 1978m 1984 Biblica, Used by permission of Zondervan. All right reserved. The "NIV" and "New International Version" trademarks are registered in the United States Patent and Trademark Office by Biblica. Use of either trademark requires the permission of Biblica.

Scripture references marked New Jerusalem Bible are from *The New Jerusalem Bible*. Copyright © 1985 by Darton, Longman & Todd Ltd. and Doubleday & Co., Inc.

Scripture quotations marked Today's New International Version are taken from the Holy Bible, Today's New International Version. TNIV®. Copyright © 2001, 2005 by International Bible Society. Used by permission of Zondervan. All rights reserved.

Trade paperback ISBN: 978-1-4335-2406-6
PDF ISBN: 978-1-4335-2407-3
Mobipocket ISBN: 978-1-4335-2408-0
ePub ISBN: 978-1-4335-2409-7

Library of Congress Cataloging-in-Publication Data

Veith, Gene Edward, 1951–
    Family vocation : God's calling in marriage, parenting, and childhood /
Gene Edward Veith and Mary J. Moerbe.
      p. cm.
    Includes bibliographical references (p.   ) and indexes.
    ISBN 978-1-4335-2406-6 (tp)
    1. Familes—Religious life. 2. Vocation—Lutheran Church. 3. Lutheran
Church—Doctrines. I. Moerbe, Mary J., 1980–   . II. Title.
BV4526.3.V45   2012
248.8'45—dc23   2011035958

Crossway is a publishing ministry of Good News Publishers.

VP		21	20	19	18	17	16	15	14	13	12
15	14	13	12	11	10	9	8	7	6	5	4	3	2	1

Dedicated to Ilona Kuchta
and
our families

Contents

Preface

This book will seem quite a bit different from other Christian books on the family. It applies Martin Luther's doctrine of vocation to the different callings within the family. This cannot be done without pulling along other aspects of Luther's theology. Readers will note here that the "gospel" does not simply have reference to conversion, what a person responds to in first becoming a Christian. Rather, the gospel—that is, the message of Christ crucified for sinners—relates to every moment of the believer's life. This book is an attempt to bring the gospel into the daily routines of family life. As such, it does not approach the issues through "law," by offering moralistic exhortations, rules to follow, or Biblical principles for successful living. Christian freedom is seen not as a grudging concession but as a positive good.

Also, Lutheran spirituality has been described as a "theology of presence," teaching not only that Christ is present in the sacraments but also in his Word and in the world. God is not just a transcendent being looking down on the universe; rather, he is actually present, closely and intimately, as he providentially works in the world and in and through our lives. God is hidden in vocation, as Luther says, and Christ is hidden in our neighbors.

It has been said that American Christians lack a theology of suffering. That cannot be said of Luther with his "theology of the cross." Thus, this book will deal with the hard issues of family life in a realistic, yet redemptive way. Also, Lutheran spirituality is very anti-gnostic; that is, it affirms the spiritual significance of matter, physical things, and the body. We hope that will not prove too embarrassing.

We must emphasize, though, that no one has to be a Lutheran (as we are) to agree with these ideas and to benefit from this book. This is the heritage of all Protestant Christians. Despite all of the theological differences that emerged soon after the Reformation, all of the various factions—Calvinists, Arminians, Zwinglians, Anglicans, Anabaptists— would probably agree with most and maybe all of Luther's teachings about vocation and the family. And though we are rather hard on monasticism and clerical vows of celibacy, even non-Protestant Christians should find much of this treatment helpful. Christians have a great resource in their own heritage, which, though often overlooked in our contemporary-flavored churches of today, is actually very helpful in addressing contemporary problems, such as those that plague many Christian families.

This is an evangelical book, exploring God's Word in depth and also permeated with the "evangel," the good news of Christ. Luther and his followers were the first "evangelicals," that is, the first to be called evangelicals. In fact, "evangelical" and "evangelical theology" is the preferred terminology, especially in Europe, for "Lutheran" and "Lutheran theology," just as "Reformed" is often preferred over "Calvinist." It may be that contemporary English-speaking evangelicals could find much to learn from those first evangelicals.

This book is a father/daughter project. Yes, it was somewhat weird going through these family issues with our own family experiences and vocational issues looming in our minds, but it was deeply meaningful for us both to work on this together.

This project had its origins in a conference entitled *In the Image of God: The Christian Vision for Love and Marriage* held on the campus of Concordia Theological Seminary in Fort Wayne, Indiana, in 2006. The event was sponsored by the seminary, LCMS World Relief and Human Care, and the Cranach Institute. The goal was to apply the considerable resources of Lutheran spirituality to marriage and the challenges that contemporary marriages face. The conference drew on the expertise and experience of many Lutheran scholars, pastors, deaconesses, and counselors, but it also featured non-Lutherans working in a similar vein. These included Christopher West, known for applying the Roman Catholic "theology of the body" to practical marriage counseling; Lauren Winner, the prominent evangelical writer on issues of sex and singleness; and staff members from Focus on the Family.

The success of the conference and the new insights it generated led the Cranach Institute, which is devoted to the application of the Lutheran theology of culture, to seek a way to make those insights more widely known. The board of the Cranach Institute provided funding for the research and writing of this book.

Preface

We, the authors, are grateful to them and to the conference partici-
pants who stimulated our thinking. Special thanks goes to Ilona Kuchta,
a board member with a true heart for the problems of families today. It
was her idea to put on the conference, it was her idea to put out this
book, and it was her encouragement that brought us into the project. To
her this book is affectionately dedicated.

We thank our families, both nuclear and extended, who have graciously and with good humor supported us in the efforts necessary for
this book. Family discussions were insightful and greatly appreciated.
We would like to mention specifically the contributions of the pastors
in our family, Ned Moerbe and Adam Hensley, who shared with us their
biblical knowledge and exegetical skills, as well as their good examples
as husbands and fathers. Also the other members of our family who
have loved and served us in their vocations and so have been models
for what we write about in this book: Jackquelyn Veith; Joanna Hensley;
Paul Veith; Samuel, Mary, and John Hensley; Elizabeth and Evangeline
Moerbe. The latter two groups have the vocation of being young children
who could not help but inspire and interrupt us with bursts of reality.

We also thank our pastors and friends, who shared sermons, articles, papers, and suggestions, in particular Rev. James Douthwaite and
Rev. Charles Lehmann. And there were others who influenced our thinking: Dr. Beverly Yahnke, Prof. John Pless, Prof. Jeffrey Pulse, and Rev.
Eric Brown. And others who helped in the making of the book, such as
Meredith Schultz. Also to Gene and Joyce Veith, whose fulfillment of
their callings is bearing fruit in the second and the third and even the
fourth generations.

1

INTRODUCTION

Confusing the Family

God settles the solitary in a home.
PSALM 68:6

The institution of the family is necessary to our very existence, basic to our culture, and critical to our happiness and well-being. As children, we were brought to life, nurtured, and shaped by our family. As adolescents and young adults, we were preoccupied with finding someone with whom we could start a family of our own. Adults who have managed to do that spend much of their time working to support their families and, if they have children, laboring to raise them. No one is more important to us than our parents, our spouse, and our children. Typically, we want to spend more time with our family, which we consider to be our haven in the storms of life. We rhapsodize over "family values" and want to bring them back. So why is family life so confusing? Why do marriage and parenthood often seem so difficult to get right?

Married couples often quarrel and fight, arguing about sex, money, and their own clashing personalities. Parents agonize over how to raise their children and often feel they have made terrible mistakes. Children sometimes break their parents' hearts, turning into ungrateful little rebels. And parents sometimes break their children's hearts, inflicting emotional wounds that make the child desperate to get away. The man, the woman, and the children often become casualties of divorce, which leaves indelible wounds of its own. If a person's family is the source of the greatest joys in life, it can also be the source of the greatest miseries.

Christians know that God looms behind the family. They know that God established the family and its different roles, that he upholds parenthood in the Ten Commandments, that Christ has something to do with marriage. But Christians have the same challenges in their families as nonbelievers. They even have additional challenges that nonbelievers do not have, such as the biblical mandate for the wife to submit to the husband, which, as it plays out in ordinary life, can drive some husbands to tyranny and some women to rebellion or despair. Christian marriages often come apart and end in divorce.

To be sure, many Christians do have strong and loving families, despite their occasional problems. What is their secret? Even those who have a good family life may not be able to explain the inner workings of a family functioning according to God's design. They may not realize that God not only established the institution of the family in general but that he also established their actual, personal family. Christian husbands and wives may assume that to say "Christ is in marriage" is a figure of speech or a pious aspiration rather than an actual presence in their relationship. Christian parents will acknowledge God as "father," but they may not recognize how God exerts his fatherhood through their own relationships with their children. Christian children, whether young or all grown up, may not see the connection between their relationship with their parents, however old they might become, and being a child of God.

God is present and active in families, bringing his gifts and working his purposes. He and his works may be hidden in the mundane-seeming details of ordinary life, but it is useful—both in times of family difficulties and when everything is going right—to catch a glimpse of him.

The Family and Contemporary Culture

Our culture, to put it mildly, is confused about the institution of the family. This cultural confusion throws off Christians as well as non-Christians. As a result, we have no consensus about how husbands and wives should treat each other or how to raise children. We are very confused about sex. We desperately want to have a strong family, and yet too often our families are falling apart, with husbands and wives, parents and children, at each other's throats.

So far we Americans still value marriage surprisingly highly, with four out of five adults getting married eventually.[1] But we have stripped away its moral significance. Marriage is no longer seen as a prerequisite for sex (61 percent of Americans believe it is morally acceptable to have sex outside of marriage[2]); or for living together (51 percent of married couples 18–49 lived together first[3]); or for having a baby (55 percent of Americans believe that having a child out of wedlock is morally acceptable[4]). There is no longer a cultural consensus that marriage should be permanent (70 percent of American adults believe that it is morally acceptable to get a divorce[5]).

If marriage is no longer necessary for sex, cohabitation, or parenting, and if it is no longer a permanent relationship, what is left? There is romance. Companionship. But romance and companionship can come in many different forms.

Thus, we have problems even knowing what marriage is. If marriage is just a matter of romantic attachment, why shouldn't same-sex couples who are romantically attached to each other be able to get married? Following this reasoning, some states and nations have changed their laws to allow men to marry men and women to marry women. Ironically, as same-sex couples clamor for marriage, an increasing number of opposite-sex couples have found that they can do without marriage altogether. In Scandinavia, which has had gay marriage for over a decade, cohabitation—"just living together"—has virtually replaced marriage as the norm.[6]

What about parenting? In one sense our culture loves children, and we value having children. Many couples go to extraordinary lengths to have a child, and reproductive technology—both in traditional medicine and nontraditional experimentation (sperm banks, egg donors, surrogate mothers, genetic engineering)—has become a big business. But so has the technology of not having children.

Contraceptives have become more than a tool for spacing children; they have had the effect of largely separating sex from procreation. If sex is just a physical pleasure, with no essential connection to having babies, why not enjoy that pleasure any way you like? Sex no longer needs to be with someone you are married to since the prospect of parenthood is no longer an issue. Sex can just as well be with someone of your own gender, or in the virtual fantasies of pornography, just with yourself. Should sex sometimes result in pregnancy—which seems strangely surprising to some people when it happens—there is always a medical procedure to take care of the problem: abortion.

Parenting too has been separated from the family. Women who do want children are increasingly raising them by themselves, without the father in the picture at all. As many as 40 percent of the children born in 2007 were to unmarried women. In 2008, one-third of America's children, 33 percent, lived without married parents.[7]

The family is the basic unit of the culture. So the instability of the family brings with it all kinds of cultural instability, from the hypersexualization of our entertainment to the alienation and misery of those who grew up feeling abandoned. This cultural dysfunction, in turn, pulls families further apart by creating unrealistic expectations that no one can live up to and by distracting people from addressing their problems.

Christians, in particular, have been concerned with the state of the family, both their own and those in the broader culture. Christians have a basis for marriage and child raising that secularists do not have. Some are saying that, given the cultural forces that are undermining the family, Christians should just pursue their own family values. Why should the state have laws regulating families at all? If the culture wants to encourage serial polygamy or same-sex marriage or out-of-wedlock births, let it. In the meantime, the church will bless lifelong marriages in which two parents will raise healthy, well-adjusted children. The church will be the place of strong families. Individuals who yearn for a rich family life will come to the church, which will thrive as an attractive counterculture in the midst of the larger cultural collapse.

But there is a rather large problem with this scenario. Christian families are often as dysfunctional and unstable and confused as the families of secularists. According to George Barna's 2008 study, 33 percent of American adults who have married have been divorced. Among "born-again Christians," the divorce rate is 32 percent. Barna has another category of "evangelicals," who not only say they have been born again but who also have a high view of the Bible and who hold to traditional Christian doctrines. These "evangelicals" do have a lower divorce rate, in fact, among the lowest of all of Barna's categories. But that rate is 26 percent. So one-third of America's Christians have been divorced. One-fourth of America's conservative Christians have been divorced. Breaking down the religion factor in more detail, 33 percent of "non-born-again Christians" had been divorced, the same as for the converted. Roman Catholics, whose church does not permit divorce at all, had a somewhat lower rate of 28 percent. Ironically, atheists and agnostics had fewer divorces than most believers, with a still substantial rate of 30 percent.[8] Sociologist Bradley Wright has taken issue with Barna's research, finding that the more seriously Christians take their faith, the stronger their marriages and the fewer divorces they have.[9]

Still, we Christians must confess that we too have problems with marriage, parenthood, singleness, and sex. What plagues and confuses the culture often plagues and confuses us, also. We need to recover, both in theory and in practice, the Biblical estate of the family.

How This Book Is Different

Many Christian books on the family offer psychological advice, practical tips, moral judgments, and pious exhortations. Much Christian discourse on the subject is preoccupied with the overriding concerns of obedience, whether of the wife or of the child, or self-fulfillment, whether through one's marriage or through one's children. Such books risk unintentionally emulating the culture in reducing marriage and parenting to the exercise of power and the pursuit of personal subjective satisfaction, both of which can be poisonous to marriage, as well as to parenting and even to being a child.

Moral exhortations, too, can have little effect if they demand external behavior without changing the heart, something only the gospel of Christ can do. But even urging couples to "put Christ in your marriage" does not always help. What does that mean, exactly, and how can this be done? And doesn't the Bible teach that Christ is already in marriage? Perhaps what we need is to discern his presence, his actions, and his self-sacrifice.

This book will attempt a paradigm shift. It will offer a different framework for thinking about and living through family-related issues. But this paradigm is not new. Rather, it draws on the history of the church, on another time that the church had to recover the significance and the disciplines of the family.

In the Middle Ages, marriage and parenthood were often treated as nothing more than a concession to the weakness of the flesh and the necessity of procreation. Those who wished to achieve full spiritual perfection would take vows of celibacy—rejecting marriage, sex, and parenthood—to enter a "holy order" in the monastery or the cloister. To be sure, marriage was a sacrament, but it was not a calling. The Latinate word for calling, "vocation" was reserved for God's summons into the religious orders, into being a priest or a monk or a nun.

Martin Luther, however, as he was recovering the gospel and the Word of God, insisted that all of life in the world is a realm for Christian service and that our everyday activities in the workplace, the culture, the church, and especially the family are vocations from God. Luther specifically described the family as a "holy order," a special realm of Christian love.[10]

Thus with the Reformation came a new emphasis on the spirituality of the family in all of its different offices and functions. What does it mean, in Christ, to be a wife or a husband, a mother or father, a child? How does each of these holy orders function together with the others? What do they all mean? What do they have to do with Christ and the life of the redeemed?

The insights of the Reformation will help us answer such questions. However, this book will not attempt to bring back the family life of the Reformation era. After all, since the family is the basis of every culture, the family is bound to that culture. Our focus will be on contemporary families and the unique challenges of our own times.

But what we can learn from the Reformation is that the solution to our family problems will not be a matter of more laws, more rules to live by, or more principles for successful living. The major contribution of the Reformation was to place the gospel of Jesus Christ—justification by grace through faith in the atoning work of Christ—at the center of every facet of Christian teaching and every facet of the Christian life, including the family. And the key to making that application and renewing contemporary families is the doctrine of vocation.

2

Vocation in the Nourishing Estate

*Only let each person lead the life that the Lord has assigned to him,
and to which God has called him.*

1 CORINTHIANS 7:17

The word "vocation" is the Latinate form of the English word "calling." In today's secular usage, the word "vocation" has become just another word for "job," but its Christian meaning is that God calls us to the different roles that he asks us to play and in which he is active. A key scriptural text on the subject is this: "Only let each person lead the life that the Lord has assigned to him, and to which God has called him" (1 Cor. 7:17). The idea is that the Lord "assigns" us to different kinds of lives, and that he then "calls" us to them.

Again, we often think of a job as our "vocation," and so it is. But the text in Corinthians is referring to marriage. God may *call* us to lead different kinds of lives—to marriage, parenthood, a job, a church, a community. It is in our various vocations that we live out our faith in love and service to the various neighbors that God brings into our lives. Not only that, God works in and through all of these vocations and the unique individuals he calls to fill them, including us.

Vocation is a profoundly biblical doctrine. But the great theologian of vocation is Martin Luther. Evangelicals of all persuasions appreciate how Luther reformed the church with his emphasis on the gospel and the Word of God. His third great contribution, however, the doctrine of vocation, has been all but forgotten. Since vocation is the key to how Christians are to live in the world, the loss of this teaching has been accompanied with the loss of Christian influence in the world. Luther considered the family callings to be the most important of all the earthly vocations.

This chapter will sketch out what the doctrine of vocation is.[1] The later chapters will then apply these teachings to the specific callings of husband and wife, father and mother, child, and the other family relationships.

God Working through Vocation

God made you. But notice *how* he made you. He made you by means of your mother and your father. God gives you this day your daily bread, and perhaps you thanked him for your food before you ate your last meal. But notice *how* he gives you the physical nourishment you need to stay alive. He feeds you by means of farmers, bakers, factory workers, and the hands of whoever prepared your meal. God heals you by means of doctors, nurses, and other healthcare workers. God protects you by means of police officers, firefighters, soldiers, and our legal system. He gives you the blessings of technology by means of scientists, inventors, and engineers. He builds up your faith by means of your pastor and other people in your church. This is the doctrine of vocation.

The doctrine of vocation has to do, above all, with the way God works through human beings. Contrary to what we might assume, vocation is not primarily about what *we* do or what *we* are supposed to do. That enters into it. But vocation is mainly about God's action. Christians are used to talking about "what God is doing in my life." Vocation emphasizes "what God is doing *through* my life." And, by the same token, "what God is doing for me through other people in my life."

We sometimes speak of God's "providence," referring to the way God governs and controls every aspect of his creation. The term comes from the word "provide." God not only rules over us all, but he also provides for us, and he has chosen to distribute his gifts through human beings. God doesn't have to go this route. He can feed us without farmers, as he did with the manna in the wilderness, and he can heal us without doctors. But his usual way of giving his gifts is through other people exercising their particular tasks that God has called and equipped them to do, that is, through vocation.

Just notice everyone who does things for you: Your parents who brought you into existence, brought you up, and cared for you. The other members of your family. Your friends. But also people you don't even know: Whoever made your clothes. Whoever built your house. The artists whose music or drawings or stories you enjoy. The experts who designed and built and programmed your computer. All the people behind the scenes who keep you safe and make your life possible. Consider that God looms behind them all, blessing you through all of these people working in their vocations, that he is as close as your neighbor.

Now consider that God also works through you. You do things for your family, your friends, the people in your church. On the job, you do things for your customers and people you work with. You provide goods or services that help others (otherwise, your employer wouldn't stay in business very long). Perhaps God has given you the vocation of marriage. That means he works through you to bless your spouse. Perhaps God has made you a parent. That means he works through you to produce one of the most amazing miracles of them all—to create new life, to engender an immortal soul—and he works through you to bring up that child. And if you are a child—and who isn't or hasn't been, no matter how old you are?—God works through you to bless your parents. According to the doctrine of vocation, God remains intimately involved in everything that he has made, and he stays close to his loved ones in part by means of human love.

God Working through the Physical Realm

Luther understood something that all Christians used to realize but that modern Christians have gotten away from—that God works through physical means. His Word is a book, consisting of ink printed on paper, that can be put on a shelf or opened and read; and yet that physical object conveys the personal saving revelation of God himself. Luther also believed that God conveys the gospel of his Son—who became physically incarnate in the real world, physically died to atone for our sins, and physically rose again to save us from our own death—through the water of baptism and the bread and wine of the Lord's Supper. Furthermore, God, who created everything, governs and rules this physical world, including ourselves in our physical lives, by providentially working through the natural order

23

and through the vocations of ordinary human beings. This means the body and things of the body—sex, childbearing, eating, drinking, working, providing for our physical needs—have profound significance and value. They are gifts to us and tools in God's hands.

Today, people, including Christians, tend to separate the physical from the spiritual. We look to the spiritual realm—by which we generally mean something interior, immaterial, and mystical—for our significance and value, while the physical, which takes up most of our attention day to day, just doesn't matter that much.[2] Non-Christians do this, as with the movie star notorious for her sexual promiscuity bragging about how she is such a "spiritual person." In her mind, what she does with her body makes no difference to her spiritual life, which is an ethereal kind of personal experience that has nothing to do with her everyday, objective, physical life.

Christians, too, can feel that their everyday lives have no meaning. They want to escape their mundane lives by means of transcendent spiritual experience. In 1 Corinthians 5, we see that believers can also imagine a disconnect between their daily lives and the faith they profess. They may try to justify immoral behavior as the movie star did, insisting that what they do in the body has no effect on their spiritual conditions. More common, though, is the notion that they have to do "spiritual things"—church work or Bible study or witnessing—in order to serve God, sometimes at the expense of their families. This devaluing of ordinary life can be so firmly rooted in our expectations that many Christians will accept only extraordinary supernatural experiences as counting for their spiritual lives, while missing God's presence in the ordinary and the everyday.[3]

The doctrine of vocation, in contrast, brings the physical and the spiritual together, so that spiritual reality becomes tangible. The ordinary doesn't need to be a burden we yearn to escape when we learn to discern God's presence in the everyday patterns of life. Physical reality, including our everyday tasks and callings, becomes transfigured with the presence of God.

The Estates of God's Love

Luther taught that God created three institutions or "estates" for human beings to live in: the church, the state, and the household. And in these estates, he gives us not just one but multiple vocations. God calls sinners, by the gospel, into his church, where they form a community in time and eternity that is no less than the body of Christ, who is truly present with his people. Here some are pastors, through whom God proclaims his Word, and some are laypeople, perhaps holding different offices as elders, teachers, musicians, and the like. Thus, all Christians have vocations in the church.

God has also ordained that we live under governments, in communities, as part of cultures. Romans 13 explains how God restrains sinful human beings by working through the vocation of lawful magistrates, thereby allowing even sinners to cooperate together and live in societies. Thus, some people have vocations as police officers, members of the military, judges, local officials, governors, legislators, and presidents. We also have the vocation of being citizens of our country and our community, with civic obligations such as, in a democracy, informing ourselves about the issues of the day and voting accordingly. This also makes us a part of the culture in which we find ourselves—that is, in which God has assigned us—and so we are called to be salt and light in our various societies. We are where we are as servants of the Lord. Thus we have vocations in the state.

But the household—that is, the family—is the primary estate and the site of our most important earthly vocations. The family is God's ongoing creation of humanity, the foundation of culture, and the image of our relationship with God on earth. God brings us to existence by means of fathers and mothers and thus assigns us to a family—including all of the siblings, aunts, uncles, cousins, grandparents, and a lineage going back to Adam and Eve. He gives us talents and opportunities and lets us grow. He even makes it possible (though not all have this calling) for us to have the calling of forming a family of our own. And all this is a gift and an earthly reflection of God the Father and God the Son, as we will explore in later chapters.

Within a single family, our vocations are multiple. A woman may have the calling to be a wife to her husband in marriage. She may also have the calling of being a mother to her children. At the same time, she may still have the calling of a being a daughter to her own parents as long as they are living. She may also be an aunt, a cousin, a grandmother. Each of these callings has its own tasks and relationships, and in each of them God is present and active. The subsequent chapters of this book will explore what that means.

Notice how personal this is. No person has exactly the same callings as anyone else. God creates us as unique individuals, and he assigns to us and calls us to unique relationships. God gives us these relationships precisely so that we can live out our faith and share his gifts, whether physical or spiritual. Through our lives, God gives personalized care to those we interact with. And he gives us personalized care through others as they carry out their vocations.

Johann Gerhard, the seventeenth-century spiritual writer, called family the "nurturing estate."[4] Husbands and wives nurture each other. Fathers and mothers nurture their children. And God nurtures everyone through these offices.

God's Economy

So if the three estates in which God assigns to us vocations are the church, the state, and the household, what about "vocation" as in job or profession? Did the Reformation writers on vocation not have a place for our more common use of the term? Is there no estate of the workplace? Luther does discuss one's work as a calling from God. Significantly, though, he includes economic activity under the estate of "household"; that is, not as a separate sphere, but as part of the family.

In his day, families generally made a living by working together. If you made a living by farming—and this holds true even today, though not as much as it used to—father, mother, and all of the kids each performed important tasks. The father would plow, cultivate the crops, and harvest them; the mother would sow the grain, pull the weeds, turn the produce into food, and preserve it for the year; each child would have his or her "chores"—tending to the animals, gathering the eggs and milking the cows, drawing water—so that they served as essential helpers to their parents and made a significant economic contribution to the family. Similarly, if you were a craftsman—a carpenter, a tailor, a shoemaker—the whole family pitched in.

The Greek word for "household" is *oikos*, which literally means "house" but included the family that lived in it, along with any servants and the land around it. The Greeks also spoke of the *nomos*, with its plural form *nomia*, meaning "laws" or "principles." *Oikonomia* referred to what it takes to manage and operate a household. This is where we get the word "economy." Originally, "economic activity" meant what you need to do to take care of your family. Economic vocations—jobs by which we make money—are thus the way we "make a living" for our families. In doing so, we also provide goods, services, and other blessings to other families.

The Industrial Revolution, of course, shattered that unity of work and family life. Men, women, and originally even children left their homes to go to work in the factories. In the modern world, people, as we say, "work outside the home." Today, the demands of work and the needs of family life are often in conflict. But it was not always so. Men, as well as women, worked inside the home, which meant that fathers were available to their children round the clock just as their mothers were. In some cases, today's Internet technology is allowing both men and women to work inside the home again. But most people today find themselves living in two different realms—the home and the workplace—and feel pulled in two different directions. Mothers torment themselves over whether they should stay home with the children or pursue their own careers. Fathers are often so busy with work that they have no time for their children. Under the doctrine of vocation, it is not as simple as just choosing either family or work; the task is to bring these realms together in God's personal calling.

The vocations of family are spouse (husband, wife); parent (father, mother); and child (son, daughter; dependent or adult). Each one serves within the relationships of marriage, parenthood, or childhood. Luther called these "offices," each of which has its own prerogatives, responsibilities, and proper work. Both the office and the individual are part of God's creation and his good will. Offices serve in a general sort of way, while individuals fulfill offices in a personal sort of way. For example, motherhood is connected with its services to children, yet every mother still is a unique woman. In the same way, vocations often have basic services associated with them that are fleshed out by the individuals and circumstances involved.

Often our interactions are determined by our vocational relationships. Pastors do not preach in church because they are sons and fathers, but because they are called to preach God's Word to his people as pastor. A wife is not usually expected to perform surgery on her husband, but to live with him, love him, and serve him in other ways. Fathers are to be fathers to their children and not simply friends or coaches. Parents should parent in ways suited to their particular children, and children should honor and obey their parents but not every adult who crosses their paths.

God lends his authority to particular vocations. Parents have authority over their children. As we will see, God also gives certain prerogatives to particular vocations. For example, husbands and wives, by virtue of God's calling them into marriage, are authorized to have sex with each other. Sexual activity apart from marriage is sinful—you have not been called to have sex with someone you are not married to—but within marriage it becomes a good work.

Loving God by Loving Your Neighbor

The purpose of every vocation is to love and serve one's neighbor. God is always calling us to love him and to love our neighbor as ourselves (Matt. 22:37–40; Mark 12:29–31; Luke 10:26–28). This is true in every estate and in every office. In the church, pastors are to love and serve their congregations, and laypeople are to love and serve their pastors and fellow Christians. In the state, rulers are to love and serve their people, and citizens are to love and serve their fellow countrymen. In the workplace, workers of every kind are to love and serve their customers. Each vocation has its own set of neighbors whom we are to love and serve with the particular tasks we are called to perform.

In the family, this means that fathers and mothers are called to love and serve their children. Children are called to love and serve their parents. The vocation of marriage is, perhaps, unique in that it entails only one neighbor whom one is to love and serve. The husband's neighbor is his wife, and his calling is to love and serve her. The wife's neighbor is her husband, and her calling is to love and serve him. As we shall see, the husband and the wife each have some distinct ways of serving each other, just as parents and children do, but mutual love and service are what characterize a strong family in God's design.

Notice that the purpose of vocation is not to serve God, as such, but to serve the neighbor. Our relationship with God is based on his service to us. "The Son of Man came not to be served but to serve, and to give his life as a ransom for many" (Matt. 20:28). "In this is love," says the apostle

John, "not that we have loved God but that he loved us and sent his Son to be the propitiation for our sins." But having done so, God sends us out to love our neighbors. "Beloved, if God so loved us," John continues, "we also ought to love one another" (1 John 4:10–11).

In Luther's day—as well as in our own—Christians sometimes had the notion that they had to do things for God in order to earn a high standing with him. They constructed all kinds of spiritual works, exercises, and pious observances and spent their time in prayers, meditations, and rituals. In order to do so, they took vows of celibacy (promising not to get married and not to have children), poverty (promising not to pursue the economic callings), and obedience (following church authority over that of the state).

Those committed to this kind of spirituality stressed that salvation was a matter of good works. In his day Luther asked, in what sense are these humanly-devised spiritual disciplines good works? Do they actually help anyone? God doesn't need our good works, Luther would insist. God needs nothing. Our relationship to him is based solely on his grace, which he offers us freely through the life, death, and resurrection of his Son. Though God doesn't need our good works, our neighbor does. Our neighbor is in need. God commands us to love and serve that neighbor.

The good works we need to do as Christians—the arena of our sanctification—are not elaborate spiritual exercises or spectacular feats of accomplishment. Rather, they are to be found in our ordinary interactions with the actual human beings whom God brings into our lives every day: the way we treat our spouse, the things we do for our children, what we do for our customers and fellow workers, how we get along with the other Christians in our church, how we treat the people we meet in the broader society. Our faith, "working through love" (Gal. 5:6), bears fruit in vocation. It is precisely in marriage, parenthood, economic activity, and life in the culture and congregation that we encounter the neighbors whom God wants us to love and serve.

Today's Christians often fall into a similar syndrome as the medieval monastics. They assume that "church work" is holier and more spiritually significant than spending time with their families or attending to their other vocations. Congregations often have so many things going on that we could spend every night of the week doing church activities. It is easy to become so busy with "spiritual" activities—Bible studies, witnessing, meetings, projects—that we neglect our marriages and our children. But the work of our vocations is also a "spiritual activity" that God specifically calls us to.

Luther believed that changing a baby's diaper is a holier work than that of all the monks in all the monasteries.[5] A holy work! Why? Because the mother and father (yes, Luther specifically talked about fathers changing baby diapers) are loving and serving their child. In God's eyes, this is holy. And so are the other works of family life, from having sex with your spouse to driving your kids to soccer practice.

Thus, in our desire to serve God we do not need to distance ourselves from the vocations of daily life. On the contrary, as Christ himself tells us, "as you did it to one of the least of these my brothers"—feeding the hungry, ministering to the sick, visiting the prisoner—"you did it to me" (Matt. 25:40). These are not always strangers—sometimes your child is the hungry, sick, and imprisoned one! But it turns out, when we serve our neighbor we are serving Christ after all.

God is hidden in vocation, and Christ is hidden in our neighbors. Thus, we love and serve God precisely by loving and serving our neighbors. We live out our faith in concrete ways, face-to-face with the people God has provided for us in our daily lives.[6]

Sacrifice by the Priesthood of All Believers

The doctrine of vocation falls under the theological category of "the priesthood of all believers." Contrary to the common perception, this does not mean that all believers get to be pastors or that we don't really need pastors. It means rather that we do not have to be pastors. The pastoral office is indeed a vocation from God through which he works, so that we speak of someone being "called" into the ministry, and churches "call" their pastors. The priesthood, though, is something different. A priest is someone who offers sacrifices.

Although Christ sacrificed himself once and for all to accomplish our salvation (Heb. 7:27; 9:26; 10:14), there are still sacrifices to be rendered: sacrifices of thanksgiving and praise, sacrifices when we "walk in love" (Eph. 5:2) and give to others (Phil. 4:18). We New Testament Christians are told specifically to "present your bodies as a living sacrifice" (Rom. 12:1). These sacrifices are offered in vocation. The father who comes home bone tired from a day on the job has presented his body as a living sacrifice for his family. The mother in the throes of having a baby, the ten-year-old helping around the house, the husband setting aside what he wants to do for the sake of his wife, the wife putting up with her husband, the couple scrimping and saving and doing without to pay for what their children need—all of these are living sacrifices. All of these are acts of priesthood, done by Christians in the service and presence of God.

Protestant churches seldom call their ministers "priests." Roman Catholic churches do so because they believe that the priest offers up in the Mass a sacrifice for sin. Protestants say that Christ was offered up as our sacrifice once and for all, so that the role of the clergy is to preach (thus, be a "preacher"); function as a shepherd to feed, guard, and care for his flock (thus, be a "pastor"); and serve his congregation (the word "minister" coming from the word meaning "to serve"). All Christians are not clergymen, but all are called to offer living sacrifices and so to be priests.

God is in vocation. As we shall see, the Bible clearly teaches that Christ is in the family. When we love and serve our neighbor, Christ is loving and serving the neighbor through us (Gal. 2:20). When we put that neighbor's need before our own, we are sacrificing ourselves. This, of course, is a pale shadow of Christ's sacrifice. And yet, Christ's sacrifice is in what we do. He takes up our sacrifice, however small, into his great sacrifice (Romans 12; 2 Cor. 1:3–5; Col. 1:24–29).

Sometimes we have difficulties in our vocations, in our families. We often fail to serve, insisting on being served instead. We thus sin in our vocations. The cross of Christ's sacrifice is there for us for our forgiveness. Sometimes we suffer in our vocations, in our families, through no fault of our own. We bear crosses, sometimes horrible ones. But, again, Christ takes our crosses into his for our healing and to restore our hope. "And we know that for those who love God all things work together for good, for those who are called according to his purpose" (Rom. 8:28). Notice that this applies "for those who are called"; thus the passage speaks of vocation. "If anyone would come after me, let him deny himself and take up his cross daily and follow me" (Luke 9:23). All of these daily self-denials are part of what it means to follow Jesus, and these take place precisely in all of our different vocations.

The rest of this book will look at what the Scriptures have to say about the different offices of family and will explore what God reveals through these vocations about his relationship with us. We will look at his constant presence and his active work through marriage and parenthood. We will explore how people within a family can serve each other in love, sharing God's gifts through his callings. Included in each part will also be a chapter on the crosses we may be called to bear in these vocations. We will thus address some of the difficulties and sufferings that are part of our lives in this fallen world. Above all, we will look for God's presence in the different vocations of the family and revel in Christ's sacrificial love that transfigures every family relationship.

Part 1

The Vocations of Marriage

3

Marriage

Let marriage be held in honor among all.
HEBREWS 13:4

At my wife's grandmother's funeral, the church was packed with her children and their families, her grandchildren and *their* families, and a fair number of great-grandchildren. Back when "grandma" and "grand-dad" were crazy teenagers, they went across the county line where two of their friends were getting married before a justice of the peace. In the hilarity of the moment, in an act of sheer impulse, they decided to get married themselves. They did, on the spot. Their parents were aghast. Nevertheless, the deed was done.

Nearly seventy years later, the consequences of that spur-of-the-moment decision, that crazy whim, filled the church. If these two had not gotten married, none of their children, grandchildren, and great-grandchildren would exist. My wife would never have been born because the particular combination of DNA that formed her father would never have come together. And although I myself would probably exist—no doubt as a lonely and bitter bachelor—my daughter and coauthor of this book would cease to exist since so much of her is from her mother.

A dreamy-eyed couple walking down the aisle faces endless possibilities. They themselves may be fixated on the moment, and they have no idea what awaits them—blessings, tragedies, bliss, conflicts, possibly children, possibly divorce, possibly all of the above. The meaning of it all will not be evident at the time. Only in looking back will the pattern emerge. But this is sure: marriage has real and living consequences determined by the God who instituted it—not only for that couple learning how to love and live together, but for countless generations that may come from them. Mary and Floyd begat Kenneth, who began Jackquelyn, who begat Mary, who begat Elizabeth and Evangeline, each with personalities, dreams, achievements, and similarly momentous families of their own. To say that marriage is a vocation means that God calls two people together to be a new family. And further, that God works in and through this couple to accomplish his purposes, both in their lives and in the lives of others.

Marriage in the Bible

Surely those "begat" passages in Scripture that we usually skip over are some of the most miraculous, tracing through centuries the ongoing creative work of God, generation after generation. Marriage itself is an ongoing theme and subject throughout the Bible. As has been said, the Bible begins and ends with a wedding—in Genesis, the marriage of Adam and Eve, and in Revelation, the marriage of the Lamb and the New Jerusalem. Brides, bridegrooms, wedding feasts, invitations, betrothals, sex, marital problems, unfaithfulness, and good marriages appear within biblical history, poetry, law, and prophecy. The Song of Solomon celebrates the intimacies and community joys of marriage. In the Gospels, we hear Christ telling parables about weddings to explain the kingdom of heaven. In the book of Revelation we are personally invited to the wedding feast at the end of the world, where Christ will come again for his bride—namely, everyone who has faith, collectively constituting his body, the church. Our relationship with Christ and eternal life itself are described in terms of marriage.

We tend to assume that the Bible here is using human institutions and relationships—marriage, fatherhood—as figures of speech to help us understand something about God and spiritual reality. The human relationships are the primary reality, which can help us understand, by analogy, certain spiritual truths. The doctrine of vocation, however, encourages us to reverse the analogy. The primary reality is in God. Our Father in heaven is the true father, of which earthly fathers are pale reflections. Christ is the true son. Christ's relationship with the church is the true marriage.

It isn't that Christ is like a bridegroom; he *is* the bridegroom. Earthly bridegrooms are like Christ. The spiritual realities can help us understand something about the human relationships.

In vocation, God calls ordinary human beings to participate in an office that is properly his, one that he continues to animate. Marriage is more than a legal formality, and more than a simple agreement between two individuals. Marriage is a tangible, living, breathing manifestation of God's love and purposes for us, and a tool within his hands. In the vocation of marriage, each spouse is God's gift to the other. This chapter will explore what marriage is—not what it is supposed to be, but what, according to Scripture, it is.

One Flesh

Some Pharisees asked Jesus about divorce. In his answer, he tells us much about marriage as a vocation: "Have you not read that he who created them from the beginning made them male and female, and said, 'Therefore a man shall leave his father and his mother and hold fast to his wife, and the two shall become one flesh'? So they are no longer two but one flesh. What therefore God has joined together, let not man separate" (Matt. 19:4–6). Jesus does not begin discussions about marriage by first addressing roles or functions; rather, he turns our focus to *God's* roles and functions within marriage: it is God who joins a man and a woman into one living flesh.

Jesus wants us to see that marriage is grounded in God's creation of human beings. Contrary to what we hear today, marriage is not a cultural construction, though of course it takes cultural forms. Nor is it a legal fiction, as if a government could pass a law to change what marriage is. Despite the rash of new laws establishing gay marriage, this passage would indicate that human governments do not have that authority. Indeed, according to this passage, God created human beings in two genders precisely with marriage in mind.

Next we see that marriage establishes a new family. A man leaves his own father and mother. Not that he no longer has a father and mother—he will always retain the office of their "son"—but he separates from them to "hold fast" to his wife. They are brought together and form a new family of their own.

Then our Lord, who has been quoting Genesis 2:24, underscores one of the most profound teachings of Scripture on the nature of marriage: The two different individuals, the man and the woman, become "one flesh." When they become married, "they are no longer two but one."

What does that mean? Is that some sort of figure of speech? I don't think so. From the use of that language in other parts of the Bible, it seems to set forth a real condition before God.

First Corinthians 6:16 says that, although sex should be reserved for marriage, joining bodies through sex unites a man and woman into one flesh. ("Or do you not know that he who is joined to a prostitute becomes one body with her? For, as it is written, 'The two will become one flesh.'") So having sex with someone creates a one flesh union with that person, which is one reason it should never be taken lightly. But being one flesh also has to do with love more broadly. "Husbands should love their wives as their own bodies. He who loves his wife loves himself. For no one ever hated his own flesh, but nourishes and cherishes it" (Eph. 5:28–29). Just as we nourish and cherish ourselves, we nourish and cherish our spouse. The wife is the husband's body. The husband is the wife's body (1 Cor. 7:3–5). That is to say, they both have one body. Not one soul, as romantics sometimes say. Not one personality, as when one spouse tries to obliterate the other's identity so that it conforms to his or her own, but one flesh. We will discuss this further in the chapters to come—especially in chapter 6 on sex—but for now we need to understand that when two people get married, they constitute before God a single physical organism.[1]

Furthermore, Jesus's statement in Matthew tells us that this marital union of a man and woman is "what God has joined together." God makes marriages. He calls the man and the woman together. He gives them their vocation. This applies not just to marriage in the abstract, as if marriage could be separated from actual flesh-and-blood husbands and wives. Jesus says that God is *still* joining together. That is to say, if you are married, God has joined you together.

How does he do that? Marriages happen in many different ways. Some couples have known each other since childhood and eventually fall into marriage. Others meet each other online and end up convinced that they should get married. Some marriages involve elaborate courtships. Others around the world are arranged by their parents. Some marry after a process of intense decision making. Others, like Mary and Floyd, marry on a whim. Jacob married Leah "by mistake" (Genesis 29), and yet God still worked through that marriage, sending Jesus through her bloodline as a direct descendant. Every couple has their own personal and unique story of how it happened. The point here, though, is that they should all understand that *God* called them together, working through the circumstances, and *he* joined them into a marriage.

Marriage is not reserved for Christians alone, but is for all human beings, by virtue of their creation. Scripture never questions the marriages of non-Israelites or non-Christians. Jesus's words say nothing to distinguish between a church marriage and one before a justice of the peace (as if either existed in those times). Rather, marriage is given to all peoples and nations and cultures.

Theologians generally say that the word "vocation" should be reserved for Christians—who have been "called" by hearing and responding to God's Word—but they admit that nonbelievers hold the same "offices," through which God also works. Non-Christians certainly get married, just as they can have children and so enter into the office of parenthood. Protestants generally deny that marriage is a sacrament, contrary to Roman Catholicism, since—unlike baptism and the Lord's Supper—marriage does not pertain to Christians only, and it does not take a church to make a marriage. To be sure, God works through the vocations of lawful magistrates to make orderly societies possible (Romans 13), so citizens under those authorities should, in general, follow their marriage laws. But this is the point: however the marriage came to be and however the wedding was conducted and whatever laws made it legal and whether the couple are believers, *God has joined the man and the woman together into one flesh.* In his providential workings, God called the couple to this estate.

A Helper

In his discourse on marriage that we have been discussing, Jesus is quoting Genesis 2:24, a passage whose context teaches us more about the nature and the calling of marriage. "Then the LORD God said, 'It is not good that the man should be alone; I will make him a helper fit for him'" (Gen. 2:18). Here we see that a major purpose of marriage is to counter isolation and loneliness, to supply our need for human love. A related purpose is to help establish dominion over the earth.

Although God could have created friendship as the first human relationship, he instituted marriage. God did not create another man or even some sort of generic woman to fulfill Adam's need for companionship. Adam didn't choose Eve out of a collection of possible partners. Rather, God crafted Eve out of Adam's own body.

At first, there was literally one flesh. From the one body, God made two human beings in two genders. And then he made them one flesh again.

Other living things could not fulfill the man's particular longing. Not animals, which are less than he is, not even the transcendent God, who is greater than he is. The man needed someone "fit" for him. Adam was allowed to participate in God's provision of his need through his own sacrifice. His body was broken. God healed the wound and made from Adam's bone a woman. At last, the man, too, was gifted according to his "kind" with a counterpart in creation, a mate, and a helper. God "brought her to the man" (Gen. 2:22).

Adam's reaction is poignant: "This at last is bone of my bones and flesh of my flesh" (Gen. 2:23). "At last"! How long had he even been in existence? And yet even in his paradisiacal state, Adam yearned impatiently for someone who was other than himself and yet was himself.

The passage describes God's creation of the two genders and his establishment of marriage from Adam's point of view. But much the same holds true for Eve. Her husband shares her bones and flesh. He is other than herself, and yet is herself. She helps her husband and is likewise not alone. Together and with their children they subdue and hold dominion over the earth: "And God blessed them. And God said to them, 'Be fruitful and multiply and fill the earth and subdue it and have dominion over the fish of the sea and over the birds of the heavens and over every living thing that moves on the earth'" (Gen. 1:28).

Luther sees the institution of marriage in Genesis as a specific calling from God:

> Marriage is a weighty matter in the sight of God. For it was not by accident that Almighty God instituted the estate of matrimony only for man and above all animals, and gave such forethought and consideration to marriage. To the other animals God says quite simply, "Be fruitful and multiply" [Gen 1:22]. It is not written that he brings the female to the male. Therefore, there is no such thing as marriage among animals. But in the case of Adam, God creates for him a unique, special kind of wife out of his own flesh. He brings her to

him, he gives her to him, and Adam agrees to accept her. Therefore, that is
what marriage is.[2]

Just as Jesus applied these texts from Genesis about Adam and Eve to the
marriages of his own time, we can do the same. A married man should
consider that God has brought his wife to him, that she is God's gift to
him. A married woman should consider that God has brought her to her
husband, that he is God's gift to her. They both should consider the old
saying to be grounded in fact, that "they were made for each other."

Does this validate the romantic notion that there is one person out
there made just for you, so that you must search and search, rejecting
possibilities along the way, until you find this ideal mate? No. Rather, it
means that *after* you actually are married, you should consider that your
spouse is the one God brought to you and so is the one he made for you.

Furthermore, we should understand that marriage involves common
work, hence "help." Husband and wife work together—tending the garden, tending the children—and they do things for each other. To be sure,
their oneness means that they can drag each other down, as happened
with Adam and Eve in Genesis 3; nevertheless, their one flesh endures,
just as Adam and Eve's marriage survived even the fall. And on this side
of Eden, husbands and wives are especially in need of each other's help
to make their way through a sin-filled world.

Christ in Marriage

Moses teaches that the two "shall become one flesh" (Gen. 2:24). Then
Jesus quotes that same passage. Then the apostle Paul, in the midst of
practical instruction for how husbands and wives should treat each
other, quotes it again. Whereupon he drops a bombshell: "Therefore a
man shall leave his father and mother and hold fast to his wife, and the
two shall become one flesh. This mystery is profound, and I am saying
that it refers to Christ and the church" (Eph. 5:31–32). Surely that passage from Genesis refers to Adam and Eve and human marriages ever
since! But now Paul, inspired by the Holy Spirit, reveals that it refers to
Christ and the church! This is no mere figure of speech. Paul's practical,
everyday advice for married couples itself derives from the relationship
between Christ as the husband and the church as his wife. Christ and his
union with those who believe in him animates human marriages.

What is the "mystery" Paul refers to? Just as a husband and a wife are "one flesh," Christ and those who have faith in him are "one flesh." That is, Christ has come in the flesh (1 John 4:2). The second person of the Trinity has become incarnate; that is, "the Word became flesh"(John 1:14)—our flesh! Jesus left his Father to be permanently united with his bride the church.[3]

The apostle Paul sometimes speaks of our life in the "flesh" as a way to describe our fallen, sinful condition (e.g., Rom. 7:5). But "flesh" is not always a negative term in Scripture. Paul emphasizes that Christ has taken on that flesh, sinful as it is, in order to redeem us: "For God has done what the law, weakened by the flesh, could not do. By sending his own Son in the likeness of sinful flesh and for sin, he condemned sin in the flesh, in order that the righteous requirement of the law might be fulfilled in us, who walk not according to the flesh but according to the Spirit" (Rom. 8:3–4). Since Christ has become one flesh with us, we— that is, the church—have become one flesh with Christ. That is to say, the church has become Christ's body (1 Cor. 12:27).

This one-flesh union of Christ and the church, of course, though imaged in marriage, is not sexual. It is a more complete unity than sex can ever be. It is one of several unions that Scripture speaks of in which different individuals constitute one body (for example, the church or the people of Israel). Christ became one flesh with humanity in his incarnation, and by faith, we become one flesh with him. "The life I now live in the flesh I live by faith in the Son of God, who loved me and gave himself for me" (Gal. 2:20).

Luther would emphasize the role of the physical sacraments in the union we have with Christ: In baptism, we are crucified, buried, and resurrected with Jesus. ("Do you not know that all of us who have been baptized into Christ Jesus were baptized into his death? We were buried therefore with him by baptism into death, in order that, just as Christ was raised from the dead by the glory of the Father, we too might walk in newness of life. For if we have been united with him in a death like his, we shall certainly be united with him in a resurrection like his" [Rom. 6:3–5]). And in the Lord's Supper, Jesus says, "Take, eat, this is my body, given for you," and we, in turn, take his body and his blood, which— however you conceive this—turns into ours. The sacraments "incorporate us"—literally, "embody" us—into Christ.

In doing so, they incorporate us into the church, which is his body.

"The cup of blessing that we bless, is it not a participation in the blood of Christ? The bread that we break, is it not a participation in the body of Christ? Because there is one bread, we who are many are one body, for we all partake of the one bread" (1 Cor. 10:16–17). That means, too, that Christians have a one-flesh relationship with other Christians—not sexual! that mode of union is unique to earthly marriage!—but all Christians are members of the same body, the body of Christ. "For just as the body is one and has many members, and all the members of the body, though many, are one body, so it is with Christ" (1 Cor. 12:12). All of these one-flesh unions involve distinct vocations, with their own kinds of callings and actions. But Christ looms behind them all, and his incarnation and his saving work of the gospel make them all possible.

As Paul shows in Ephesians 5, which we will discuss in the following chapters, this sublime revelation that marriage "refers to" Christ and the church is manifested in the ordinary day-to-day dynamics of married life. And, as we will see, the gospel of Christ's sacrifice for the church is at the essence of the vocation of marriage. Not only that, the very texture of married life—from enjoying sex to resolving conflicts—involves responding to that gospel.

Let Not Man Put Asunder

The discourse of Jesus that began this chapter was in specific response to a question about divorce. "And Pharisees came up to him and tested him by asking, 'Is it lawful to divorce one's wife for any cause?'" (Matt. 19:3). Then Jesus quoted the passage from Genesis about the two becoming one flesh. He followed that with his resonating words: "What therefore God has joined together, let not man separate" (19:6).

So Jesus is teaching against divorce. But the Pharisees come back at him: "Why then did Moses command one to give a certificate of divorce and to send her away?" (19:7). The law of Moses, as we see in Deuteronomy 24:1, *allows* divorce. Jesus replied, "Because of your hardness of heart Moses allowed you to divorce your wives, but from the beginning it was not so" (19:8). Jesus then equates divorce and remarriage to adultery: "And I say to you: whoever divorces his wife, except for sexual immorality, and marries another, commits adultery" (19:9).

What is going on here? The Bible indicates that the disciples were astonished, as we must be also. We are no longer under the Levitical law, but surely the words of Moses in Scripture are likewise the revelation of God. For Jesus to cancel the Law of Moses and to replace it with an even more sweeping law is a breathtaking example of Christ's authority. But how can we explain the contradiction? So is it permissible to get a divorce or not?

Obviously, divorce is *possible*, since Jesus refers to "man" causing it. But divorce is a rending of the one flesh, the tearing apart of a living organism. In the words of the King James translation, divorce is to "put asunder"—to rip into its separate parts—the one flesh that God himself has joined together. Moses does allow divorce "because of your hardness of heart." In the beginning, though—at the creation, where we see God's essential design for marriage—"it was not so." God joins two human beings into "one flesh." This is a reality. Divorce rends that asunder. Adultery rends that asunder. This is why Jesus seems to permit divorce and remarriage in the case of adultery. But apart from that rending, remarriage—becoming one flesh with someone, divorcing, and then becoming one flesh with someone else—is another kind of adultery.

So God hates divorce (Mal. 2:13–16). He never intended it. God the Son says not to do it. Tearing asunder what God has made one flesh is never God's will and is always the work of man. And yet, the Bible *does* permit divorce—not only in the Old Testament but also in the New Testament. The apostle Paul seems to allow it in the case of believers married to nonbelievers, if the unbelieving spouse no longer consents to the marriage (1 Corinthians 7). And Jesus himself, in the very words in which he condemns divorce, makes an exception ("except for sexual immorality") that allows it.

Again, what are we to make of all of this? Try this: Divorce is not necessarily a violation of the moral law. The Bible allows for divorce. There can be innocent parties in a divorce. But sin generally causes divorces even if divorce itself is not necessarily a sin. Divorce is not an absence of law. It is, however, an absence of gospel. It occurs in the absence of forgiveness. Divorce is a rejection of God's gracious gifts. It happens when the husband no longer plays the role of Christ to his wife, or when the wife ceases to emulate the church—when one (or both) refuse to let Christ and his marriage animate the earthly marriage with repentance and forgiveness.

Forgiveness is always a free gift, a matter of grace. It is not an entitlement. God has no *moral* obligation to forgive, and neither do wronged spouses. We know of a case in which a husband repeatedly committed adultery until his wife finally divorced him. Being Christians, under the authority of their congregation, they were subjected to church discipline. The husband who had wronged his wife and torn apart their one-flesh union made a tearful repentance before the pastor and the elders. He was restored to the Christian fellowship. But the pastor and the elders excommunicated the *wife*, even though she was the innocent party, because she did not forgive him quickly enough! Instead of disciplining the sinner, the church punished the one who was sinned against, the one wounded, rent apart, by the sin.[4] This was a travesty of church discipline.

There is sometimes an inability to forgive. When a marriage comes apart, as both Moses and Jesus observe, the heart hardens against the spouse. One or both begin saying no to God's calling. Often healing is needed in order to forgive, and healing takes time. For Christians, this rending of their one flesh becomes a cross they must bear, one of great anguish and torment. This breaking of the marriage is also a kind of crucifixion of Christ, who is in that marriage, and who is also one flesh, one body, with the couple. And yet, his crucifixion on the cross is also the healing they need, before and after the divorce.

In a marriage based only on law—following rules, standing on principles, determining who is more righteous, standing on the authority of Moses—divorce remains a possibility and a moral option. But in a marriage based also on the gospel—that is, animated by the relationship between Christ and the church, exercising repentance and forgiveness— divorce is impossible.

When couples discern Christ and his church in their marriage, when the husband and wife respond to him accordingly, their entire marriage becomes a fruit of their faith in Christ. So conscious are they of their own forgiveness in Christ that forgiveness for each other comes naturally. They no longer have a hard heart toward each other. Their oneness with Christ makes possible the oneness they have with each other.

4

The Office of Husband

Your Maker is your husband, the LORD of hosts is his name; and
the Holy One of Israel is your Redeemer, the God of the whole earth
he is called.

ISAIAH 54:5

So what is the vocation of the husband? To answer that question, we must consider how God is present in the office of husband and how God works through husbands to bless their wives. Scripture addresses these questions in highly explicit terms. As we have seen, Christ is in marriage. And he is specifically in the office of husband. What the husband is called to do is to be Christ to his wife.

Little Christs

In his classic treatise "The Freedom of the Christian," Luther said that all Christians are liberated from the bondage of sin through the gospel, whereupon they are called to be "little Christs" to their neighbors.[1] Thus, all vocations are ultimately Christological. But husbands are put into the position of Christ in the clearest possible terms:

> Husbands, love your wives, as Christ loved the church and gave himself up for her, that he might sanctify her, having cleansed her by the washing of water with the word, so that he might present the church to himself in splen-

dor, without spot or wrinkle or any such thing, that she might be holy and without blemish. In the same way husbands should love their wives as their own bodies. He who loves his wife loves himself. For no one ever hated his own flesh, but nourishes and cherishes it, just as Christ does the church, because we are members of his body. "Therefore a man shall leave his father and mother and hold fast to his wife, and the two shall become one flesh." This mystery is profound, and I am saying that it refers to Christ and the church. (Eph. 5:25–32)

Here again is the teaching that husband and wife constitute one flesh and that marriage is the image of Christ and the church. It is perhaps not too difficult to appreciate the imagery of Christ being the bridegroom to his bride, the church, come for our sake, for our salvation. But the apostle Paul is not simply using marriage as a metaphor to explore the relationship between Christ and the church. Rather, he is doing the reverse, using that relationship to explore the relationship between husbands and wives. The context of Ephesians 5 is to give practical instruction for how Christians are to carry out the whole range of their different vocations: husbands and wives, parents and children, servants and masters. So when the apostle Paul says that husbands are called to play the role of Christ to their wives, he is offering practical instruction.

At first glance, this teaching appears incredible, even absurd. We are used to thinking of husbands in terms of the guy who takes out the trash and fixes things around the house, in between watching football on TV and putting in too many hours on the job. At best he is a lovable lug who remains mostly clueless about women. At worst he is an insensitive brute. Such is the husband as portrayed in our popular culture, in television sitcoms, and even pop psychology marriage books. And sometimes, let it be admitted, this *is* what husbands often seem like. To exalt such husbands, in general, to the role of Christ seems ludicrous. And I can hear women thinking, *Oh, great. Not only do men get all the breaks, but the husband also gets to be Jesus.*

But what does it mean to say that husbands are to be Christs to their wives, or more broadly, that all vocations involve being Christ to one's neighbor? It is a commonplace of Christian teaching that we should be "Christlike," that we should imitate Christ. This is often construed as being morally and spiritually perfect, as he is. But his is a standard that no human being can attain. When I hear a Christian going on about how being saved is not enough, that we also must act the way Jesus did, my response—under my breath but sometimes out loud—is, "and how are you doing with that?" Jesus is not primarily a new lawgiver, a new Moses with even higher standards. As much as we should imitate Christ, and his apostles ("Be imitators of me, as I am of Christ" [1 Cor. 11:1]), still we need Christ primarily as our savior from the consequences of our *not* obeying his law and for *not* imitating him. Jesus sacrificed himself for us. In vocation we are little Christs because loving and serving our neighbors means *sacrificing ourselves for them*. In the workplace we are sacrificing ourselves for our customers. In the church and in the state, we sacrifice ourselves for our fellow members and our fellow citizens. As we shall see, this is what parenting is, sacrificing—time, money, attention, energy—for our children. Children sacrifice for their parents. And in marriage, husbands are called to sacrifice themselves for their wives.

What Christ Does for the Church

Christ saves the church. Does that mean that the husband saves the wife? Certainly not in the way that Jesus has saved her. It is surely possible for marital love to become idolatrous for husband or wife as other earthly loves can be. Christ alone is the wife's savior from sin. Christ's relationship with her, as a member of his church, is deeper and more profound than any she could have with any human being.

And yet, can it be that a husband can, in a sense and as a shadow of the greater reality, be a sort of savior to the woman he has married? This is a theme in many of the old tales. A young woman is held captive by a dragon, is mired in poverty, or is oppressed by her wicked stepmother. A prince rides in on a white horse, rescues her, marries her, and they live happily ever after. Of course, this motif is widely derided today, to the point that *Cinderella* is often considered inappropriate reading for young women who, it is said, need to become self-reliant rather than hope for a man to solve their problems. And yet, old tales often contain primal wisdom. In the olden days of the fairy tales, marriage often was a way for a young woman to leave her problems behind, escape a bad family situation, or otherwise improve her condition. So it is, sometimes, today.

But if it is wrong to think of a man "saving" a woman by marrying her, it has become commonplace to hear that a woman has "saved" a man. The stereotype now is of the man who had a wild, dissolute life until he was saved by a good woman. This is the theme of countless popular songs

(Ray LaMontagne singing, "I've saved by a woman"[2]), especially country music songs. ("I used to have a wild side," sings Brooks & Dunn, "I'd burn those beer joints down," but now "You've turned my life around," to the point of being "baptised/by the fire in your touch/and the flame in your eyes."[3]) High-powered scholars write about the "civilizing effect" of women on men. Christian books, too, can try to explain masculinity in terms of a wildness that women are to tame.

It is certainly true today that in man/woman relationships, the man often plays the role of the needy one. He presents himself as troubled, unhappy, and emotionally vulnerable. The woman feels sorry for him, and is attracted by the prospect of helping him, even saving his life or saving his soul. But what these men are doing is appealing to a woman's *maternal* instincts. The woman is asked to play the role of the mother, not the bride. The man is playing the role of the child, not a potential husband.

It is certainly a good thing for a woman to help a man. This often happens in marriage, when the wife is a good influence on her husband. Indeed, as we have seen from Genesis, Eve as the primal wife was very specifically to be a "helper" to her husband. This is part of a wife's calling. But the man also needs to love and serve his wife, to the point of sacrificing himself for her and, in some sense, saving her. That is the husband's calling.

Christ needed nothing. The bride whom he sought, in her filthy rags and in thrall to Satan, needed everything. Christ put his life on the line to rescue her. Similarly, in marriage the woman is free to be the needy one. The man is called to be strong for her, to rescue her, to deny himself—setting aside his own needs—to do her good.

This is doubtless what looms behind the traditional roles of the husband as protector and provider. In the olden days and in more dangerous cultures, the husband often was called upon to fight, literally, to protect his wife and family. He was called upon to provide the food that was the difference between life and death for his wife and children. In carrying out his duties as husband, he saved their lives. This sometimes happens today, though the threats to wife and family are more commonly emotional, economic, and moral. Today a husband still must sometimes work to deliver his wife from her emotional malaise that, if not dealt with, can destroy her. He may be called to take on an extra job to get his family through economic problems. He may have to be vigilant in battling the moral assaults that will threaten his family from a godless culture. In each case, he will have to "give himself up" for his family but specifically for his wife—setting aside his own emotional needs to give his wife the support she needs; taking on the extra job that leaves him physically exhausted; turning his back on what he himself might enjoy to safeguard the moral sanctity of his household. In such personal sacrifices, he is playing the part of Christ, who, in turn, is working through him with his deeper sacrifice.

The Authority of the Husband

Most discussions of the husband being to his wife as Christ is to the church fixate immediately on the issue of authority. Who has to obey whom? The church must obey Christ; therefore, the wife must obey her husband. The biblical teachings about marriage are reduced to external laws, and the marriage relationship itself is reduced to the imposition of power. This causes some women, who see these teachings as unjust and oppressive, to throw out the biblical teachings altogether. And it causes some men to lord it over their wives, demanding their obedience, to the point of ruining their marriages. Now it is certainly true that the Bible teaches that the husband has authority over his wife. As we will see in the next chapter, she is called specifically to "submit" to her husband, as the church does to Christ. She responds to the self-sacrifice of her husband with her own self-sacrifice. But what so many of us miss is, first, the nature of authority according to the Bible, and second, the nature of Christ's relationship with the church.

Jesus himself teaches that, at least for Christians, authority must manifest itself not in the exercise of power but in service that finds its ultimate expression in sacrifice: "And Jesus called them to him and said to them, 'You know that those who are considered rulers of the Gentiles lord it over them, and their great ones exercise authority over them. But it shall not be so among you. But whoever would be great among you must be your servant, and whoever would be first among you must be slave of all. For even the Son of Man came not to be served but to serve, and to give his life as a ransom for many'" (Mark 10:42–45).

In the world and among nonbelievers, rulers "lord it over" others. They are above those they rule, and the rulers act as their lords. They "exercise authority" over the ruled. This describes the conventional status hierarchy by which power is exercised over others. "But it shall not be so among you," Jesus commands. His kingdom is not without hierarchy, but everything is turned upside down.

"Whoever would be great . . . must be your servant." And whoever would be the greatest of all, "first among you," must be the lowest sort of servant, the "slave of all." Then Jesus applies everything that he said to himself. Even the Son of Man—the one who truly is Lord, who as God is exalted above all things (Col. 1:15–20), the one who is actually entitled to "lord it over" all things—"came not to be served, but to serve." And in doing so, he lowered himself below all things, giving "his life as a ransom for many" (Matt. 20:28), which entailed emptying himself (Phil. 2:7–8), being rejected and despised, being tortured, becoming *sin* ("For our sake [God] made him [Jesus] to be sin who knew no sin, so that in him we might become the righteousness of God" [2 Cor. 5:21].), and dying. This, Jesus teaches his disciples, is how you must exercise your authority, whatever its extent. Christian rulers and great ones must self-sacrificially serve those under their care.

This passage applies to all Christians in authority. Again, the purpose of every vocation is to love and serve the neighbors that the vocation binds you to. The vocation of a ruler—a king, a magistrate, a government official, an employer—is to love and serve those under his authority. To be a tyrant, to exalt yourself over others by crushing or controlling them with your power, is to sin against your vocation. God did not give you his own authority for you to do *that*, to use it for yourself instead of for your neighbor. To insist on being served rather than serving is also to violate vocation. To be sure, the one in authority *is* served—part of the calling of subjects, citizens, and employees is to love and serve *their* neighbors to whom their vocation binds them, which includes the one in authority—but receiving service is never the goal of the calling. God does not call you to a position of responsibility so that people will bow and scrape to you, but so that you will have a sphere of service to them. Authority is vested in order to give, not to take. A husband does have authority over his wife, but not to "lord it over" her or even "exercise authority" as nonbelievers do; rather, the husband is to use his authority in service to his wife, as Christ does for the church.

52

"That She Might Be Holy"

We have examined the first part of Ephesians 5 on marriage, which teaches that the relationship between husband and wife is to be like that between Christ and the church. It is time now to consider the rest of that text, which teaches specifically what Christ does for his bride, the church, and what husbands, in turn, are called to do for their wives:

> Husbands, love your wives, as Christ loved the church and gave himself up for her, that he might sanctify her, having cleansed her by the washing of water with the word, so that he might present the church to himself in splendor, without spot or wrinkle or any such thing, that she might be holy and without blemish. In the same way husbands should love their wives as their own bodies. He who loves his wife loves himself. For no one ever hated his own flesh, but nourishes and cherishes it, just as Christ does the church, because we are members of his body. (Eph. 5:25–30)

The passage teaches us that Christ is the divine husband married to the church, and then it describes the services he gives as a husband to his bride. We see him committed to his bride in several specific ways. He cleanses, nourishes, cherishes, and presents her as perfect. He does so by sacrificing his very life to sanctify the church; that is, to make us holy. Similarly, husbands are called to love their wives "in the same way," to give themselves up, to sacrifice themselves, to make their wives holy.

They cannot do that of themselves, of course. Only Christ can do that. But husbands are charged with their wives' spiritual welfare. This will entail bringing Christ to her—seeing that the family goes to church (something wives tend to take the lead in today), initiating prayer with her and for her, and the like. But recall that in vocation, God uses and works through human beings in their callings. So the husband must also serve as something of a channel for Christ. This means that Christ will love and serve the man's wife as he loves and serves her. And Christ's goal for all of us in his church is to make us holy.

Holiness and the process by which we are made holy, sanctification, is more than just moral perfection. Holiness in the Old Testament was ascribed to the furnishings of the temple and other inanimate objects, and people were made holy not by their virtues but by the application of sacrificial blood. Being holy certainly includes living and acting in ways that accord with God's will, but the holiness that makes this possible seems to involve contact with the Holy God or with something he has set aside for himself.[4] For Luther, God's Word is the holiest thing that we have, and that Word has the power to make other things holy—such as the Sabbath Day, the work of our callings that we do in response to that Word, and our own lives as we follow that Word.[5]

How can an ordinary human being, such as a husband, help make someone holy? Consider forgiveness. When a husband forgives his wife (or, yes, when she forgives him, but we are focusing on husbands right now), he is directly imitating in his faint, shadowy way, what Christ has done and continues to do for all of us in the church. But consider this often ignored text, recounting Christ's action and his promise on the evening of the day he rose from the dead: "Jesus said to them again, 'Peace be with you. As the Father has sent me, even so I am sending you.' And when he had said this, he breathed on them and said to them, 'Receive the Holy Spirit. If you forgive the sins of any, they are forgiven them; if you withhold forgiveness from any, it is withheld'" (John 20:21–23).

The Holy Spirit connects earthly, Christian forgiveness with heavenly forgiveness. Evidently, a marriage characterized by forgiveness is going to manifest the presence of Christ and be a place of sanctification.[6] The Ephesians passage zeroes in on certain actions Christ has accomplished to sanctify his bride, the church, that are applicable to the relationship between a husband and his wife. He "cleansed her by the washing of water with the word" (Eph. 5:26). Here we see Christ's gift of baptism. Christ applies his love to his bride through tangible water and audible word. And by doing so, he sets her apart in valued status with the full strength of his authority. According to the Reformation theologians, the Christian's vocation begins with baptism. In that rite, the new Christian is called by name, joined with the name of the triune God, and having been cleansed of sin as imaged in the baptismal washing, begins the Christian life, which, again, is the life of vocation.

So how does baptism relate to the husband's vocation to his wife? While Christ expresses his love through "the washing of water with the word" (Eph. 5:26), husbands do so through their own tangible actions and their own words. In Scripture, we see husbands and fathers bringing their families to be baptized (Acts 16:33, 18:8). Husbands participate in the day-to-day family life, listening to God's Word and receiving his gifts, but also adding their own words and deeds of "cleansing"—forgiving, solving problems, righting wrongs, doing what is right. Meanwhile, through conversations, joined prayers, or simply driving to church and worshiping together, God is working with and through the husband to convey spiritual blessings to his wife.

Perhaps the reference to baptism, which marks the beginning of the Christian life and the Christian's vocations, might find a parallel in the wedding, when the couple first got married. Some churches consider the rite of matrimony to be a sacrament, like baptism. Though the Reformers, as was said, did not; they believed that marriage is "made holy by the word of God and prayer" (1 Tim. 4:5).[7] Just as the newly baptized is given a new name (the "Christian" name and that of the Father, the Son, and the Holy Spirit), the newly married woman in many cultures, including our own, is given the new name of her husband. And just as Jesus sees the new Christian, cleansed and incorporated into his bride, the church, in a new way, so the husband sees his wife, the two having been called together, in a new way.

The Ephesians passage says that Christ looks upon his bride, the church, whom he has cleansed and sanctified, so that he sees her in "splendor, without spot or wrinkle or any such thing, that she might be holy and without blemish" (5:27). Of course, the church and its members do have spots and wrinkles and blemishes, but Christ has taken care of those. When his work is complete, at the great wedding supper of the Lamb described in Revelation 19, he will see nothing but "splendor." Despite the sins and weaknesses in our lives, through his saving work, Christ will present us "without spot or wrinkle" or "blemish" in his eternal kingdom.

For husbands to love their wives "in the same way," as the next verse says, it must mean that the husband should similarly see his wife apocalyptically. Of course he will be aware of his wife's faults, as she is of his, and together they help each other to know Christ better and to grow in holiness. But the husband sees beyond those faults, glimpsing his wife as she is in glory, as she is in Christ's eyes: "In splendor." Because she is his wife, by virtue of their wedding in which their relationship—yes, even their sexual relationship—was made holy by the Word of God and prayer, the husband "presents her to himself" in her splendor, "without spot or wrinkle or any such thing."

Headship

This chapter would not be complete without addressing the headship that God gives to husbands. But again we must first look to Christ and our heavenly Father for clarification on what this means. Christ is the head over the church and husbands are head of their wives, each as "his body." But Christ also has a head: God the Father. "But I want you to understand that the head of every man is Christ, the head of a wife is her husband, and the head of Christ is God" (1 Cor. 11:3).

Thus, the scriptural metaphor that someone is "head" in relation to someone else does not denote inequality. In the Trinity, the Son of God is equal to the Father. ("God of God, Light of Light, very God of very God, begotten, not made, being of one substance with the Father," as the Nicene Creed puts it.) But to be "Son" to the "Father" involves—as we shall see when we discuss parenting—a relationship of authority and obedience, giving and receiving, love and the reception of love.

Within the Trinity, within that state of perfection and love and total unity, there is headship and authority. God the Son obeys God the Father and clearly says so to all creation. He is not weakened by obedience. He is no less God because of it. He is not inferior in his divinity. There is no shame or injustice or competition in this. The Son submits because he is Son to the Father.

Headship, then, reflects something about God. It does not need to be a term that brings to mind sin; much less can it be an excuse for cruelty or abuse. Nor does headship prove any sort of superiority of the male gender. Jesus is the primary character and eternal theme in biblical headship discourse. Consider this text: "And [the Lord] put all things under [Christ's] feet and gave him as head over all things to the church, which is his body" (Eph. 1:22–23). Here Christ, whose head is the Father, is made by the Father "head over all things" and then given, as a gift, "to the church, which is his body." Here the levels of headship multiply, but the bottom line is that Christ's headship is a gift to the church—which means that the husband's headship also must be a gift to his wife.

Part of our problem with the image is that today we often think of someone being the "head" over someone else as a metaphor from the business or bureaucratic world, in which the "head" of a division makes the decisions and exercises power over everyone "beneath" him or her on the organizational chart. But headship is an organic analogy used by God in

Scripture. It is not the business term that developed later, but a very physical one that expresses life itself. The head only lives as long as it is connected with the body, and the body lives only as long as it is connected with the head. Here again is the rich language of the one-flesh union. The needs of the head are not more significant than the needs of the rest of the body, nor does the head exist to repeatedly tell its counterpart, "I'm the head! I'm the head!"[8] God has joined "head" with "body" for the sake of life. The head and body are meant to benefit each other. They are meant to live together, work together, rest together, rely on each other, and be one with each other. They are to constitute a union that is greater than each of them separately. This union is to be so complete that, in the words of Richard Eyer, there is no "his problem" or "her problem" in marriage, but "our problem."[9]

Levels of authority are built into everything that dimly reflects God and his relationships. Authority on earth exists to serve God and our neighbors, not our own selfishness or personal interests. Authority, as is spoken about in Scripture, is not arbitrary power amassed because of strength, intellect, or even worth, but it belongs to God and is delegated through human beings in their vocations. But all authority, whether in government, family, or church, ultimately does not belong to the person but resides in God himself (Rom. 13:1).

Christ is the head of all authority (Col. 2:9–10), and Christ himself goes so far as to say his authority—and therefore all authority—is bound directly to the Father's (John 5:19). He demonstrates with his own life and death that authority is never given for the sake of selfishness but for service to others (Matt. 20:25–26; Mark 10:42–43). In Jesus, we can see that even when God gives authority to someone, that person may not abuse it by using it for his own sake (Rom. 15:1–3).

Christ retains all his authority, but uses it in service to his Father and his bride. Christ looks after his church because he cares about her and to protect her from the very real dangers around, or even within, her. In passages such as Ephesians 1:22 and Colossians 2:9–10, we see that Christ's headship puts other powers under his feet.[10] Christ has dominion over all creation—even over dark powers—yet he does not use force or power to coerce his church, but to protect her. And in Ephesians 5:23–29, we have already seen that Christ's headship encompasses providing and nourishing.[11] In Ephesians 4:15–16, headship equips the body. In 2 Corinthians 10:8, authority is to build others up.

Yes, the headship of a husband gives him authority, but it is not about absolute control and certainly cannot be an excuse to demean his wife, whom God has put under his care. Headship has implications for how husbands should interact with their spouses, but also for how they ought to speak about and act toward their wives and marriage publicly: sensitively and protectively. Headship is part of the living intimacy of a husband and wife, and headship is part of an authority given within creation for purposes even larger than the couple.

In a healthy human being, the head and body are not at odds with each other. There are no power struggles or mind games. The head does not ignore the needs of the rest of its body. In the body and in marriage, any need the wife has becomes her husband's special need, precisely because they are now one flesh by God's hand.

Not only that, the very sacrifices that husbands and wives make for each other are returned back to the one who sacrifices. As if Paul were not clear enough with his emphasis on the body and one-flesh union, he states, "He who loves his wife loves himself" (Eph. 5:28). This is how closely a husband and wife are joined together. Selfless love reflects back upon the self. The husband's love affects the wife's love and it also affects the husband himself. "No one ever hated his own flesh" (Eph. 5:29). Ultimately people do not hate themselves. They may hate what they look like, what they've become, or what seems to be hindering their happiness, but even those who succumb to suicide presumably want escape for themselves. Scripture ties our flesh with our very selves. So now in marriage, the two selves become one self.

The Great Exchange

Whether husbands are "good" or not, believers or unbelievers, God uses them to point to his own relationship with his people. Every day they demonstrate to their wives—whether overtly or in their faults—that they should trust in Christ above all people and all things, including themselves. Sinners simply do not handle sacrifice and authority in the superb ways God does, yet no matter how awful (or how good) a husband may be, he cannot diminish the husband he is called to reflect and who is present in his office.

When a husband does something as small as taking out the trash, he is showing that his wife is worth getting dirty for. Christ showed his love by getting dirty for us—washing his disciples' feet, being spit upon, taking the sins of the world upon himself—but he also continues to show his love by listening to us, mourning when we mourn, stimulating our thoughts, and building up our faith. He knows us. He loves us. He directs his love outward. So do husbands.

Marriage is not easy. But we are not alone when we struggle or sacrifice: Christ is present! Through his providing, husbands provide. His sacrifice overflows our shortcomings and empowers our sacrifices. In themselves, sacrifices cannot promise happy endings, but when Christ gave himself up to death, he did much more than suffer and die. He joined us in our suffering. He offers us cleansing, forgiveness, healing, and safety in his care. And he laid the foundation so that he can work all of our suffering and sacrifices together for good. He has given us marriage and one-flesh unity, and it is he who builds up the house through his vessels, through husbands and wives (Psalm 127).

That is another metaphor that some women find irritating, but whose point is often lost: "Likewise, husbands, live with your wives in an understanding way, showing honor to the woman as the weaker vessel, since they are heirs with you of the grace of life, so that your prayers may not be hindered" (1 Pet. 3:7). Weaker vessel? The imagery is that of a vase or piece of pottery and suggests that women are susceptible to damage. But the point is that the wife is an honorable *vessel*.[12] What does this vessel contain? She is an heir with her husband of the grace of life. She contains the Holy Spirit. And she also has work to do, being "a vessel for honorable use, set apart as holy, useful to the master of the house, ready for every good work" (2 Tim. 2:21). Husbands are to understand their wives and to show honor to them. If they do *not*, if they violate their vocation by refusing to treat their wives as Christ does the church, their own spiritual lives will be weakened. Their prayers will be "hindered." Luther asks, how can a husband pray, "Father, forgive us our trespasses as we forgive," if he remains caught up in constantly finding fault or assigning blame regarding his wife?[13] Many Christian men today are struggling spiritually and praying futilely precisely because of the way they are treating their wives.

Husbands are not called to love their wives as long as they meet a certain set of requirements. Is that how God loves us? Instead, a husband's love is to be Christlike, encompassing, patient, forgiving, and diligent. Even her weaknesses and problems—serious enough that Christ died to heal them—provide opportunities to express love by sharing her burdens (Gal. 6:1–2).

The vocation of marriage is for a husband and wife to live together in love, service, and faithfulness for life. To cherish and nourish. Spouses are to recognize each other as a fellow vessel of the Holy Spirit. The spouse is a precious gift personally given by God himself. Marriage is the place where love surrenders itself to the other. In this vocation, spouses put the other first and sacrifice for each other. Sometimes confessing your sins is the most powerful sacrifice that can be made for your spouse and marriage. Sometimes forgiving your spouse's confession is your sacrifice instead. As sinners, we are pointed to something, Someone, far greater than any sin: Christ, who came as the Bridegroom of the church. In brief, marriage is to be an icon of the gospel.

5

The Office of Wife

Come, I will show you the Bride, the wife of the Lamb.
REVELATION 21:9

God is present and at work through the office of husband, and he is also present and at work through the office of wife. As Luther explained in "The Freedom of the Christian," Christians in all vocations are called to be "little Christs" to each other. That is, every vocation—including those of the highest authority—involves some kind of voluntary self-sacrifice for the neighbor.

In Ephesians 5, as we have seen, in the vocations of marriage are hidden the relationship between Christ and the church. The husband loves and serves his wife by giving himself up for her, as Christ gave himself up for his bride, the church. The wife loves and serves her husband by submitting to him, as the church submits to Christ.

If we can understand the calling of the husband by contemplating Christ, as we did in the last chapter, we should be able to understand the calling of the wife by contemplating the church. Though in her multiple vocations—including that of a wife—she too is called to be a "little Christ" to her neighbors (including her husband), the uniqueness of marriage summons her specifically to be a "little church."

The Bride of Christ

Without belittling or undermining the two sexes within creation, we can consider that all Christian men and women are collectively called

Christ's bride, his wife (Revelation 21). Scripture calls all people feminine in relationship to the masculinity of God. And so there is a sense in which the office of wife stands as an embodiment of the natural order for everyone. In particular, she embodies the vocation of the church.

The immediate parallel between Christ's marriage to the church and our earthly marriages is that both wives and the church are, above all, recipients of love, sacrifice, and commitment. The Ephesians 5 passages about wives and husbands speak of love and not judgment, centering not primarily on rules or sin but on Christ and forgiveness. Wives are like the church. Simply put, one's understanding of wives will be colored by one's understanding of the church.

The Christian emphasis on receiving begins and ends with God's goodness and mercy toward us sinners. Faith is dependent only on Jesus and receiving his gifts. And from this standpoint, receiving is at the essence of the Christian's condition.

This is true spiritually, and it is also true in our lives in the world. Marriage and the home are primary places where individuals receive. Everyone receives something, whether it is nourishment from meals, quiet for sleep, support for thoughts or activities, etc. Our whole lives can be classified as time spent receiving from God and others.

We receive outside the home as well, of course—our food, shelter, clothing, and everything else we need for our lives—but those gifts, which we receive from God through our own and others' vocations, are given and received in a system of exchange. I exercise my vocation, for which I receive money, the medium of exchange that quantifies my labor, and then I give that to buy the fruits of other people's labor. Justice and economic laws are operative in that realm.

But in the family, giving and receiving are free. Children do not have to pay for the food, shelter, or clothing that their parents give them. Nor do husbands and wives expect any kind of payment for the things they do for each other. Thus family is designed as an earthly manifestation of the gospel. It is the realm of free gift, the icon of Christ and the church.

Scripture particularly applies this icon to marriage, to the relationship of husbands and wives. Husbands, of course, also receive—as human beings, as members of the church—but they are specifically called in marriage to play the Christlike role as a giver. Wives, playing the churchlike role, are called to receive from their husbands.

Yes, this is imaged in the sexual relationship (which we will discuss further). It is also found in the traditional role of the husband as provider, with the wife receiving from him the fruits of his labor, which she then turns into sustenance for the entire family. It is also manifest in the obligation of the husband to give his wife emotional support and to *"give himself up"* for his wife.

The usual emphasis in discussions of vocation is, What does this particular vocation make or create or do? We often fail to recognize the vocational elements of receiving. The giving/receiving relationship established by God is about love. The lover gives; the beloved receives. This precisely describes Christ's relationship with the church. In fact, this is how the apostle John defines love: "In this is love, not that we have loved God but that he loved us and sent his Son to be the propitiation for our sins" (1 John 4:10). We did not love God, not at first; but he loved us and gave us the gift of his Son. In response, though, to God's love in Christ, we *do* love God. And our love of God overflows to love of our neighbors. "We love because he first loved us. If anyone says, 'I love God,' and hates his brother, he is a liar; for he who does not love his brother whom he has seen cannot love God whom he has not seen. And this commandment we have from him: whoever loves God must also love his brother" (1 John 4:19–21). This plays out, of course, in vocation, as God's love for us creates faith toward God, which bears fruit in love and service to our neighbor.

But it also explains a curious Biblical teaching about marriage. Husbands are told to love their wives. But wives are not told to love their husbands. "Husbands, love your wives, as Christ loved the church," exhorts the apostle Paul (Eph. 5:25). "Husbands should love their wives as their own bodies," he says later. "He who loves his wife loves himself" (Eph. 5:28). Then he concludes his whole discourse about marriage in Ephesians with this: "Let each one of you love his wife as himself, and let the wife see that she respects her husband" (Eph. 5:33).

Husbands are to love their wives. But wives are only enjoined to "respect" their husbands. Of course, this parallels the relationship of Christ to the church. The Christian responds to the love of God expressed in Christ's sacrifice in faith ("not that we have loved God but that he loved us"), which then manifests itself in love for God ("we love because he first loved us"). Similarly, the wife responds to her husband's love with respect, which then grows into love for him. It is probably futile to change the romantic language and conventions so that we speak not of a woman's love for a man, but of her faith in him. But the model surely applies when a man is looking for a wife and not a mother. "She loves because he first loved her."

Submission

Part of the problem in discussing marriage or any vocation is that qualities the Bible upholds as virtues our contemporary culture holds in contempt. That vocation teaches our dependence on others contradicts our American ideals of autonomy and self-sufficiency. And the notion that we should sacrifice ourselves for anyone flies in the face of the Western ideals of self-aggrandizement, from the "enlightened self-interest" of our economic system to the "self-fulfillment" mandate of our popular ethics.

As for "submission," as in the New Testament injunction for wives to submit to their husbands, that concept tends to be dismissed at once as unjust and oppressive. Terms like "submit," though originally a neutral, organizational word, elicit reactions as though it means "brainless slavery"! But Ephesians 5 does not describe slavery, but the relationship between Christ and the church—which entails Christ liberating his people from slavery and giving them freedom (Gal. 5:1)—as the pattern for the relationship between husband and wife.

It is understandable that women who have been fighting against the low status assigned to them by their culture should recoil at the discipline of submitting to their husbands. And it is clear that this injunction has been misused as a way for husbands to exert power over their wives. But the husbands are called to a similar sacrificial discipline, namely, giving themselves up for their wives.

Submission is, in fact, a discipline that all Christians are called to. Immediately prior to the teachings on individual vocations in Ephesians—the treatment of wives and husbands, children and parents, masters and servants—the apostle Paul, as if writing a thesis sentence for what comes next, says that *all* Christians should be "submitting to one another out of reverence for Christ" (Eph. 5:21).

This principle of denying one's self for others—specifically sacrificing one's own desires for the desires of others—runs throughout the New

Testament: "Let no one seek his own good, but the good of his neighbor" (1 Cor. 10:24). "If anyone would come after me, let him deny himself and take up his cross daily and follow me" (Luke 9:23). The "daily" relates this cross bearing to everyday vocations.

Not only are all Christians supposed to submit to each other, Scripture also teaches that Christ himself submits to his Father. As a child, Jesus is described as being "submissive" to his parents (Luke 2:51). Thus, Jesus places himself under vocation, with his calling as a child responding to Mary and Joseph's calling as parents. Jesus submitted himself to his heavenly Father in fulfilling his own calling to be Savior of the world. In the garden, his own will was in tension with the will of the Father, but in this struggle, he manifests the very essence of submission: "Father, if you are willing, remove this cup from me. Nevertheless, not my will, but yours, be done" (Luke 22:42). And finally, when he returns, he again submits to the One who causes all things to submit to him: "When all things are subjected to him, then the Son himself will also be subjected to him who put all things in subjection under him, that God may be all in all" (1 Cor. 15:28). (The Greek verbs translated as "be subject to" and "submit" are the same.)

Similar to what we saw with the concept of headship, for one person to be submissive to another does not mean that the two are unequal to each other. After all, the Son is equal to the Father in essence and deity. To think otherwise is heresy. Similarly, that the wife submits to her husband by no means implies her inequality to him, but a distinction from him.

Submission is christological. And, in its various guises, it is an intrinsic part of every vocation. One cannot love and serve one's neighbors without some kind of submission to them. The employee may not "want" to go into work, but he does. The new mother may desire to sleep late, but she gets up to attend to the inarticulate desires of her baby. The citizen may not want to stop at the light, but he does. A church member may not agree with the rest of the congregation's choice for the new carpet, but goes along with the decision of the group. The sacrifice of one's personal desire in favor of following the desire of someone else is asked of us in every vocation.

To understand submission in marriage, we always must have recourse to the relationship between Christ and the church. This is not primarily a relationship of power or even status, since Christ saved the church precisely by humbling himself and emptying himself on the cross (Phil. 2:5–8). Furthermore, Christ continues to relate to his church in grace and love. Is Christ oppressive to those who have faith in him? Is he cruel to the church? Christians do need to submit to him to receive his gifts. In fact, submitting to Christ is something of a definition of what faith is. It appears that God's design for marriage asks wives to have something like faith in their husbands.

"Wives, submit to your own husbands, as to the Lord" (Eph. 5:22). The wife is called to submit to her husband–not because of who her husband is, and certainly not because her husband is always right, but because Christ himself stands hidden behind her marriage. The phrase "as to the Lord" reminds both husbands and wives that marital authority ultimately belongs to the Lord. In fact, when a wife submits to her husband—saying, in effect, "not my will, but yours, be done"—she is submitting to Christ, who is hidden in her husband.

Husbands dare not abuse Christ's authority, nor should wives disregard it. The purpose of vocation is to love and serve, and God promises to be present and active through that love and service. The wife fulfills her calling by loving and serving her husband. Submission is simply her expression of love and her acts of service. Submission finds its fulfillment in receiving the husband's sacrifice of himself for her (Eph. 5:25).

The Australian theologian John Kleinig makes several profound (yet practical) connections. He notes, "Surprisingly, the call for subordination of a Christian wife to her husband does not focus on her obedience to him, but on her respect for him as her head (Eph 5:22, 33; 1 Pet 3:2). Its purpose is for her to receive his love (Eph 5:24-27), and, if she is married to an unbeliever, to gain his conversion (1 Pet 3:1-2)." Kleinig goes on to say:

> In the ancient world the ideal person was an independent man, with economic resources and political clout, a self-sufficient autonomous person. Yet in the Church this is reversed. There the ideal human being is a dependent person, someone who is subordinate and reliant on others, such as a wife or a child or a servant. Thus the Church is the bride of Christ; all Christians are children of God and servants of Christ. The ideal state for the Christian is now no longer to be a master, with legally assured status, wealth and power, but to be a servant, free from enslavement to social status, wealth and power (1 Pet 2:16). Subordination has therefore become the normal condition in the Church. All

> Christians are subordinate to Christ (Eph 5:21, 23), to God the Father (Heb
> 12:9; James 4:7), and to the orders that God has established (1 Pet 2:13). So,
> every Christian is in subordination to someone else. All are under headship
> and authority. None are self-sufficient and autonomous.[1]

He concludes: "In sum: the apostolic teaching on subordination does not establish a chain of command for the exercise of power by those who sit at the top; it promotes a chain of transmission from the triune God for the delivery of blessings through his appointed agents in the church and in the world."[2]

Submission is then also a transmission of God's blessings toward humanity. Headship or authority passages in the Bible are not encouragements for tyrants to crack their demanding whips harder, but are for the good of the ones under authority. It is our God, who "shows his love for us in that while we were still sinners, Christ died for us" (Rom. 5:8), who stands behind authority, even the earthly authority of a husband. And it is our God who calls for submission, not in order to harm, but to build up; not in order to wound, but to heal. The patterns of submission described in Scripture—God the Son to God the Father; the church to God the Son; wives to husbands; Christians to each other—involve receiving and giving grace.

Submission does not mean that the wife has no influence with her husband or in her family, or that her will has to be broken, nor does it mean that wives have no say in family decisions. It does mean that a wife is part of a mission (sub-mission) with her husband. *Missio* is the Latin term for "send." A wife is sent with her husband in a particular vocation by a loving God actively involved in both of their lives.

Submission can be daunting and difficult. And to an extent, it should be, even as headship and "giving himself up" are daunting to husbands. These are spiritual disciplines, exercised not in a monastery, with its vows of obedience, but in everyday life.

Submission has to do with denying oneself and taking up the cross (Mark 8:34). It is an act of faith, of trusting God above our own perceptions. Here again we can remember just how close our God is to us. Vocation emphasizes "what God is doing through my life" and "what God is doing for me through other people in my life." God is with us—as close as our spouse and closer. He is working for us and through us. To the point that, because Christ is hidden in her husband, when the wife submits to her husband, she is submitting to Christ.

If husbands would always treat their wives the way Christ treats the church—and this is precisely what the husband is called to do—there would be little problem, with submission coming easily and freely as a joyful response to the husband's own self-denial for her. This does not always happen, of course. Rather, one or both spouses try to dominate each other. The result is conflict, resentment, and marital discord. Because of our sinful nature, such violations of vocation happen in all marriages; but if they continue unrepented and unforgiven, they can destroy a marriage.

The selflessness required of both the husband and the wife in a marriage according to God's design comes as the fruit of faith. And it is not just the wife's faith in the husband—trusting his judgment, trusting him to do the right thing—but faith in Christ, who is in marriage. And for the husband to resist misusing his office, he himself must submit in faith to Christ.

The result of this submission on the wife's part and "giving himself up" on the husband's part is that the two become unified—being "one flesh"—so that together they constitute something larger than either of them individually: they are a family. Christ's submission to his Father inheres in the unity of the Trinity. Citizens submit to lawful authority, which establishes a social and national unity. Christians submit to one another out of reverence for Christ to maintain the unity of the church.

Everyone must, at one time or another in their various vocations, say with Jesus, "Nevertheless, not my will, but yours, be done." All Christians must say this to God the Father, as we pray in the Lord's Prayer ("thy will be done on earth as it is in Heaven"). Workers have to say it or think it to their bosses, their colleagues, and their customers. Children have to say it or think it to their parents. A husband sometimes says it to his wife, in the course of "giving himself up" for her. A wife is called to say it or think it to her husband.

This does not mean that they will always be in agreement. The "nevertheless" in Jesus's words shows a genuine conflict of wills even within the Godhead. Arguably, submission *requires* a conflict of wills; otherwise, there is common agreement rather than submission. When this happens, the wife is called to "give in." What prevents this from being tyrannical is that her husband is called to "give himself up" for her. What makes this possible is that Christ hidden in marriage, so that both the wife and the husband are submitting to him.

What the Church and the Wife Do

If the wife has the role of the church, what is the wife to *do*? Certainly the church, in the faith that comes from submitting to Christ, is active in the world. God himself works through his church to spread the gospel, to build up the faith of those whom he has called to himself, and to carry out the implications of his kingdom in ministry to the world. In the same way, God works through wives to spread his love, mercy, and care. The church responds to what she receives with tangible action, her "faith working through love" (Gal. 5:6); so does the wife.

The church receives from Christ, but does that mean that is all there is to their relationship? No, because in that receiving there is also unity, a powerful and productive unity. In their union, the church does as Christ himself does. The church receives from Christ and together she can bear him fruit: love, joy, peace, patience, kindness, goodness, faithfulness, gentleness, and self-control (Gal. 5:22–23). This fruit is directed toward others. This love, joy, peace, and patience is manifested within our relationships—that is, within our vocations.

A wife then is far from an inactive person. Her office as wife certainly emphasizes how God works through his people receiving his gifts, but receiving becomes part and parcel of actively living out her faith. The fullest detailed picture of the wife's activities that Scripture gives is found in Proverbs 31:

> An excellent wife who can find?
> She is far more precious than jewels.
> The heart of her husband trusts in her,
> and he will have no lack of gain.
> She does him good, and not harm,
> all the days of her life.
> She seeks wool and flax,
> and works with willing hands.
> She is like the ships of the merchant;
> she brings her food from afar.
> She rises while it is yet night
> and provides food for her household

and portions for her maidens.
She considers a field and buys it;
   with the fruit of her hands she plants a vineyard.
She dresses herself with strength
   and makes her arms strong.
She perceives that her merchandise is profitable.
   Her lamp does not go out at night.
She puts her hands to the distaff,
   and her hands hold the spindle.
She opens her hand to the poor
   and reaches out her hands to the needy.
She is not afraid of snow for her household,
   for all her household are clothed in scarlet.
She makes bed coverings for herself;
   her clothing is fine linen and purple.
Her husband is known in the gates
   when he sits among the elders of the land.
She makes linen garments and sells them;
   she delivers sashes to the merchant.
Strength and dignity are her clothing,
   and she laughs at the time to come.
She opens her mouth with wisdom,
   and the teaching of kindness is on her tongue.
She looks well to the ways of her household
   and does not eat the bread of idleness.
Her children rise up and call her blessed;
   her husband also, and he praises her:
"Many women have done excellently,
   but you surpass them all."
Charm is deceitful, and beauty is vain,
   but a woman who fears the LORD is to be praised.
Give her of the fruit of her hands,
   and let her works praise her in the gates. (Prov. 31:10–31)

Notice the emphasis here, as in Luther, on "household," the estate that brings together both the family and the economic vocations. She does good to her husband and does not harm him (an excellent formulation that is applicable for all vocations: love and serve your neighbors, and, conversely, do not harm them!). Her husband trusts her. He praises her. He calls her "blessed," which must mean that God blesses him through her (another all-vocational concept). But the wife's work extends beyond just her relationship with her husband. She is a mother, and her children also recognize that God is blessing them through her. She herself bears authority in the household, not just with her children but with the servants whom the household employs. She contributes economically to the household. She is engaged in productive labor, working with "willing hands." She makes profitable merchandise. She makes clothing for her family but also sells it to outsiders. Her work has a scope beyond her family. "She considers a field and buys it." She helps the poor.

This is to say, she has other vocations. She is a wife. She is also a mother, a creative worker, a businesswoman. Of course, economic vocations are very different today than they were in Luther's and Solomon's days. And yet this passage and the doctrine of vocation surely address the vexed issue of women "working outside of the home." Evidently, they may be called to do so. And that work is not necessarily in conflict with her family vocations. In the Proverbs text, her economic activity contributes to the prosperity and well-being of her family. It also benefits her: "Give her of the fruit of her hands."

This does not mean that a woman has to "do it all." Women today have problems balancing the demands of family and work. So do men, if they properly understand their family vocations. In Luther's and Solomon's day, family and work were more fully integrated than they have become since the Industrial Revolution. And yet, the doctrine of vocation applies today just as it did in the past. In today's culture and today's economy, the majority of women do work outside the home. This often produces angst and guilt, especially in Christian women. But the doctrine of vocation teaches that some women may well be called by God to serve in the world outside of their households, whether in the workplace or in the state, as we are seeing today with Christian women who are activists, lawmakers, and public officials. Women in any of these positions must see them as Christian vocations, as realms of love and service.

What should be done when the obligations of our different vocations pull us in different directions? When the demands of parenthood, marriage, and the workplace—as well as church and social obligations—conflict with each other, which vocation should have priority? The answer: Since all vocations involve loving and serving the neighbor, the most urgent "calling" will be from the neighbor with the greatest need. This applies to all of our multiple vocations. Sometimes a woman's child may need her, to the point that her husband, her job, and her church have to be put on hold. Sometimes her husband needs her most, and it will be time to find a babysitter for the child and to put off a project at work. Sometimes, though, her job or the church may need her most, and her husband and children will need to be patient. It can also be helpful to remember that some vocations are temporary—like jobs, which may change or even end—while others, including the vocation of spouse, are permanent.

Obviously, being able to discern which neighbor needs you most will not always be obvious or clear cut. And navigating these conflicts will never be easy. But this handling of conflicts—like submission—is necessary in every vocation.

Love Spills Over

We have been discussing different vocations, each in its turn, and will continue to do so. But we must always remember that vocations do not exist in isolation. They exist in dyads with other vocations[3]—husband and wife, parent and child, employer and employee, ruler and subject—and these all together form complex and interlocking webs of love and service.

God has ordained vocations because he delights in men and women giving gifts of loving service to one another. God has organized the world in interlocking but not strictly reciprocal ways. Simply put, love spills over. God's love spills over into creation. This happens in the complex patterns of giving and receiving that characterize all vocations, which work together to make a society and an economic order possible. It certainly happens in the family. The husband gives to the mother, which enables her to give to her children. Or the husband gives to his children who in turn give toward their mother.

In marriage, love spills over. Husbands and wives love and serve each other in ways that spill out into the rest of their lives. This spilling imagery reminds us that God has not promised any kind of 1:1 ratio of blessings or gifts, a karmic system of payback with everyone getting just what they have coming and no more; rather, he promises an abundance, a superfluity of grace. That is to say, marriage is an image of the gospel. As such, it is a realm of forgiveness and freedom. Ultimately, that is what it means to say that marriage is about Christ and the church.

6

Sex and Vocation

But because of the temptation to sexual immorality, each man
should have his own wife and each woman her own husband.

1 CORINTHIANS 7:2

Every vocation has its particular and defining work. Farmers grow crops. Doctors heal the sick. Rulers rule; judges judge; preachers preach. Every vocation is authorized—that is, has the authority—to do that work. The proper and unique work of marriage is sexual intercourse.

Sex is an overwhelmingly powerful reality in the human condition, but it is fraught with difficulties, moral dangers, and confusions. This is true for both non-Christians and Christians, single people and married couples. The doctrine of vocation helps us to understand sex in a completely different way, one that clarifies the moral issues and helps restore sex to its rightful place in life.

The Authorization for Sex

Why is it that sex outside of marriage is considered to be wrong, while sex inside of marriage is all of a sudden moral? As people say, what difference does a piece of paper—the marriage license—make? The answer, in vocational terms, is that God calls and thus authorizes husbands and wives to have sex with each other. God confirmed that calling through civil laws and, yes, even that piece of paper, the marriage license. He does not call and authorize people to have sex apart from the vocation of marriage.

In an important text for the doctrine of vocation, we are told, "There is no authority except from God, and those that exist have been instituted by God" (Rom. 13:1). Strictly speaking, only God has authority in himself, but he gives his authority to certain vocations that he established and through which he works.

Immediately prior to the text we just quoted, we are told, "Never avenge yourselves, but leave it to the wrath of God" (Rom. 12:19). Then we learn that the way God punishes wrongdoers on earth is through the vocations of "the governing authorities." The ruler is described as God's "servant" and God's "*avenger* who carries out God's wrath on the wrongdoer" (Rom. 13:4). We ordinary citizens may not avenge ourselves, but there are lawful, God-ordained vocations that "bear the sword" (Rom. 13:4)—police officers, soldiers, other members of our legal system and military orders—who have the authority to use that sword to protect the innocent and to enforce justice, something the rest of us are not authorized to do.

Thus, the same action can be a sin when done outside of vocation and a good work when done inside a vocation. We are forbidden to kill, and yet a soldier operating in a Romans 13 chain of command can do so in love and service to his neighbor. We are forbidden to take someone else's property, and yet the tax collector has a divine sanction (Rom. 13:6–7). The proper work of a physician is to heal, and in doing so, he can do things with the bodies of his patients—including cutting them open—that no one else is authorized to do. By virtue of his medical license, another "piece of paper" conferred upon him by the state, he has a vocation, a calling manifested in the opportunities and talents that brought him through medical school and that ultimately derive from God himself.

The basic meaning of the word *license* means formal, usually written, permission. The state—a set of vocations through which God governs the social order—issues marriage licenses. But this is no mere "piece of paper." It is a legal contract establishing the man and the woman as constituting a new family, with specific legal rights due to the foundation of society. Some societies, of course, do not bother with a marriage license as such, but there is nearly always some kind of public and external declaration—a legally binding verbal contract, a statement of mutual consent, a wedding ritual. Strictly speaking, it is not the state but God who joins a man and a woman together in marriage. The state can issue "pieces of paper" and legal conventions apart from God's design, as we see in states that permit same-sex marriage. But in general, the marriage license, the wedding, or the equivalent are symbols of the objective calling, an authorization ultimately deriving from God himself confirming that the man and the woman have the vocation of marriage.

Sex as a Family Value

Sexual relations make a man and a woman "one flesh." They literally share one body and constitute one organism. This significance of sex holds true, according to Scripture, even in extramarital sex. "Do you not know that he who is joined to a prostitute becomes one body with her?" asks the apostle Paul, "For, as it is written, 'The two will become one flesh'" (1 Cor. 6:16). This is why sexual morality is so crucially important. Sex creates unions, imposes obligations, and establishes responsibilities in ways far beyond our comprehension.

For one thing, sex is the means through which God performs one of his most astonishing miracles, something no less miraculous because it is so commonplace: the engendering of new life. Sex belongs in the family because it creates the family. The man and woman desire each other and come together in marriage, where they become "one flesh." Then the same act that makes them one physical organism can bring into existence a new immortal human being. This ushers in an additional calling for the husband and wife: the vocation of father and mother, which we will discuss in a later section. The point for now is that God situates sex within the family and nowhere else.

Yes, it is possible to have sex with someone you are not married to, just as it is possible to have a baby without being married. But both are violations of vocation—rejections of the responsibility a man has even to a prostitute, a one-night hookup, or the horribly exploited woman on a porn video; and rejections of the responsibility a man has to be a father to his own child.

Sex is not just a spasm of pleasure. It cannot be reduced to recreation, the release of pent-up lust, or a private passion. That sex creates one-flesh unions means that promiscuity of every kind is destructive. That sex creates new life is not an unfortunate side effect, but its God-given biological nature. To be sure, sexual desire is enormously powerful, capable of sweeping away the best intentions and all self-control. It can channel itself into all sorts of perversities and transgressions. But its fulfillment and its true nature can only be found in marriage.

Today, of course, sex *outside* of marriage has become not only accepted but is also almost, in the pop culture, the norm. Judging from our entertainment industry, sex is primarily for single people. Marriage is derided as "settling down," as the giving up of sexual pleasure. The reality is very different, as research shows that married people have far more sex and sexual satisfaction than singles.[1] Still, so dominant is the fantasy of single sex that it even shapes sex within marriage!

One of the best books on the subject is surely Lauren Winner's *Real Sex*.[2] She shows how the qualities associated with single sex—being secretive, transgressive, and out of the ordinary—are reflected in the expectations of married couples. Egged on by sex manuals, including Christian sex manuals, they too look for sex to be seductive, forbidden, and exotic. Married couples are urged to "date"—which is what unmarried couples do—and to "spice up their relationship" by leaving the home and checking into a hotel. (Certainly, it is a good idea for married couples to schedule time together and to get away together sometimes. The point here is the implications of the language and the mind-set behind it. Married people pretend to be single so as to recover a sense of romantic attraction. Sex in a hotel is more romantic than sex in the home.)

Dr. Winner points out that what we have lost is the sense of sex being a normal, regular, accepted part of the household. Notice her use of the vocation term "household," which is the estate of the family and all its associated callings. In the vocation of marriage, sex is part of ordinary life. Thus, the desire for sex is neither repressed nor disordered; rather, it is satisfied.

Marriage as the Cure for Sexual Sin

To be sure, sexual sins are deadly. No wonder, since sex is the foundation for both marriage and parenthood, for the family itself. Certainly being able to engender new life may be human beings' most miraculous power. Misusing sex—making it into something trivial, self-centered, and destructive of the family—is a violation akin to sacrilege.

The Bible is clear on the subject. "The body is not meant for sexual immorality," says the apostle Paul, "but for the Lord, and the Lord for the body" (1 Cor. 6:13). Notice that the prohibition against sexual immorality is *not* a rejection of the body in favor of being "spiritual." Rather, the body is "for the Lord." Not only that, "the Lord" is "for the body." The Lord made, sustains, and cares for our physical natures. Sexual immorality is described here as a violation of our bodies, a sin against what the body *means*.

The apostle continues, underscoring the point that sexual immorality is not valuing the body too much, but valuing it too little. "Every other sin a person commits is outside the body, but the sexually immoral person sins against his own body" (1 Cor. 6:18).

Paul had in mind the gnostics at Corinth who rejected the physical realm—to the point of rejecting the creation, its Creator, Christ's incarnation, his bodily death, and his physical resurrection—in favor of an elaborate hyperspirituality. Ironically, while some gnostics practiced an extreme asceticism, others felt free to indulge in sexual vice. This is because, in their way of thinking, "the body just doesn't matter." What they did in and with their bodies had no bearing on their true spiritual identity, a view that has also become common today. Gnosticism, of course, has come back big-time in the twenty-first century, both explicitly as an alternative religion, and implicitly as a continuing heresy in the church.[3] Paul will have none of that. He repeats the "one flesh" teaching that we have discussed, saying that we ought not to become one flesh with prostitutes (1 Cor. 6:16). Then he says that when we are joined to God, we have a similar unity with him: "But he who is joined to the Lord becomes one spirit with him" (1 Cor. 6:17). And the locus of this unity is *the body*. "Or do you not know that your body is a temple of the Holy Spirit within you, whom you have from God? You are not your own, for you were bought with a price. So glorify God in your body" (1 Cor. 6:19–20). Because the Holy Spirit indwells the believer—specifically, the believer's *body*—we are literally temples, physical structures in which God is actually present.

This passage also completely dismantles the rationalization that we keep hearing over and over again today: "But it's my body. I should be able to do what I want with my own body." No, it isn't your body. You didn't bring it into existence and you don't own it. God does. In fact, "you were bought with a price" (6:20); that is, the blood of Christ (1 Pet. 1:18–19). Therefore, God has every say over what you do with "your" body; especially since, as Paul develops later in the epistle, if you are a Christian incorporated into his church, you are also part of "his" body (1 Cor. 12:12–27).

Thus, because sexual immorality is sin against the body and against the Holy Spirit, it must be evaded at all costs. "Flee from sexual immorality" (1 Cor. 6:18). Run away from it, as Joseph did when Potiphar's wife tried to seduce him (Genesis 39). Avoid letting yourself even be in a situation that could lead to sexual sin, as in Solomon's warnings against adultery and "the forbidden woman" (Prov. 6:20–7:27).

But what is the cure for sexual immorality? How, exactly, can it be avoided, given the strength of sexual passion and desire? Paul treats this in the next chapter of his epistle: "Because of the temptation to sexual immorality, each man should have his own wife and each woman her own husband" (1 Cor. 7:2). Marriage is the cure for sexual sin.

Paul does say that "it is good for a man not to have sexual relations with a woman" (1 Cor. 7:1). Singleness, like marriage, is a divine gift. When the disciples heard Christ's teaching against divorce, they thought the high view of marriage that Jesus was insisting upon was too difficult. "If such is the case of a man with his wife," they concluded, "it is better not to marry" (Matt. 19:10). And Jesus did not disagree with them: "But he said to them, 'Not everyone can receive this saying, but only those to whom it is given. For there are eunuchs who have been so from birth, and there are eunuchs who have been made eunuchs by men, and there are eunuchs who have made themselves eunuchs for the sake of the kingdom of heaven. Let the one who is able to receive this receive it'" (Matt. 19:11–12). Both marriage and singleness are states that are "given" by God. They are gifts. Jesus's teachings about marriage are not to be "received" by those who do not have that calling. Not everyone has sexual desires, which is presumably what Jesus meant with the imagery of "eunuchs," including those who sacrifice them for the kingdom of God. But such celibacy is also a gift to be received, not a commandment. Those who do have sexual desires that go beyond the disciplines of self-control evidently do not have the gift of celibacy.[4] While Paul values very highly the single state and evidently was so gifted himself, he is forthright about those who do have strong sexual desires: "But if they cannot exercise self-control, they should marry. For it is better to marry than to burn with passion" (1 Cor. 7:9). This sounds very unromantic. How crass! Getting married for sex—rather than loftier reasons such as romantic love, spiritual communion between a man and a woman, and the civilized benefits of a happy family—sounds unworthy of the noble state of matrimony.

Paul's recommendation for marriage is not at all for the reasons we might expect. He might have encouraged people to get married in order to have children, what with the necessity of propagating the species and the importance of caring for children in a two-parent family. He might have drawn on Genesis, saying that it is not good for man to be alone, emphasizing the need for a "helpmate." He might have talked about God's institution of the family as the basis for all culture. Instead, he says that people should get married "because of the temptation to sexual immorality" and so that they will not have to "burn with passion."

Paul's recommendation for dealing with sexual sin is also unexpected. He advocates "self-control," but for those who cannot manage that, he does not stress abstinence. He does not give advice for extinguishing the fires of passion—working out at the *gymnasium,* contemplating diseases, or plunging into the *frigidarium* at the Roman baths. Rather, Paul says that those passions should be satisfied in marriage.

Paul's directive is morally lucid. Scripture defines sexual immorality as sex outside of marriage. Therefore, the ultimate way to attain sexual morality is sex within marriage. His directive is also pastoral, realistic, and compassionate: You do not need to be ascetic, denying yourself and suppressing your God-given desires. Get married.

We realize that it is not that simple, especially today. If you want to get married—as opposed to burning—how do you find someone who will marry you, or who will be good for you to marry? In Paul's time and through much of the world's history and in most of the world's cultures, if you wanted to get married, you would tell your parents, and they would arrange a good match. In our time and in our culture, each person is on his or her own to find a spouse. We do not make this easy.

Adolescence, the awkward age of being mature sexually but still treated as a child, is a modern invention.[5] It used to be that when young people were sexually ready, they were married. Now, we make them wait until they are out of their teens, have finished college, and are established in their careers. This means a protracted period of time—when the fires of passion are at their highest—when they are not supposed to have sex or to get married. During this decade or two, it is little wonder that young people fall into sexual sin. Many young people, inflamed further by a sexually charged pop culture, just give in to their sexual desires. Even among Christian young people and others who take vows of abstinence, many eventually break those vows.[6]

If we were serious about promoting the sexual morality of young people, we would encourage and facilitate earlier marriages.[7] Not because sexual morality is the only consideration for entering into marriage, but because it is one so commonly, if absurdly, overlooked. If the culture—or the church—were serious about combating sexual immorality, we would make it easier for men and women to find each other, moving away from the dating culture to a renewal of family courtship customs (as some Christians are doing), to intentional matchmaking efforts (as is happening online), and to the cultivation of true communities in which men and women can form personal ties in a natural, supportive way (as some churches are attempting).

Do realize that we are not denying the necessity of abstinence and the discipline of celibacy before marriage. The point is simply that the biblical answer to extramarital sex is marital sex. The former is a sin; the latter is a good work. It is the defining mark of the vocation of marriage.

Loving and Serving Sexually

Is it possible to sin sexually with one's own spouse? This was an ancient question in the church. The answer usually given was yes. The theologians spoke of "concupiscence," the notion that human desires by their very nature are tainted with sin. This means that sexual desires of every kind—even for one's spouse—have a primal impurity. When a husband and a wife use the evil of lust for the good purpose of propagating children, this is not sinful, said Augustine. But to have sex without the intention of having a baby is sinful, though it is only a minor, non-condemning "venial" sin.[8]

Part of the problem of drawing on the church's history of teaching about sex is that for many centuries the church had lost the doctrine of vocation. Virtually all of the theologians were clergymen of one kind or another, and up until the Reformation, this status required the vow of celibacy. Thus, they labored under the disciplines of fighting their sexual desires, which in light of their vows, would indeed lead them to sin. Marriage was not an option for them. If they married, that too would be a sin, a so-thought deadly violation of their clerical vows. So they tended to operate with the assumption that sex is bad in itself, as indeed, it would be for them. Add in the climate of neo-Platonism, which assumed that the physical realm is inferior to the nonmaterial realm, and the unfavorable stance of the early and medieval church to sex is understandable.

But this does not seem to accord with the teachings of Scripture. "Because of the temptation to sexual immorality, each man should have his own wife and each woman her own husband" (1 Cor. 7:2). Marriage is presented as a way to avoid sexual immorality, not as another occasion for sexual immorality. Moreover, the "one flesh" unity of husband and wife, with its clear connection to sexual union, is commended in Scripture. Furthermore, with the exception of Genesis 4:1 (which we will discuss later), the Bible generally addresses sex within marriage and having children separately. Scripture does not condition the one-flesh union or the moral satisfaction of sexual passions on begetting children.

It is dangerous to disagree with a theologian of the stature of St. Augustine, so let us agree with him on this: it is possible to sin sexually with one's spouse. Sexual desires are indeed tainted by the concupiscence of the fall. But sinning sexually with one's spouse happens only when the vocation is not fulfilled but violated. Again, the purpose of every vocation is to love and serve the neighbor. In the vocation of marriage, husbands and wives are to love and serve each other. It is certainly possible to use sex to violate this love and service. A man who uses his wife sexually against her will—for example, forcing her to do something he saw in a pornographic movie that she does not want to do—is not loving and serving her. He is sinning against her and against his vocation.

This is another manifestation of the sin that plagues all vocations: wanting to be served, rather than to serve.[9] And yet, just as marriage is the solution to sexual immorality, the Bible spells out a solution to sexual immorality within marriage. Not only to the misuse of one's spouse, but also to the other temptations that even married people are susceptible to: not only overt adultery, but mental adultery (Matt. 5:27–28) in all of its guises, from pornographic indulgence to sinful fantasies. Let us return to 1 Corinthians 7: "The husband should give to his wife her conjugal rights, and likewise the wife to her husband. For the wife does not have authority over her own body, but the husband does. Likewise the husband does not have authority over his own body, but the wife does. Do not deprive one another, except perhaps by agreement for a limited time, that you may devote yourselves to prayer; but then come together again, so that Satan may not tempt you because of your lack of self-control" (1 Cor. 7:3–5).

This describes a profound mutuality when it comes to sex. The husband has authority over the body of his wife—the ancient world would have had no problem with that. But, at the same time, in a concept unprecedented for the ancient world, the wife has authority over the body of her husband. Neither should deny the other sexually. If they both agree, they might resolve not to have sex "for a limited time" in a kind of sexual fast. "But then come together again." Otherwise, Satan will be at work, bringing temptation and exploiting the spouses' weaknesses.

This is also a description of vocation, of the husband and the wife both loving and serving each other sexually. They both employ the lawful sex of marriage to save the other from sexual immorality. The wife loves and serves her husband by satisfying his sexual desires. The husband loves and serves his wife by satisfying her sexual desires. Neither is fixated on self-satisfaction, but on satisfying the other. But both thereby receive satisfaction.

This is neither patriarchy nor feminism. If this is a strange teaching for the ancient world, in which men dominated women, it is no less strange today. The model now is autonomy. The husband expects the wife to "meet his needs," and the wife expects the husband to "meet her needs." But the biblical and vocational model is about self-denial and meeting the other person's needs.

But can't this be abused? If the husband is sex crazy, surely the wife should not have to give in to him every time he wants her. But if the husband is loving and serving his wife, he will be considerate even of her desire not to have sex. She will try to please him, even at the sacrifice of her will, but he will also try to please her, even at the sacrifice of his will. The two will have to work out their sexual relationship in active consideration of each other.

But they must not "deprive one another." As the stewards of each other's bodies, they feel a responsibility for the sexual morality of their spouse. Sexual temptations have little allure to those who are sexually satiated, just as emotional flirtations are less tempting to those emotionally served. And when the husband is concerned above all to please his wife sexually, and his wife is concerned above all to please her husband sexually, both experience the highest level of pleasure and fulfillment.

Conclusion

Sex is difficult to talk about, as you may have noticed in this chapter. Sex is so hedged around with taboos—like other powerful, mysterious, even sacred things—that we lack a language for it. All of our words that have to do with this primal passion and need are either obscene (meaning not to be uttered in public) or they are euphemisms (meaning expressions that avoid naming the thing directly). Even seemingly neutral words are actually euphemisms. "Sex" technically refers simply to biological gender. "Intercourse" means "conversation." "Making love" is a romantic euphemism, which used to mean simply "courting" or "flirting." (Keep that in mind when reading nineteenth-century novels, which are not as steamy as they sound today when they speak of couples "making love in the parlor"; rather, that expression could be said with complete Victorian propriety.) Even the obscene words are euphemisms, of a sort; they are technically "dysphemisms," words that make things sound worse than they are. The most offensive obscene word for sex derives from an ancient word meaning to strike or beat up, perhaps an association with rape.

But the Bible uses a different kind of language and a different kind of imagery: "Now Adam knew Eve his wife, and she conceived and bore Cain, saying, 'I have gotten a man with the help of the LORD'" (Gen. 4:1). The husband *knew* his wife.

The English Standard Version, used here, like the King James Version and other literal translations like the New American Standard Version, preserves the Hebrew metaphor. Something is missing in the translations that try to put the Bible into contemporary English by translating "meanings" rather than the language. The Holman Christian Standard Bible keeps the metaphor but adds a coy adverb: "Adam knew his wife Eve intimately." The New International Version (1984) uses a strangely old-fashioned euphemism: "Adam lay with his wife Eve." *The Message* uses a related euphemism: "Adam slept with Eve his wife." The New

Living Translation is clinical: "Now Adam had sexual relations with his wife." The New Jerusalem Bible is even more so: "The man had intercourse with his wife Eve." Today's New International Version tries to be romantic, while ending on a clinical note: "Adam made love to his wife Eve, and she became pregnant." The Contemporary English Version leaves out the embarrassing sex stuff altogether: "Adam and Eve had a son." The very difficulty modern translators have with these lines—the primness, the prudishness—demonstrates the difficulty Christians have with sex today, having forgotten the doctrine of vocation.

But if the words of the Bible are inspired, surely its metaphors are also. And Christians should certainly not presume to have more propriety than the Bible. Adam and Eve "knew" each other. The word expresses perfectly the unity, the intimacy, and the familiarity that exists between two people in the vocation of marriage. Their knowing each other defines their sexual relationship, but it is much more than that. A man and wife live together, go through trials together, and raise a family together. And so they come to know each other better than any other human being—better than friends, better than parents. This includes knowing each other sexually, knowing the other's needs, desires, and limits.

7

The Crosses of Marriage

As the ark of the LORD came into the city of David, Michal the daughter of Saul looked out of the window and saw King David leaping and dancing before the LORD, and she despised him in her heart.

2 SAMUEL 6:16

Vocation, according to the old theologians, is also where we bear our crosses.[1] So since marriage is a vocation, we should not be surprised or disillusioned to find ourselves bearing crosses in marriage. But what does that mean? We usually think of our crosses as some kind of suffering, especially suffering that we cannot do anything about. "That is the cross I have to bear" is a statement of fatalism and grim resignation. But surely in the New Testament the cross has a far more specific meaning than that.

Consider the text where the saying comes from: "If anyone would come after me," said Jesus, "let him deny himself and take up his cross and follow me" (Matt. 16:24). Taking up the cross has to do with self-denial. That is, it has to do with sacrifice. This does not mean that followers of Christ must sacrifice themselves for their sins. Christ has offered, once and for all, the only sacrifice necessary for the forgiveness of sins. On the cross, he became both our High Priest and the sacrificial victim (Hebrews 9–10). And yet Jesus says here that his followers will have personal crosses of their own. These must be related to what the apostle Paul says after explaining the saving work of the cross to the Roman Christians: "Present your bodies as a living sacrifice" (Rom. 12:1).

There are many occasions for Christians to deny themselves and to offer themselves as living sacrifices, and this certainly applies to every vocation. Again, the purpose of vocation is to love and serve the neighbor. That involves denying oneself in order to put the neighbor first. Every act of love and service is thus a living sacrifice. Since Christ dwells in believers and their vocations, our sacrifices and our crosses are taken into his. Notice how the apostle Paul defines love in terms of both Christ's sacrifice and our own: "Walk in love, as Christ loved us and gave himself up for us, a fragrant offering and sacrifice to God" (Eph. 5:2).

Just as Christ sacrificed himself for us, in vocation, we sacrifice ourselves for our neighbors. Many of these sacrifices are small, and our self-offerings are joyful and satisfying. But these sacrifices can also be enormously difficult and painful. Christ's cross certainly was one of suffering, and at least some of our crosses may be as well.

All of this is true in the vocations of the family. This book draws out what God is calling us to in the different family offices. But we will also comment on at least some of the conflicts and problems that arise in these vocations. Please understand, though, that we will not necessarily be able to eliminate the conflicts and solve the problems. They are crosses that are inherent to the vocations. For example, even the best marriage ends with the cross of death. A problem is something to solve; a cross is something to bear.

Some Christians have the expectation that they should not have any difficulties in their families, and if they do—that is, when they do—they assume that there must be something wrong with their faith or their morals, or with the faith and morals of their spouse. It may be that the embarrassingly high divorce rate among conservative Christians comes at least in part from this perfectionism. When they find themselves arguing with their spouses or falling short of complete happiness in their marriages, they become disillusioned and want to leave and start over, seeking another chance for that perfect Christian marriage. But there must be no illusion in vocation.

Differences

The husband and the wife are distinct human beings, with different personalities, beliefs, feelings, and desires. And yet they are brought into the unity of marriage. Thus, the differences between them—which would mean nothing if they were simply the differences between acquaintances or even friends—can become distressing and hurtful. The differences find expression in disagreement and then in conflict. Couples fight over money. After all, due to their marital unity, they hold their bank accounts in common, and yet they differ about priorities in spending. They fight over sex, over in-laws, even over dishes. Often, a single decision is necessary—Where shall we live? What shall we do today?—and yet the couple has two distinct wills.

So how can the couple resolve their differences when they need to act in their marriage as one? If they are Christians, they might try to apply the scriptural teaching that the wife is to submit to her husband (Eph. 5:22). Some women may do so easily and gladly. Other women, though—and even the first group on some issues—might submit, but they resent having to do so, storing up bitterness against their husbands and sometimes against God, whose Word seems to subjugate them. This syndrome is intensified when husbands lord it over their wives, flaunting their authority, ordering their wives to obey, and making artificial demands just to test their wives' submission. The phenomenon of overbearing husbands and resentful wives is surely another factor that contributes to Christians' high divorce rate.

The unity of marriage does require wives to submit to their husbands, but it also and at the same time requires husbands to "love your wives, as Christ loved the church and gave himself up for her" (Eph. 5:25). When husbands do not treat their wives in a loving and Christlike way, when they do not give themselves up for their wives, they are sinning against their wives, their vocation, and God's command. Of course, sometimes the husband *does* give himself up for his wife—denying his own beliefs and desires for her sake—but instead of submitting to him, she takes his self-denial for weakness and dominates him. This, in turn, makes the husband resentful and bitter, another contribution to the divorce rate.

God's design for marriage requires *both* the wife's submission *and* the husband's giving himself up—at the same time. Both deny themselves, sacrificing their own desires for the other, but both thereby have their desires met. But, a rationalist or a utilitarian might ask, How does that work? Doesn't that just result in a stalemate, a stasis of mutual giving in? "We'll do what you want." "No, we'll do what *you* want." "No, I just want you to be happy." "But I just want *you* to be happy." And nothing gets done and no one is happy.

In reality—as is evident in most actual marriages—the couple *just work it out*. The husband does not insist on his own desires but is considerate of what his wife needs. And she does not insist on her own desires but is considerate of what he needs. Together, they find a way forward. It may be that one of them has a weakness or an issue that is especially urgent, whereupon the other gladly gives in. Or perhaps they discover that one of them really doesn't care that much after all, or that they can find a solution that works for them both, or they compromise. Or maybe there is no solution, but one of them ends up getting his or her way, and the other just accepts it in a spirit of resignation and mutual respect. The point is—they work it out together.

It is easier for a wife to submit to her husband when he is acting in a Christlike way toward her. And it is easier for a husband to be Christlike to his wife when he knows that she will submit, church-like, to him. In that God-given unity, that back and forth, they help each other to fulfill their callings.

Unequally Yoked

The big problems, of course, come when only one of them plays a biblical role. How does a wife get her husband to be Christlike and sacrificial to her? How does a husband get his wife to be submissive? Nagging and demanding clearly do nothing but make the conflict worse. The problem is compounded when the two do not share a common faith. And yet the Bible addresses this issue.

The apostle Paul admonishes, "Do not be unequally yoked with unbelievers" (2 Cor. 6:14). Though this text is often used to discourage Christians from marrying non-Christians, the immediate context makes no reference to marriage. "For what partnership has righteousness with lawlessness? Or what fellowship has light with darkness? What accord has Christ with Belial? Or what portion does a believer share with an unbeliever?" (2 Cor. 6:14–15). As a general principle, the text emphasizes the incompatability of belief and unbelief, righteousness and lawlessness, light and darkness, Christ and false gods. Still, marriage is surely one of those "partnerships" that poses profound difficulties when being "unequally yoked."

Nevertheless, the apostle does not exclude the possibility of believers being married to unbelievers:

> If any brother has a wife who is an unbeliever, and she consents to live with him, he should not divorce her. If any woman has a husband who is an unbeliever, and he consents to live with her, she should not divorce him. For the unbelieving husband is made holy because of his wife, and the unbelieving wife is made holy because of her husband. Otherwise your children would be unclean, but as it is, they are holy. But if the unbelieving partner separates, let it be so. In such cases the brother or sister is not enslaved. God has called you to peace. For how do you know, wife, whether you will save your husband? Or how do you know, husband, whether you will save your wife? (1 Cor. 7:12–16).

Believers should not divorce an unbelieving spouse because of his or her unbelief. And yet, an unbelieving spouse might divorce the believer. If this happens, the believer is free and is apparently allowed to remarry. Again, the unity of marriage is not absolutely indissoluble. But the unity of marriage is real, to the point that "the unbelieving husband is made holy because of his wife, and the unbelieving wife is made holy because of her husband" (v. 14). Remember that in marriage, the two individuals become one flesh. This unity is not restricted to a Christian marriage. But the couple's corporate identity is such that the faith of either one of the spouses is enough to make the other spouse, as well as their children, "holy."

What, exactly, does that mean? The Scripture is not altogether clear, but being "holy," in the case of children, is contrasted with being "unclean." Clearly, a family has a special status before God if even one member is a Christian. Does this mean that the unbelieving spouse is "saved"? No. Salvation comes from faith in Christ. But this passage suggests that there is a good possibility that the unbelieving spouse might come to a saving faith as a member of this "holy" family. "For how do you know, wife, whether you will save your husband? Or how do you know, husband, whether you will save your wife?" (v. 16).

How can a Christian win over an unbelieving spouse? This is addressed by another apostle, Peter: "Likewise, wives, be subject to your own husbands, so that even if some do not obey the word, they may be won without a word by the conduct of their wives, when they see your respectful and pure conduct" (1 Pet. 3:1–2). The apostle Peter is saying that the wife's conduct—her respect, even for an unbelieving husband, and her purity—may "win" her non-Christian husband to the faith. Even, remarkably, without saying anything. The apostle Peter goes on:

> Do not let your adorning be external—the braiding of hair and the putting on of gold jewelry, or the clothing you wear—but let your adorning be the hidden person of the heart with the imperishable beauty of a gentle and quiet spirit, which in God's sight is very precious. For this is how the holy women who hoped in God used to adorn themselves, by submitting to their own husbands, as Sarah obeyed Abraham, calling him lord. And you are her children, if you do good and do not fear anything that is frightening. (1 Pet. 3:3–6)

Parts of this text are often wrenched out of context, turned into a rule about what women should or should not wear. But the context has to do with how wives might win over their husbands who "do not obey the word" (v. 1), which must apply to both unbelief, rejecting the gospel, and immorality, refusing to follow God's law. Apparently, it is sometimes possible for a wife to get through to a nonbelieving or sinful husband by her radical self-sacrifice and cross bearing. This is not a matter of outward appearance but of cultivating "a gentle and quiet spirit" (v. 4). Her intentional submission and the respect she shows to her unworthy husband can provoke a response in him. It is as if, by playing the role of the church to him, she might call forth the Christ, who is hidden in the husband's office, so that the husband can know him.

This is indeed asking much of the woman. Some might say, too much. How can she be expected to suffer in meek submission to an ungodly husband? We will address the most extreme cases shortly. Certainly a Christian woman in this situation is truly enduring the cross, actually suffering to redeem her sinful husband. The only way she can do so is in faith. That last clause is especially curious and far reaching: "Do not fear anything that is frightening" (v. 6). There is indeed much to be frightened of—her vulnerability to her godless husband, the difficulties of her marriage, the possibility that he might never be converted despite everything—and yet she has Christ's promises: "In the world you will have tribulation. But take heart; I have overcome the world" (John 16:33). "Fear not, daughter of Zion; behold, your king is coming" (John 12:15).

The apostle Peter goes on to address husbands: "Likewise, husbands, live with your wives in an understanding way, showing honor to the woman as the weaker vessel, since they are heirs with you of the grace of life, so that your prayers may not be hindered" (1 Pet. 3:7). We already mentioned this passage in the chapter on husbands, but as a parallel to the verses immediately before it, could this be a similar instruction to husbands on how they might win over wives who are "weaker" in faith and good works? Here the husband is responding to his wife in a Christlike way, honoring her in her very weakness, treating her as an heir of grace. Again, much is asked of the husband. He must sacrifice himself for his wife in all of her weakness. And because he bears the role of Christ, he is judged severely if he does not carry out that role—God will not hear his prayers. But it is clear that the husband, too, must bear the cross for his wife. By playing Christ to his unbelieving wife, the husband may bring out the church in her, helping her to know the Christ who inhabits his vocation.

Satanic Marriages

The connection of marriage to Christ and the church seems intrinsic to its institution and applies to all marriages, not just those of Christians. As we have just seen, one believing spouse makes the entire family holy. It is possible for the believing spouse, in the faithful exercise of his or her vocation, to "save" the unbelieving partner. And yet, the unbelieving partner may want no part of this holiness.

In the very text in which the apostle Paul talks about the Christian spouse making the unbelievers in the family holy with the possibility of bringing them to faith, he admits that the unbeliever may want out of a spiritual unity like that: "But if the unbelieving partner separates, let it be so. In such cases the brother or sister is not enslaved. God has called you to peace" (1 Cor. 7:15). The unbelieving spouse may repudiate completely his or her calling, perhaps especially as the presence of Christ and the church are disclosed in the relationship.

A husband who does not "obey the word" (1 Pet. 3:1) may not follow his God-given vocation at all. That is, he may refuse to act anything like Christ to his wife. Instead of loving and serving her, he harms her. He abuses her. He emotionally torments her. He physically hurts her.

Notice that under the doctrine of vocation, a husband is not called by God to hurt his wife. God called him to be her husband so that he could love and serve her. Therefore, the husband has no authorization to be cruel to his wife. A husband who treats his wife in this way is violating his vocation. It does no good for the husband to claim his authority and demand that his wife submit to him. The only authority in vocation comes from God (Rom. 13:1), and an authority in the service of sin, who refuses to be "God's servant for your good" (Rom. 13:4) and rebels against his will, is no authority at all. In the specific vocation of marriage, husbands are to emulate Christ. If the husband harms his wife—something Christ never does to his church—he is emulating not Christ but Satan.

Satan does harm the church, as well as everyone outside the church. He is cruel. He abuses us. He accuses us. Instead of loving and serving, Satan hates and dominates. All sin, of course, is satanic, partaking of his pride, his self-centeredness, his rebellion, and his malice. But if a husband sins against his wife to the point of there being nothing left of Christ in his office, he may become a little Satan to her. In that case, no one is being a husband to her, and—in our opinion—she would be right to leave the marriage.

More than wanting to hurt, Satan wants to corrupt and to damn. In addition to physically abusive marriages, there are morally and spiritually abusive marriages. Some husbands want to corrupt their wives morally. There is a whole subculture of wife swapping and multiple-partner orgies. Some husbands pimp their wives or turn them into subjects of pornography. A husband who pressures his wife into such practices is trying to cause her to commit adultery, thus breaking her own marital union with him! There are some husbands and some wives who make their spouses complicit in other sins, such as child abuse and other overt crimes.

Some husbands and some wives are harmful to their spouses spiritually. They pressure them to join cults or abandon the Christian faith for a different religion. Less dramatically but still perniciously, they might prevent a Christian spouse from going to church.

Recall that the calling of the husband is to parallel Christ in working for the sanctification of the wife: "Husbands, love your wives, as Christ loved the church and gave himself up for her, that he might sanctify her, having cleansed her by the washing of water with the word, so that he might present the church to himself in splendor, without spot or wrinkle or any such thing, that she might be holy and without blemish" (Eph. 5:25–27).

There can be no divine approval of a marriage that renders the wife unclean and unholy, or that wrenches her from her baptism and from God's Word. In such cases, in our opinion, she would be right to leave the marriage. This might even be an act of sacrificial, loving service on her part: removing from the husband the occasion and the temptation to continue in sin. And perhaps such radical surgery might wake him up to his bondage to Satan and to his need for a Savior.

We have been talking about husbands who act like Satan to their wives. Wives can also act like Satan to their husbands, though the analogy cannot be so exact. Christ loves and sacrifices for the church precisely in its sinfulness. Husbands should not abandon a wife just because of her sins. It is his responsibility to bring her to holiness if he possibly can. But in the 1 Corinthians passage we have been quoting, the apostle Paul applies his principles to both sexes, saying that "the unbelieving wife" is being made holy by her believing husband, as well as vice versa, and that "the brother or sister" is not bound to the marriage if the "unbelieving partner separates" (1 Cor. 7:12–16). So evidently, just as a person can reject Christ and his sacrifice, a wife can reject the Christ in her husband, despite his sacrifices for her.

In positing the category of a satanic marriage, we do not wish to pro-vide yet another excuse to justify divorce. Such overtly evil or spiritually harmful marriages are extremely rare. Again, Scripture allows Christians to be married to non-Christians. Even when both spouses are unbeliev-ers, God's working in marriage remains, and the connection to Christ and the church still holds. Even a neglectful, unbelieving, sinful hus-band is likely in some way to act as Christ to his wife. And a neglectful, unbelieving, sinful wife is certainly acting like the church to Christ.

Luther, the great theologian of vocation, believed that marriage has a power of its own. So often, husbands and wives are kind and good to each other, not because they feel like it, but simply because something within marriage compels them. The "station" of marriage itself acts as an ethi-cal agent to lessen selfishness for the sake of the spouse.[2] Not because marriage suddenly stops sin dead in its tracks—it doesn't—but marriage itself can and does play a real and legitimate role as one of God's tools for preserving and sustaining creation by creating a civil righteousness even among unbelievers.[3]

And again, Scripture says that a Christian wife can make her nonbelieving husband holy, with the possibility of eventually bringing him to faith; and a Christian husband can make his nonbelieving wife holy, with the possibility of bringing her to faith (1 Cor. 7:14, 16). What we are calling a satanic marriage is one that threatens to make the believing spouse unholy and that undermines the believing spouse's faith. A satanic marriage is one that is harmful to the spouse's body or soul. A satanic spouse, in this sense, has violated the calling and thus broken the marital union. This would seem to constitute a separation such as the apostle Paul addresses: "But if the unbelieving partner separates, let it be so. In such cases the brother or sister is not enslaved. God has called you to peace" (1 Cor. 7:15).

Remember that the word "call" in Scripture speaks of vocation. It is not that vocations, such as marriage, always involve "peace," or that the lack of "peace" means an absence of vocation. But even in times of cross bearing, callings from God point ultimately to the gospel, which brings the peace from sins forgiven, including the sins of broken marriages. Leaving a satanic marriage may well be a case of leaving "house or wife or brothers or parents or children, for the sake of the kingdom of God" (Luke 18:29).

Unhappy Marriages

Of course, most marriages that are unhappy—and most marriages that end in divorce—do not involve such dramatic violations of vocation. Christian psychologist Beverly Yahnke describes the majority of the troubled marriages she deals with in poignant terms:

> The single most frequent suffering that I observe in my clinical practice is two people living in a marriage that appears to have died long ago; two people, each empty, each living in an orbit apart from the spouse, living lives of whispered resentment and disappointment. They are enslaved to their history of hurts. They recite to one another the injustices each has suffered at the hands of the other. After years of exchanging those litanies, silence is all that they continue to share. These are people who are perpetually grieving for the Godly marriage that might have been. These are people who have grown weary of pretending.[4]

The familiarity that comes from years of marriage can bring greater and greater intimacy, but it can also breed contempt. Couples stop respecting each other. They stop loving each other. They stop serving each other.

Their dissatisfaction with each other is often accompanied with the sense that they could do better, that they could be happy with some-one else. Christian marriage counselor Michael Eschelbach observes, "Every temptation has this thought in common: 'God is hiding a better life from you; you could do better if you would choose/act for yourself.' Listening to that temptation has and is still killing everyone and every marriage."[5] Sometimes this temptation leads to overt adultery—or to the mental adulteries that also damage the union of marriage (Matt. 5:28): illicit sexual fantasies, Facebook flirtations, indulgence in pornography. In the meantime, the petty annoyances and dissatisfactions of everyday life keep building. Often couples get a divorce, with one or both think-ing they will find the happiness and fulfillment they crave with another partner, only to find the same syndromes reoccurring in their new marriages.

Such problems are not, of course, limited to bad and broken mar-riages. Even when couples love each other deeply, there are still mis-communications, annoyances, disagreements, and problems. Every marriage experiences forms of tension and inner boiling. Even in solid, committed marriages, such discord and frustration are draining and discouraging.

We might assume that these kinds of marital discord are unique to our own time. But they seem to be universal. The Bible itself speaks of them. Michal was King David's first wife and at first she loved him so much that she risked her life and defied her father and king for his sake (1 Sam. 19:11–17). David loved her, too. He fought bravely at war to pay the steep and bloody bride-price her father, Saul, asked (1 Sam. 18:20–27). Still, when trials arose in their marriage, and they did more than once, her heart fell to contempt. "As the ark of the Lord came into the city of David, Michal the daughter of Saul looked out of the window and saw King David leaping and dancing before the Lord, and she despised him in her heart" (2 Sam. 6:16). Her embarrassment at her husband's zeal led to their permanent estrangement (6:23).

David's son—with Bathsheba, with whom he committed adultery (and for whom murder)—was the wisest of men, but even Solomon's wisdom did not result in good marriages. His grotesque polygamy (he married seven-hundred wives!) combined with insatiable unfaithful-ness (he had three-hundred concubines!) was a travesty of God's inten-tions for marriage (1 Kings 11:3). And those wives were more than sexual playthings. Instead of King Solomon leading them to know the true God, they "turned away his heart after other gods, and his heart was not wholly true to the LORD his God" (1 Kings 11:4).

One hopes that he returned to faith. He must have, since the Holy Spirit lived in him so as to inspire him to write two books of the Bible. Inspired by the Holy Spirit, Solomon wrote the book of Ecclesiastes, which looks back on a vain, wasted life from an eternal perspective, and the book of Proverbs, which says much about marriage, as well as other vocations. Solomon there praises the "excellent wife" (Prov. 12:4; 31:10–31), but he also describes the misery of marital sniping and arguing. "It is better to live in a corner of the housetop than in a house shared with a quarrelsome wife" (Prov. 25:24). "A continual dripping on a rainy day and a quarrelsome wife are alike; to restrain her is to restrain the wind or to grasp oil in one's right hand" (Prov. 27:15–16). The constant quarreling goes on and on, like water torture, and seemingly nothing can be done about it.

And yet, the Holy Spirit, speaking through Solomon, tells husbands to "rejoice in the wife of your youth" (Prov. 5:18). The context is a stern warning against committing adultery, of going after a "forbidden woman" and being unfaithful to one's wife (Proverbs 5). Do not scorn or neglect the woman you married when you were young. Rather, look to her and her alone for your sexual pleasure and for your love. "Let her breasts fill you at all times with delight; be intoxicated always in her love" (Prov. 5:19).

This requires a particular perspective. The solution to the numbing drip-drip-drip of marital quarreling and the allure of the honeyed lips of the adulteress, which eventually turn "bitter as wormwood" (Prov. 5:3–4), is to realize the action of God. "He who finds a wife finds a good thing and obtains favor from the LORD" (Prov. 18:22). If a man has found someone to marry him, he is blessed, and God promises him more blessings. Not only that, his wife *is* a blessing from God. "House and wealth are inherited from fathers, but a prudent wife is from the LORD" (Prov. 19:14). The fruits of other vocations are obtained from belonging to his parents' family, but starting a new family is God's work. A man's wife is a direct gift from God. (We are given the male point of view here, from Solomon and the young man he is instructing, but the genders could easily be reversed. A woman's husband is a direct gift from God.)

In the book of Ecclesiastes, Solomon confronts all of the dreariness and frustrations of life. He then concludes with the only possible response to the vanities of existence: "The end of the matter; all has been heard. Fear God and keep his commandments, for this is the whole duty of man" (Eccles. 12:13). That is, turn away from dependence on this world and have faith in God. Second, do his will. That means to do your duty in your vocations, specifically in your work and your marriage: "Enjoy life with the wife whom you love, all the days of your vain life that he has given you under the sun, because that is your portion in life and in your toil at which you toil under the sun. Whatever your hand finds to do, do it with your might" (Eccles. 9:9–10). Embrace what God has given you. Embrace—and enjoy—the "portion in life" that God has assigned you. Do your work and whatever else God gives you to do "with your might." That includes working on your marriage and enjoying your spouse, understanding that you have received your spouse from the hand of God.

This is exactly what Luther, the theologian of vocation, teaches about how we should respond to the difficulties of marriage. "If it weren't for sin, marriage could be a blissful surrender of self to the other," says Paul Althaus, summarizing Luther, "but because of sin 'each seeks to satisfy his desire with the other.'"[6] Luther, in fact, back in the sixteenth century, zeroes in on a condition commonly associated just with our time—couples get bored with each other. Boredom, Luther says, is the work of the Devil: "At first everything goes all right, so that, as the saying goes, they are ready to eat each other up for love. But when their curiosity has been satisfied, then the devil comes along to create boredom in you, to rob you of your desire in this direction, and to excite it unduly in another direction."[7] The Devil can distort marriage to the point "that hate is never so bitter as there."[8]

"Marriages fail because people do not recognize that the marriage estate is created and ordered by God and do not observe his purpose in instituting marriage," says Althaus, summarizing Luther. "As a result, when their marriage is unhappy they become impatient and are not ready to forgive each other. But patience and forgiveness are the most effective defense against the thoughts of divorce."[9]

Happiness in marriage comes when "husband and wife cherish each other, become one, and serve each other."[10] What is needed in marriage is the same mutual love and service that must animate every vocation. "The station of marriage is comprehended in the law of love," says Luther. "For the love among Christians should be the same kind of love as that of every member of the body for every other one . . . each one accepting the faults of the other, sympathizing with them, bearing and removing them, and doing everything possible to help him."[11]

So what is the remedy for feeling bored or dissatisfied with one's spouse? Luther recommends thinking along these lines: "In my wife at home I have a lovelier adornment, one that God has given me and has adorned with his word beyond the others, even though she may not have a beautiful body or may have other failings. Though I may look over all the women in the world, I cannot find any about whom I can boast with a joyful conscience as I can about mine: 'This is the one whom God has granted to me and put into my arms.'"[12] That is to say, God has called you to this woman, and he has called her to you. She is the one whom God has given you. And the same holds for her: she should consider that God has called her to this man, and that he has called him to her. Husbands and wives can realize how precious is their relationship, despite all trials, when they understand that, in their vocations, they are God's gifts to each other.

Conclusion

No conversation about marriage crosses would be complete without addressing the verdicts to Adam and Eve in Genesis 3:

> To the woman he said, "I will surely multiply your pain in childbearing; in pain you shall bring forth children. Your desire shall be for your husband, and he shall rule over you." And to Adam he said, "Because you have listened to the voice of your wife and have eaten of the tree of which I commanded you, 'You shall not eat of it,' cursed is the ground because of you; in pain you shall eat of it all the days of your life; thorns and thistles it shall bring forth for you; and you shall eat the plants of the field. By the sweat of your face you shall eat bread, till you return to the ground, for out of it you were taken; for you are dust, and to dust you shall return.'" (Gen. 3:16–19)

Regarding vocation, we see that the man is going to need more help than ever, yet the woman, his helper, now has her own suffering and complications to think about. The ground is cursed. Work is made hard. And Adam and Eve find themselves a sinner married to another sinner.

Specifically, wives struggle because they are sinners married to sinners, and are also sinners under the authority of a sinful husband. As sinners themselves, wives may resist and strike out against their husbands. Husbands have struggles and temptations as sinners and as sinners with authority over a wife. They may be tempted to abuse or belittle the authority God gave them, authority intended for loving service. Sin is ultimately the reason for discord within marriage—not just the sins of one or the other, but given the one-flesh unity of married couples, sin that entwines and entraps them both. And the solution to sin is forgiveness.

We cannot emphasize enough the centrality of forgiveness within marriage. When God uses marriage language, he is speaking of the gospel, so the passages are replete with forgiveness, emphasizing love and mercy. Marriage is the great proving ground for forgiveness. The greater the intimacy between two people, the greater the knowledge of faults and weakness, and thus the greater the occasions for forgiveness. This is more than a precursory "No harm done; it doesn't matter; no apology needed." Forgiveness exists exactly because harm is done. Something was wrong, but forgiveness allows the relationship to move on. Forgiveness is a huge aspect of our relationships with each other and our relationship with our Lord. In fact, Jesus—who, remember, is present in our neighbor—connects his forgiveness with our forgiving each other. We are to pray, "Forgive us our debts as we also have forgiven our debtors" (Matt. 6:12).

Spouses should make a practice of forgiving each other. But forgiveness, like Christ's forgiveness, must be a free gift. We cannot coerce forgiveness, nor can we presume that anyone is *owed* forgiveness. "Forgiveness that is coerced from the mouth of an adult or child victim meets neither God's requirements for a forgiving heart," says Dr. Yahnke, "nor does it meet very real emotional requirements of readiness. This is particularly true for individuals who have been victims of sexual abuse."[13] We cannot coerce forgiveness, nor can we presume that anyone is *owed* forgiveness.

Spouses should also realize that in this fallen world, not all problems can be solved. A cross cannot be made to disappear by applying some simple formula or technique. A cross has to be borne. Distinguishing between problems and crosses can be very helpful, practically speaking.

A problem, such as a disagreement, may indeed have a solution. But something like grief or a disability or an intransigent characteristic of one's spouse cannot be "fixed" but only borne.

To say that bearing a cross involves accepting suffering does *not* mean, in Dr. Yahnke's words, that "we may falsely bludgeon the sinned against with the glories of suffering."

> The inference is that we should simply deal with any pain privately, suck it up, and move on. I'm reminded that if one member of the Body of Christ suffers, all suffer together. I know for a fact that the phrase, "suck it up" just doesn't appear in many Scriptural concordances because the concept is foreign to our doctrine. . . . There is little gained from elevating suffering to an art form and pronouncing it to be "good." That invites misinterpretation that the power for "good" rests in the experience of suffering rather than in God who works through it. We would be wise not to glorify the pain of the wounded, but instead to glorify God. Otherwise, we adopt a bizarre and fatalistic explanation that God does want us to suffer and we become resigned to the belief that it is God who wills that our pain continue.[14]

Suffering, though, does not have to be borne alone. The hidden blessing of suffering is that it calls forth mercy, that is to say, love. One of the glories of marriage is that it offers daily occasions to "bear one another's burdens, and so fulfill the law of Christ" (Gal. 6:2).

Sin and forgiveness, suffering and love, sacrifice and reconciliation come together and find resolution in the cross. That of Christ, that of vocation, and that of Christ hidden in vocation—this is what it means to bear the cross.

Part 2

The Vocations of Parenthood

8

Parenthood

And when Esau lifted up his eyes and saw the women and children,
he said, "Who are these with you?" Jacob said, "The children whom
God has graciously given your servant."

GENESIS 33:5

When you ask people about their "religious experiences," they often bring up one particular event: when their baby was born. This is true for both mothers and fathers. The delivery room is a place of unparalleled agony and fear and excitement. The woman in labor is indeed laboring, but that is a relatively weak word. The old word "travail" is better: she is in travail. Her body is completely taking over, and her conscious mind has no control over it. Meanwhile, the father in the delivery room is in anguish with sympathy for his wife, which is intensified by his feeling that there is nothing he can do for her. He wants desperately to help her and does whatever he can.

Looming behind the timing of the contractions, the doctors and nurses coming and going, and the often long vigil of labor is the awareness of something that is almost never stated: What is going on in the delivery room is a matter of life or death. Will the baby live? Will the mother live? What if both of them die? The woman in labor is, literally, bearing a cross. She is suffering for her child. She is offering herself as a sacrifice, risking death to bring forth new life. Everyone in the delivery

103

room is too frantic and busy to think about it—except, perhaps, the father—but the stakes could not be higher.

And then, in the midst of this intense human drama, the baby comes. Attention shifts immediately. It's no longer about the pain. As Jesus said, "When a woman is giving birth, she has sorrow because her hour has come, but when she has delivered the baby, she no longer remembers the anguish, for joy that a human being has been born into the world" (John 16:21). According to what Jesus said, childbirth is emblematic of existence itself and the resolution of the maddening problem of suffering in a world presided over by a loving God. As in childbirth, so in our lives after death, our "sorrow" will turn to joy, so much so that our earlier suffering cannot compare with it. "So also you have sorrow now, but I will see you again, and your hearts will rejoice, and no one will take your joy from you" (John 16:22).

The birth of a child is indeed a miracle. One can hardly imagine a greater miracle, akin to creation itself. "A human being has been born into the world!" The baby is a new life, a new immortal soul! Childbirth is commonplace and ordinary, but it is no less miraculous. It is God who creates this immortal soul—and also nourishes it and equips it for heaven—by means of vocation, that is through commonplace and ordinary human beings whom God has called into their office as parents.

Our Flesh and Blood

A man and a woman become one flesh. In doing so, they engender a child, who is made from that flesh and who is part of the fleshly union that constitutes the family. The Bible uses "one flesh" to describe both sex (1 Cor. 6:16) and marriage (Matt. 19:5–6). In God's design, the two amount to the same thing. So then children "share in flesh and blood" with their parents (Heb. 2:14).

In this fallen world of sinful men and women, of course, it is now possible for man to separate the one-flesh union of husband and wife (Matt. 19:6). It is also possible to separate marriage and sex and marriage and having children. (In fact, our new reproductive technology makes it possible to separate any form of sexual activity from having children.) Today it is becoming increasingly common and socially acceptable to have children outside of marriage, so that one can hold the office of father or mother without being a husband or wife. Single parents hold a true and valid vocation from God. The single mother struggling to take care of her child and the single father who may never know his own child both have been used by God to bring a new life into the world. As a result, like it or not, unless the child is adopted into another family, they have a calling from God that brings both authority and responsibilities.

But the very physiology of reproduction demonstrates the connection between the offices of marriage and the offices of parenthood. The father's DNA—in which is encoded every aspect of his body—combines with the mother's DNA, in which is encoded every aspect of her body. The result of this combination is a completely new, individual human being. And yet, the child, while having his or her own uniqueness, nevertheless shares the flesh—quite literally—with the mother and father. The Bible affirms what scientists have discovered: "The children share in flesh and blood" (Heb. 2:14).

This common physical flesh defines a family. The man and the woman are unified in the act of sex—in which, as far as reproduction is concerned, they become a single organism—and they are unified again in the person of their child, who consists of both parents. This one-flesh family goes back through all generations. Parents have parents, and they have parents with parents. All parents pass along themselves to their children along with their DNA. We each are part of a family that goes back through time. We have a lineage, a family tree, which itself has many branches. We can say of every member of our family, including our remotest ancestors whom we may only know by researching our family's history, "You are my flesh and blood."

Everyone's ancestry goes all the way back to our first parents, Adam and Eve. As the apostle Paul told the Athenians, "He made from one man every nation of mankind to live on all the face of the earth, having determined allotted periods and the boundaries of their dwelling place" (Acts 17:26). In this sense, though we have our separate families—with their God-given boundaries—we human beings are all related. We have a corporate identity as a member of a particular family. (The word *corporate* comes from the Latin word for "body.") We also have a corporate identity—a unity of flesh—as a human being.

God often treats us in terms of our corporate identities. His promise to Noah applied not just to that one righteous individual but to his wife, sons, and their wives—to his "household" (Gen. 6:18; 7:1). He told

Abraham that his covenant applied not only to "you" but also to "your offspring after you throughout their generations" (Gen. 17:9).

And our corporate identity with the entire human race as members of Adam's family means that his fall is ours (Romans 5). We have the same flesh that he did. Now our flesh shares in his sin (Rom. 7:18).

And yet, just as we are one with the body of Adam, we can also be one with the body of the second Adam. What Adam lost for us all, Christ has won for us all. "For as by a man came death, by a man has come also the resurrection of the dead. For as in Adam all die, so also in Christ shall all be made alive" (1 Cor. 15:21–22). The apostle Paul goes on to speak of our natural inheritance from Adam and our spiritual inheritance from Christ, so that now we not only have a "natural body" but "a spiritual body."

> If there is a natural body, there is also a spiritual body. Thus it is written, "The first man Adam became a living being"; the last Adam became a life-giving spirit. But it is not the spiritual that is first but the natural, and then the spiritual. The first man was from the earth, a man of dust; the second man is from heaven. As was the man of dust, so also are those who are of the dust, and as is the man of heaven, so also are those who are of heaven. Just as we have borne the image of the man of dust, we shall also bear the image of the man of heaven. (1 Cor. 15:44–49)

In Christ, then, we have yet another corporate—that is, bodily—identity. We are members of Christ's body, which is the church (1 Corinthians 12). This is another kind of family. Our fellow Christians are our "brothers and sisters." We belong to "the household of faith" (Gal. 6:10).

God animates all parenting. As the Creator, he is the ultimate and true Father, who continues to create new life. He does so not out of dust anymore, as he made Adam, but from flesh, as he made Eve; not out of the man's rib but out of the one flesh of both parents.

Adoption

All children come into existence from the one flesh of a man and a woman. And yet this is not the only way a child can come into a family. Nor is it the only way a man and woman can be called into parenthood.

It is possible for someone to be "grafted" into a family, as Gentiles through Christ were grafted into the family of Abraham (Rom. 11:17–24). A branch from one tree can be cut off, an incision made into another tree, and the branch implanted, whereupon the branch and the tree grow together as a single organism. This agricultural technique, used in the ancient world—Paul talks about grafting a "wild olive branch" into a domesticated olive tree—and also today, is an image of adoption. An adopted child belongs to the family union just as the child born into that family does. And the parent who has adopted a child is his or her father or mother just as surely as with a child born from their bodies.

We can say this with certainty because every human vocation takes its shape and its meaning from God, who inhabits each office that he calls people to. For Christians, adoption is the prime model of God's parenthood. As executive director of Lutherans for Life, James Lamb, has observed, "God only has one 'natural' child. He adopted all the rest" (Gal. 4:4–5).[1] That is, Jesus Christ is the "only begotten" Son of God (John 3:16).[2] The rest of us have God as our Father because he adopted us. Thus, the apostle Paul writes, "For all who are led by the Spirit of God are sons of God. For you did not receive the spirit of slavery to fall back into fear, but you have received the Spirit of adoption as sons, by whom we cry, 'Abba! Father!' The Spirit himself bears witness with our spirit that we are children of God, and if children, then heirs—heirs of God and fellow heirs with Christ" (Rom. 8:14-17). The Holy Spirit makes us God's sons by adoption. But this is a genuine sonship. We can cry affectionately to our new Father, and we have all of the rights of inheritance that natural sons have. Moreover, we are "fellow heirs with Christ." That is, we adopted children will inherit what Jesus, the only-begotten Son, inherits! Namely, "the glory that is to be revealed to us" (Rom. 8:18).

Thus, adoption is a powerful image of the gospel. We do not receive the inheritance of everlasting life because of our works but because of our status as God's children, which we share with Jesus. This status was none of our doing. Rather, God chose us to be his children. Just as adopting parents choose the child who will be made a part of their family, so God has chosen us. The apostle Paul makes this connection explicit: "He chose us in him before the foundation of the world, that we should be holy and blameless before him. In love he predestined us for adoption as sons through Jesus Christ, according to the purpose of his will, to the praise of his glorious grace, with which he has blessed us in the Beloved" (Eph. 1:4–6). Even the Israelites, God's chosen people through Abraham, were adopted (Rom. 9:4).

In his book *Adopted for Life: The Priority of Adoption for Christian Families and Churches*, Russell Moore explores the connection between the gospel and the concrete realities of adopting children and being their parents.[3] "You are designed to love 'your own flesh and blood,'" he says, "but your design is redeemed in Christ to see as your flesh and blood those who you previously didn't recognize as such."[4] That we have all been adopted into the family of the church means that our fellow Christians really are our "brothers and sisters." And this understanding of our own status before God means that Christians should be in the forefront of adopting "the fatherless," a group God has a special heart for, as evident throughout Scripture.[5]

Conversely, an adopted child is a gift of God. Those who have adopted children know how true this is. Whether or not a couple has other children, including natural-born children, adoption is one way that the Lord makes a woman "the joyous mother of children. Praise the LORD!" (Ps. 113:9).

Just as the God who created the world and sent his Son to be our Savior adopts from all races, all nations, all physical conditions, and all degrees of brokenness, so can we. Adoption is a way to love and serve one of the approximately 145 million orphans in the world.[6] It is a way to love and serve the young casualties of dysfunctional or oppressive foreign countries. Adoption is also a way to be pro-life at the deepest level and to participate in a particularly powerful earthly image of the gospel.

Our culture naively permits sex outside of the vocation of marriage, leading, by necessity, to untold numbers of women conceiving children and untold numbers of men rejecting their calling to serve as fathers. Abortion is the great sin of our culture, and it is a supreme sin against vocation, with parents pursuing the death of their own children, doctors using their God-given gifts to kill rather than to heal, and governments violating their Romans 13 mandate by refusing to protect the innocent. Adoption gives women with unwanted pregnancies an option to abortion. True, the prevalence of abortion has meant many fewer children to adopt—so that it is often extremely difficult for those who wish to adopt to find a local child—but many mothers draw back from abortion precisely because they know their babies, if they let them live, will find a good home.

Even the woman who gives her child up for adoption holds the office of mother. We can be thankful for every mother, every conception, and every birth, whether that woman is able to mother the child into adulthood. We dare not belittle what God has done through her, conceiving the child and bringing that child into the world. Likewise, whether the two individual parents live and remain together to raise the child need not detract from the fact that God has worked through both of them to bring a new life, a breathing soul, into the world. Sometimes the way to love and serve the child is to make an adoption plan for him or her

Adoption is no less a call to parenthood than conception. The call is to specific parents for a specific child, who is brought into that family as a full member, offered the family name, publicly accepted, and placed under the guidance and authority of his new parents. And it is God who cares for his adopted child by giving him parents of flesh and blood. Thus, a vocation to parenthood for adoptive parents is just as valid as for biological parents.

Controlling Birth?

Thus far we have discussed men and women entering into the calling of parenthood, whether from creating a child from their own bodies or from adopting a child into their family. But what about men and women, husbands and wives, who do not want to be parents, at least not yet, or who do not want to be parents of more children than they already have? Is it legitimate—or is it sinful—to practice birth control? This is a controversial issue, but we can hardly avoid it in a discussion of marriage, sex, and parenting. Thinking about the issue in terms of vocation—rather than seeking blanket prohibitions or permissions—gives us a different way of approaching the questions.

First of all, we can appreciate the force of the Roman Catholic position that condemns all types of birth control except for periods of abstinence. The Roman Catholic Church bases its prohibition not on arbitrary dogmas but on natural law, which is one of the pillars of Catholic ethics. Biologically, sex exists to make children. The entire physiology of sex in its every detail, from the microscopic level to the glands and organs of the reproductive system, are oriented to making babies. There can be no question about that. Roman Catholic ethicists, drawing on Aristotle, teach that anything that interferes with something's purpose is, literally, "unnatural" and thus immoral. Homosexual acts cannot possibly conceive children and so violate the purpose of human sexuality; therefore, they are immoral. The same can be said for birth control pills, condoms, and other technologies for preventing the conception of children. They violate the purpose of sex—which is a particularly good purpose, the creation of new life—and so they are sinful.

The Roman Catholic position is based on reason, not just moralistic rules. Roman Catholics are certainly right about the cultural consequences of generally accepted contraception. Sex really has been separated in people's minds from having children. Thus, it is hard for many people to see what is so wrong with extramarital sex, or homosexuality, or pornography. Sex is just seen as an intense pleasure. Why should it be denied anyone? As far as our contemporary culture is concerned, as we see in the way it is depicted in the entertainment industry, sex is to be pursued with no reference at all to its biological purpose. People speak of "birth *control*," as though conception is something we can control. And when a baby is conceived, despite everything, it comes as a surprise. Or a problem. Or a tragedy. Or a disease. Women with an "unwanted pregnancy" can go to a doctor for an abortion, often funded by the child's own father. Some of the worst evils of our culture can be traced to the unmooring of sex from having children.

So Catholics deserve credit for their analysis. Their position was held by most Christians, including Protestants, throughout history. Since the opposition to contraception is grounded not in revelation but in natural law and reason, even non-Christians should, theoretically, acknowledge its validity. And yet a biblical and vocational ethic approaches the issue differently.

When the Bible directly addresses sex in marriage, it says nothing about doing so to conceive children. Certainly, it relates sex to procreation ("Now Adam knew Eve his wife, and she conceived" [Gen. 4:1]). But the foundational text on marriage that is repeated throughout Scripture ("A man shall leave his father and his mother and hold fast to his wife, and they shall become one flesh" [Genesis 2:24; Matt. 19:5; Mark 10:7; Eph. 5:31]) does not mention children. Nor do the detailed instructions for marriage in Ephesians 5 and 1 Corinthians 7.

The sexual "one flesh" union is said to create a separate family, so that marriage, and not parenting, constitutes the family. Marriage is presented as the cure for sexual immorality, and married couples are commanded to give each other their "conjugal rights" (1 Cor. 7:3). They are not to be celibate. "Do not deprive one another, except perhaps by agreement for a limited time, that you may devote yourselves to prayer; but then come together again, so that Satan may not tempt you because of your lack of self-control" (1 Cor. 7:5).

It sounds as if sex has another purpose, in addition to engendering children: to bind husband and wife together. Sex in marriage is also described as a protection against sin, since Satan otherwise can exploit our "lack of self-control" when it comes to sexual passions. Yes, sex in nature exists for reproduction, but sex for human beings is also profoundly emotional and relational. Biblically, it would seem that sex within the vocation of marriage has moral value in itself. Thus, sex in marriage for the purpose of binding husband and wife together and to finesse sexual immorality would be in accord both with the law of the Bible and with natural law. Sex would not have to be directed to conceiving a baby to fulfill its purpose.

Again, a vocational approach to moral issues recognizes, first, that certain vocations are authorized to do things that may be unlawful outside the vocation. Sex is authorized within marriage and nowhere else. Second, the purpose of vocation is to love and serve the neighbor.

It may sometimes be an act of love and service for the husband *not* to get his wife pregnant. At the same time, it may be an act of love and service for the wife to continue to have sex with her husband. In those situations, as worked out between them, in our opinion, they might practice contraception—nothing that would harm a child they might conceive, not morning-after pills or abortifacients of any kind, but methods that would prevent a conception from ever happening. Conversely, in some cases, using sex only for procreation could possibly harm the unity of marriage. A couple that does not want to have any more children—because they cannot afford them or because the woman's body is exhausted from childbearing—may well simply stop having sex. That would not be good for the marriage. They would not be enacting their "one flesh" union, and the man in particular might well be led into sexual immorality. The couple might agree to abstain for a while as part of a discipline of prayer and fasting, but only "by agreement" and only "for a limited time." "Do not deprive one another," says the Bible. "Come together again" (1 Cor. 7:5).

Here is the bottom line, in our opinion: In general, parenthood follows marriage naturally. Sex in marriage should indeed lead to engendering children. The one-flesh union that is the vocation of marriage leads to the new vocation of parenthood. And yet at some stages of the marriage, use of contraceptives is preferable to restricting sex in such a way that the unity of marriage is harmed or that either partner becomes subject to sexual temptations. It is better to use contraceptives than to burn with passion. A couple's mutual acceptance of some form of contraceptive may be a way for them to love and serve each other: the husband, so that he does not overburden his wife with pregnancies; the wife, so that she continues to satisfy his sexual passions lest they become sinful. Having said that, though, we want to stress that contraception should not be thought of as the norm in marriage.

Begotten, Not Made

Many wives and husbands are struggling with the opposite problem of control: wanting children but not having them. The plight of infertile couples who earnestly yearn to have a baby is poignant and often heartbreaking. They crave the vocation of parenthood. And yet, vocations cannot be summoned at will. They must be received from God's hand. Infertile couples, though, today have the recourse of new technology. They must try to discern, though, whether the new reproductive technologies are gifts of God that can heal their barrenness and make them parents or temptations to evade his will.

Certainly, the Bible shows great sympathy to husbands and wives who are "barren." Abraham and Sarah (Gen. 17:17), Elkanah and Hannah (1 Samuel 1), and Zechariah and Elizabeth (Luke 1:7) suffered in this condition until God miraculously intervened. It is difficult, and can even seem unjust, when many Christians, who are loving and in seemingly ideal situations and would seem to make wonderful parents, cannot get pregnant, while other men and women become parents of children they do not even want.

And yet, vocations do not come from our desires, our choices, or our demands. We cannot earn them. We do not have a right to any particular vocation. Our callings come from outside ourselves, and they are not contingent upon our will. Vocation is a call from God's voice and orchestration. This applies to every vocation, and certainly to parenthood. Wanting a child is no sign that a person is called to be a parent.

Understanding vocation may mean coming to the realization that God has not called me to parenthood, or marriage, or another particular vocation. Faith in God sometimes involves accepting his will, however much one would like it to be different.

Children do not come simply from a choice. Whether we choose to have one or not to have one, having a baby is, to a large measure, outside of our control. Despite the "pro-choice" rhetoric of the abortion industry, pregnancy is not a matter of choice. A woman may choose not to have a baby, but find herself pregnant. A woman may choose to have a baby, but not conceive. When a woman finds herself pregnant, it nearly always comes as a surprise. The gift of a child and the calling to be a parent come from God alone. He is at work, granting children as he chooses. And though this may do little to soothe the pains of infertility, it is worth remembering that no one is ever born a parent or has a right to be a parent or deserves to be a parent. Vocations are not so much an indication about ourselves as a revelation of how our Lord is currently at work, sustaining and preserving the world.

God does allow us choices in this life, including in regard to marriage and parenthood, but Scripture predominately speaks of *God choosing*. And God's choices often go against our expectations. "God chose what is foolish in the world to shame the wise; God chose what is weak in the world to shame the strong; God chose what is low and despised in the world, even things that are not, to bring to nothing things that are, so that no human being might boast in the presence of God" (1 Cor. 1:27–29). Too often our choice language detracts away from God as the divine Chooser. It replaces his choices with our own. But the Christian life is always a matter of following *his* will. We pray "your will be done, on earth as it is in heaven" (Matt. 6:10). And Jesus himself exemplified the life he calls us to, praying in his agony in the garden, "not my will, but yours, be done" (Luke 22:42). And embracing God's will, rather than our own, is the way of the cross, and it is the way of faith.

It may not seem like much of a consolation to exhort infertile couples to pray, have faith, and embrace God's will, to the subjugation of their own, but all Christians have to do that in whatever crosses they have been called to bear.

And yet vocation means that God offers his gifts—including healing from afflictions—through others working in their vocations. That certainly includes the medical callings. Christians who are healed through the ministrations of doctors and nurses are no less the recipients of God's healing than those who are healed by a direct miracle. Infertile couples do indeed have recourse to medical procedures and medical technology that are among God's greatest blessings to our modern age. Many couples who were not able to have children due to some physical problem can now have children after all.

The doctrine of vocation would certainly allow for infertile couples to pursue the new medical treatments. A few caveats, though: The treatments should be in accord with their one-flesh union. In vitro fertilization, in which conception happens outside of the womb, may not violate this union as long as the genetic material that is combined comes from both parents. The child that is so conceived will still be made of the flesh of both parents. To use a sperm donor or an egg donor would go outside the marriage unity and be a kind of adultery. Using surrogate mothers to carry one's child was a bad idea for Sarah and Abraham (Genesis 16), and it is still a bad idea. Though motherhood begins at conception, the woman who gives birth to the child would have a conflicting claim to that vocation.

Also, couples should be aware that in vitro fertilization, as normally practiced, can result in the conception of multiple embryonic children, only one of which will be brought to term. The "extra" embryos then are typically discarded, frozen, experimented upon, or killed for their stem cells. Parents have a calling to protect all of the children they conceive.

One of the great Christian services of our time, however, is to adopt one of these unwanted frozen embryos. It is possible to implant one of these embryos in the womb of a woman, letting her bear the child. This is called having a "snowflake" baby. There is no violation of the one-flesh union, since there was no extramarital mingling of DNA. This is an adoption. All adoptions, as we have shown, are images and examples of God's grace, and this kind is especially so—a snowflake adoption is also a rescue.

Christians need to resist the mind-set, which unfortunately sometimes accompanies the new reproductive technology, that children are consumer goods to be manufactured. The very term "reproductive technology" turns a baby into a product and has the sound of a factory. Some women who are not even infertile—such as single women who want to be mothers—are patronizing sperm banks that sell the seed in Nobel Prize winners or Nordic athletes. "Genetic engineering" holds out the promise of constructing "designer babies," made to order to be beautiful, athletic, smart, and however else the parents would like them.

The sense that children exist solely for the gratification of their parents, as their property and adornment, is a misunderstanding of the vocation of parenthood. But sadly, this dehumanizing of the child can start with his or her conception, artificial or not. "Genetic screening" often means identifying an imperfection so that the developing child can be aborted. On the other hand, some genetic therapy does hold promise for identifying and treating specific diseases in a forming child, resulting not in death but in healing. The difference between good uses of the new reproductive science and sinful uses hinges on whether they love and serve the neighbor, that is, the little developing child.

Children—like the Son of God, according to the Nicene Creed—are "begotten, not made."[7] They are not to be thought of as commodities or possessions, much less as designer accessories or purebred pets. They are begotten, coming into existence from the union of two imperfect human beings, resulting in another imperfect human being. "Begotten" means that like comes from like. As the comedian Stephen Colbert put it, arguing with an atheist, the son of a duck is a duck; the son of God is God.[8] God "made" things that are different from himself. His "only-begotten son" shares his very essence. And so do the children of human parents.

Parenting As a Calling

When Jacob first met Esau, after years apart, long after Jacob's deception, Esau asked, "'Who are these with you?' Jacob said, 'The children whom God has graciously given your servant'" (Gen. 33:5). The context of the passage is about family values gone terribly wrong, a tale in which virtually every member of the family has been in conflict with each other and has been deceiving each other. And yet this dysfunctional family is that of the patriarchs of the twelve tribes of Israel and is nothing less than the family line of Jesus Christ. Clearly, God is at work, making his purposes unfold even through a family like this. But this is also the line of faith, as we see in Jacob's answer to his estranged brother. We hear a powerful testimony that it is *God* who gives children, and not men and women who produce them. These children are not objects but are "graciously given," bestowed on a "servant."

Much later, Jacob's descendant Jesus said not to make too much of ancestry, as the Pharisees did who based their hope on their physical lineage from Abraham rather than sharing his faith: "I tell you, God is able from these stones to raise up children for Abraham" (Luke 3:8). God can make children from stones. He can make human beings from dust, as he did with Adam. And yet, God sends children through the bodies and souls of men and women. God knits the child together from the parents. God creates the space for the child, in the womb and the world. Through the parents, God feeds and cleans the little one and curbs the child's crawling away into dangers. And through the child, God grants opportunities for the parents to love and serve, expressing their faith.

Parenthood is a God-given extension of the one-flesh union. A family is one flesh! The parents are unified in marriage and sexual union, and children spring from that union. The fleshly connection continues to express itself in the cohesion of the family around the fleshly needs that are addressed in service to one another. Through the mother, God works through her body to nourish and protect the child both before and after the baby is born. Through the father, God works to protect and support the mother and the child. God joins them together to share the work of parents: providing daily bread, protection, guidance, and instruction.

Thus, the vocation of parenthood for us is very physical. It begins with our flesh and results in another mouth to feed and a body to protect. It means holding the child, soothing the child, and meeting the needs of the child. Caring for a child can be dirty, exhausting, and stressful. Changing diapers, potty training, keeping the child fed, buying clothes, tending the child through sickness, getting the child educated, driving the child to one activity after another—it is all loving and serving.

Luther said that changing a baby's diaper is a holy work, holier than what all the monks in all the monasteries do.[9] How can that be? Babies have to be changed, but changing them is a vile and repellant task. There is nothing more grossly physical. What could possibly be spiritual about a dirty diaper? But in doing this for the baby, the parent is loving and serving the child. God is loving and serving the child, even changing and cleaning the child, through the parent's love and service. And so the parent is fulfilling a holy vocation.

9

The Office of Father

For this reason I bow my knees before the Father, from whom every family [or, all fatherhood] in heaven and on earth is named.
EPHESIANS 3:14–15

In his earthly ministry, Jesus used "Father" more than any other name for God.[1] And God has been father since before the foundations of the world were laid—in the mystery of the Trinity, he has always been Father to the Son. Yet, too often we forget what being a father *is,* what fatherhood *means.*

Some have assumed that by using that term Jesus is helping us understand God, something we do not know, by comparing him to something we do know, namely, human fatherhood. God is not a literal father, of course; rather, he has certain remote similarities to fathers. But actually, the associations are reversed: God *is* the literal father. Earthly fathers have certain remote similarities to *him.* The essence of fatherhood is found in God, not in human beings. And an awareness of vocation goes further: God exercises his fatherhood, in part, by means of human fatherhood.

Our Heavenly Father

Scripture is clear that all earthly fatherhood finds its origin in our heavenly Father, but it also reveals more than that. When Jesus referred to his Father during his earthly ministry, "father" expressed his particular child-parent relationship, which he then extends to us. The word also captures an important aspect of who God is. Our God is not a distant creator or one who occasionally dabbles in history; he is a *father.*

Just as Ephesians 5 describes Christ's connection with marriage, Ephesians 3:14–19 describes our Lord at work *as a father:*

> For this reason I bow my knees before the Father, from whom every family in heaven and on earth is named, that according to the riches of his glory he may grant you to be strengthened with power through his Spirit in your inner being, so that Christ may dwell in your hearts through faith—that you, being rooted and grounded in love, may have strength to comprehend with all the saints what is the breadth and length and height and depth, and to know the love of Christ that surpasses knowledge, that you may be filled with all the fullness of God. (Eph. 3:14–19)

From this Father "every family in heaven and on earth is named." The word for "father" in the original Greek is *pater;* the word in this verse rendered here as "family" is *patria.* The two words are closely related. Greek scholar Marvin Vincent explains that "family" in our sense would be expressed in Greek as *oikos,* that is, "house." (Compare the Reformation vocation of the "household.") But *patria* means a set of individual families, all of whom have a common father. "Observe the play of the words," comments Vincent, "which can scarcely be reproduced in English, *pater, patria.*" The verse is saying that from God the Father all lineages of fathers are named.[2]

What does our Lord do as our Father, according to this text? He grants according to his riches, strengthens with power, reaches even into our inner beings, and desires our eternal salvation through Christ. This is not a checklist, neither for him nor for human fathers, but it expresses the essence of loving service to children. When our Lord describes himself as a father, he does more than reward or chide or discipline. He even does more than teach. He who instituted family in the first place now draws us into his own family, where he reveals himself to us in love and generosity.

In the parable of the loving father and his two sons—also known as the prodigal son—Jesus talks about a father who has every right to be disappointed in his younger son (Luke 15:11–32). His son wants to leave his father and spend all his money and time in reckless living. This son valued money and pleasurable living over having a father. While the younger son was still a long way off, his father saw him. Recognizing him in spite of dirty clothing and extreme poverty, he was moved by compassion. Without another thought, he ran to, embraced, and kissed him. The father restored the prodigal to his former status and prestige as his son. In this parable God clearly connects fatherhood with his own abundant and unearned love and forgiveness.

When this same father learned that his older son was not rejoicing, he sought him and found him. He entreated him. He spoke graciously with him. He withheld nothing: "Son, you are always with me, and all that is mine is yours" (Luke 15:31). This father loved his two sons, in spite of pain, disrespect, and discontent, a picture of our heavenly Father with his generosity, patience, mercy, and tenderness. Our heavenly Father is constant. He does not leave us. He does not strike us down when we are angry or already defeated. He restores what is lost. This parable is very frank about how our heavenly Father sees and responds to us *as our father*.

God is not just our Maker—again, what we make is different from ourselves—but "when the fullness of time had come, God sent forth his Son, born of woman, born under the law, to redeem those who were under the law, so that we might receive adoption as sons" (Gal. 4:4–5). God becomes our father and fully incorporates us into his family: "See what kind of love the Father has given to us, that we should be called children of God; and so we are. The reason why the world does not know us is that it did not know him. Beloved, we are God's children now, and what we will be has not yet appeared; but we know that when he appears we shall be like him, because we shall see him as he is. And everyone who thus hopes in him purifies himself as he is pure" (1 John 3:1–3). That God is our father means that, as his children, we have a special status. Families—*patria*—are one flesh with the father. This will be manifested fully in eternity. "We shall be like him."

Fatherhood and Husbandry

In very real ways, marriage prepares a man for parenthood. In marriage, he enters one-flesh union, the nature of which he cannot fully perceive. Then that union extends to another flesh unseen—the small child within his wife. At conception, when husband and wife come together, that new father has become a source of life for his tiny child. In the vocation of father, God calls men to serve their neighbor, their child. Early on, unlike with mothers, there are times when fathers can only serve their children indirectly. For example, during pregnancy the father best serves the child by serving the mother. The vocations of husband and father overlap to affect the child immediately as well as work together to prepare a place for that child.

With his wife, the husband is positioned to put another before himself and to make sacrifices. He first bears the intimacy of authority with the person he is closest to, his wife. In parenthood, his authority and care is broadened to serve his children. His headship, once a matter between his wife and himself, expands to serve and unify his growing family.

In the vocation of father, God is at work, giving a great gift through the father and to the father. He unites the parents in their common task of parenting. God embodies his love through fathers for the sake of children and mothers. And as fathers express their love, they reflect parts of God's perfect fatherly love.

Not that earthly fathers will be perfect or that they will always display that perfect fatherly love. Certainly not. But it sounds as if God will compensate for their shortcomings. "Or which one of you, if his son asks him for bread, will give him a stone? Or if he asks for a fish, will give him a serpent? If you then, who are evil, know how to give good gifts to your children, how much more will your Father who is in heaven give good things to those who ask him!" (Matt. 7:9–11). Even "evil fathers" give good gifts to their children—at least that initial gift of life—and usually much more, in the routine work of making a living and providing for the family—giving bread and fish—which keeps that life going. "How much more," though, will the Father in heaven, who exercises his love through even sinful fathers, give "good things"—such as the Holy Spirit (Luke 11:13)—to his children.

His Instruments

God calls earthly fathers to reflect what God does as father. Playing off Ephesians 3:14–19, which we quoted earlier, that would suggest that earthly fathers should grant things to their children according to *their* riches, strengthen *their* children with power, reach into the inner beings of their children, and hold *their* children's eternal salvation through

Christ foremost in their prayers and actions. The Lord wishes fathers to love their children, as he does—to provide for their children and to strengthen them as they are able, and to relate with their children in such a way that they can run to their father, as the Prodigal Son does, confident of his help.

That fatherhood denotes tenderness was emphasized also in the early teachers about vocation. In the exposition of the Lord's Prayer in his *Small Catechism*, Luther teaches, "With these words [Our Father who art in heaven] God tenderly invites us to believe that He is our true Father and that we are His true children, so that with all boldness and confidence we may ask Him as dear children ask their dear father."[3] With the picture of "dear children" crowding around "their dear father," the earthly father and the heavenly Father come together.

To be sure, the heavenly Father and the earthly father are also disciplinarians. The text in Ephesians that specifies the duties of the various vocations says only this to fathers: "Fathers, do not provoke your children to anger, but bring them up in the discipline and instruction of the Lord" (Eph. 6:4). Fathers must walk a fine line, disciplining their children without provoking them to anger. But Scripture makes clear that the father's discipline is to emulate God's discipline, in that both are to be expressions of love:

> "My son, do not regard lightly the discipline of the Lord,
>   nor be weary when reproved by him.
> For the Lord disciplines the one he loves,
>   and chastises every son whom he receives."

> It is for discipline that you have to endure. God is treating you as sons. For what son is there whom his father does not discipline? If you are left without discipline, in which all have participated, then you are illegitimate children and not sons. Besides this, we have had earthly fathers who disciplined us and we respected them. Shall we not much more be subject to the Father of spirits and live? For they disciplined us for a short time as it seemed best to them, but he disciplines us for our good, that we may share his holiness. For the moment all discipline seems painful rather than pleasant, but later it yields the peaceful fruit of righteousness to those who have been trained by it. (Heb. 12:5–11)

After quoting Proverbs 3:11–12, the author intertwines what earthly fathers do and what the heavenly Father does. The former can, indeed, be arbitrary in their discipline, but even then "we respected them." God the Father "disciplines us for our good." He "chastises every son whom he receives" so "that we may share his holiness." Again, God's purpose even in afflicting us is to give us what he has. "We shall be like him" (1 John 3:2).

The other duty of fathers related in Ephesians 6:4, in addition to discipline, is to bring their children up in the "instruction of the Lord." Fathers are to teach their children the Word of God. They are to evangelize them. They are responsible for the family's spiritual well-being.

In the Old Testament, according to God's directions, fathers functioned like priests within their families. There were specific father-child rituals (namely circumcision, Passover, and the redemption of the first-born) at which the father would preside. The entire family would also eat, pray, and meditate on God's Word together, under the father's leadership. The father was a primary teacher of Scripture to his children.

Today, Christian fathers should do everything they can to bring their children to Christ. They can do that by taking their children to church; making sure their children learn God's Word, both by ensuring their Christian education and by teaching their children themselves; seeking their baptism; and establishing a Christian home that lives and breathes the grace of God. In that climate, God's Word and the gospel of Christ work on a child to create faith. Most Christians came to faith directly as a result of their upbringing and by the personal influence of their fathers and mothers. Some evangelicals who never can remember a time when they did not trust Jesus as their Savior worry about whether they were properly converted! But in reality, the evangelism that happens through parents, in the natural course of everyday life, is especially effective.

Again, God is pleased to give his gifts by means of human vocations, and this includes the gift of salvation. "Fear not, little flock, for it is your Father's good pleasure to give you the kingdom" (Luke 12:32). He often does that through earthly fathers. In the book of Acts, when a man was saved, he brought his whole household with him (Acts 10–11, 16, 18). Mothers did, too (Acts 16), and God definitely uses mothers to bring their children to faith. Often today, mothers take the lead in the religious life of the family, which can be fitting, especially if the father cannot or will not do so. But the father's spiritual influence is especially profound.

Statistically the single most important factor in whether a child will go to church as an adult is whether the child's father did. That was the conclusion of a 1994 study of church attendance in Switzerland. Granted, the Swiss have a different culture than Americans do, so perhaps the findings are not completely transferable. But the findings were startling evidence for the impact of fathers on the spiritual lives of their children. Among adults whose father and mother both attended church regularly, 74 percent attended church (33 percent regularly and 41 percent irregularly). When the father attended irregularly and the mother attended regularly, only 3 percent of their children became regular churchgoers, though 59 percent would attend sometimes. When the father never attended at all, but the mother went to church faithfully, only 2 percent became regular worshipers, with 37 percent attending sometimes, which meant 61 percent never attended.[4]

But when the father attended church regularly and the mother attended only sometimes, 75 percent of their grown children attended church (38 percent regularly; 37 percent sometimes). And if the father attended regularly but the mother did not attend at all, the likelihood of their children becoming *regular* churchgoers becomes even higher: 44 percent will attend church regularly, and 22 percent will attend sometimes. Somehow, the father's spiritual influence increases in proportion to the mother's lack of interest in church. Robbie Low sums up the findings: "In short, if a father does not go to church, no matter how faithful his wife's devotions, only one child in 50 will become a regular worshipper. If a father does go regularly, regardless of the practice of the mother, between two-thirds and three-quarters of their children will become churchgoers (regular and irregular). If a father goes but irregularly to church, regardless of his wife's devotion, between a half and two-thirds of their offspring will find themselves coming to church regularly or occasionally."[5]

It is as if the Lord is making it ridiculously simple for fathers to fulfill their duties to bring up their children in the faith. All fathers have to do is take their children to church. And yet many fathers find that too difficult to manage.

If fathers do such a simple thing as take their children to church on Sunday mornings, their children will be likely to continue to go to church when they are grown up. But it has to be the father who goes to church with them. When the mother takes the kids to church while the father stays home, the message the children receive is that church is not all that important. When it comes to religion, children, for better or worse, tend to emulate whatever their father does.

The Fatherless Child

Fathers have an impact whether they realize it or not. Simply being present in their children's lives exerts a powerful influence. This is especially evident today as we see the consequences of children being raised without a father.

Though God connects the vocations of marriage with the vocations of parenthood, today it has become culturally acceptable to be a parent without being married. To be sure, as we will discuss in the next chapter, single mothers still hold the office and the vocation of mother, despite their having no husband or father in the picture. But the marginalization of fathers is devastating, both culturally and in the lives of the children.

The number of children being raised without a father is staggering. In 2009, some 41 percent of the children born in America were to unmarried mothers.[6] That represents a jump since 1946 of over 1,000 percent.[7] Most of these pregnancies were not merely accidents. Nearly half of all births outside of marriage are now *intentional.* Slightly over one-third of the pregnancies occurred earlier than the mother had planned, but only 14 percent were not wanted.[8] That is to say, women are *choosing* to have children without getting married. Factor in divorce, and nearly half of the children in America spend at least part of their childhood living only with their mothers.[9]

So what is the impact of children growing up with no fathers in their lives? We want to emphasize that the pathologies we are going to cite *need not happen.* Many boys and girls grow up in single-parent households, that parent nearly always being the mother, and they turn out fine. In fact, as we shall see, God offers a special promise for faithful mothers raising their children alone. But we all need to face up to the problems. Just as single mothers have the vocation of motherhood, the men who engendered their children have the vocation of fatherhood, which they violate by abandoning their own children.

Fathers are called to provide for their children. When there is no father present, the family struggles economically. One study found that children born out of wedlock are poor 51 percent of the time, whereas children born to parents who are married to each other are poor only 7 percent of the time. The absence of a father increases the likelihood of child poverty by 700 percent.[10]

Fathers, as we have shown, are called to discipline their children and to form them morally and spiritually. What happens to children who grow up without that influence?

A study of prison inmates found that 87 percent of those incarcerated were from single parent families.[11] One important study demonstrated that neither race nor poverty is correlated to crime, but that virtually *all* of an area's crime rate can be explained by the illegitimacy rate.[12] According to another study, a child raised in a never-married family is twenty times more likely to end up in prison than a child raised by parents who are married to each other.[13]

Not that all fatherless children end up in prison, by any means, but the lack of a father poses specific challenges for a child. A boy without a strong male role model does not know how he is supposed to act. His mother may try to discipline him, but he may not respect her efforts in the way he would those of a man. Studies have found that fatherless children struggle with lower impulse control—they feel like doing something and they do it—and thus increased behavioral problems. This, in turn, means that they often do poorly in school, which impacts them later in the workforce. Their social development is also thrown off without a father's example.

Children outside of marriage lack so many of the finessed social experiences that children have through their parents' marriage, which acts as a stabilizing and perspective-forming background. Their parents argue but then compromise, fight then make up, struggle but remain committed. So that marriage can actually affect a child's ability to interpret situations, empathize with others, and cope with frustrations. Children who must struggle apart from marriage may see the arguments and fights but not have a larger picture through which to view them. Fewer examples— and less practice—may mean that boy who never sees his father interact positively with his mother may not learn how to treat women with respect and love.[14] Sometimes, boys crave a masculine presence in their lives so much that they revert to what psychologists call "hypermasculinity." That is, they adopt the macho stereotype of being physically aggressive, emotionally cold, and brutal towards women. This is often accompanied by seeking masculine role models, as happens in criminal gangs. Here they find a hypermasculine brotherhood characterized by status hierarchies, arcane codes of honor to be defended with blood, and elaborate rituals of revenge. But they also find discipline, structure, emotional support, and protection—things they should have received from a father.[15]

What about fatherless girls? Without a father's love and protection, girls can grow up to be insecure and self-loathing. Without a father's model of what a man and a future husband should be, girls can have problems in their relationships with men, often getting into bad relationships and getting hurt in the process. Some girls try to fill the father void in their lives by trying to attract a man, any man. They crave a masculine presence in their lives so much that they revert to "hyperfemininity." They become obsessed with trying to be physically beautiful; they dress in sexually provocative ways; they often become sexually promiscuous.[16]

Finally, the lack of a strong, emotionally connected father seems to be associated with homosexuality. The causes of homosexuality, of course, are elusive and controversial. Most of the controversy has concentrated on whether same-sex attraction is a lifestyle choice or whether it is genetic or otherwise innate. Another possibility, though, is that homosexuality is a cultural construction. Christian ministries to gays have drawn the connection to family relationships.[17] Many who describe themselves as gay will tell about bad relationships with their fathers. In many cases, the father was still present in the family. But he was emotionally distant. He was not involved in his son's life. Or he was involved only to be harsh, judgmental, and derisive. Some suggest that mothers play a role, too. The combination of a dominating, smothering mother with a distant father seems to be a formula for homosexuality. In this scenario, boys begin to identify with their mothers rather than their fathers. More poignantly, the boys crave a man in their lives so much, not having a loving father, that they become highly attracted to men. This yearning, not sexual at first, can be felt even at a very young age and can become entwined with how they understand and identify themselves after puberty.

We hasten to say, though, that homosexuality is not always caused by bad parenting. There are too many exceptions, with some gay people coming out of very strong families and some well-adjusted heterosexuals reporting distant fathers and smothering mothers. Ultimately, parents do not determine how their children turn out. The children bear their own responsibility, including for how they deal with the difficulties in their lives.

But because God works through the vocation, vacating the office of father has serious consequences. Whether we are culturally belittling fatherhood, socially experimenting with it, or historically pretending its irrelevance, we cannot manipulate God away from the channels he has chosen to provide. The needs for a father will remain.

Young people who are casualties of being fatherless may never go to these extremes. But they often live with a profound pain nonetheless. Mary Eberstadt studied the dark, violent, tormented music that is so popular among teenagers of all social groups today. She found that the dominant subject matter of this music—from misogynistic hip-hop to angst-ridden alternative rock—is the pain of being abandoned by one's father, a theme that resonates deeply with its young audiences from across the social spectrum. "If yesterday's rock was the music of abandon, today's is that of abandonment. The odd truth about contemporary teenage music—the characteristic that most separates it from what has gone before—is its compulsive insistence on the damage wrought by broken homes, family dysfunction, checked-out parents, and (especially) absent fathers."[18] It thus appears that many of our "culture war" issues—sexual permissiveness, homosexuality, crime, abortion, even twisted music—can be traced to fathers who are not fulfilling their vocations. And as the number of single-mother homes keeps growing, we can only expect those issues to intensify.

But there is hope. *Any* presence of a father in the child's life is enough to forestall many of these dire consequences. In the case of divorce, a father with visitation rights who stays in his children's lives can still exercise his fatherhood. In a strange grace, when the father *dies*, the effect of his absence is not so harmful. Again, it is the sense of being abandoned, having the feeling that my father doesn't love me, that a child finds so devastating. A father who dies, by contrast, loved me and, in Christian hope, still loves me. In the complete absence of a father, other male role models can step in to give the child stability: a grandfather, an uncle, a church leader, a coach. All of these are very effective in preventing the worst dysfunctions of growing up fatherless as God simply works through alternative vocations.

But the greatest hope is that the Source of all fatherhood will move into the child's life and personally fill the void left by the earthly father. Psalm 68, while describing God's righteous power in scattering evildoers and protecting his people, makes this promise:

> Father of the fatherless and protector of widows
> is God in his holy habitation.
> God settles the solitary in a home;
> he leads out the prisoners to prosperity,
> but the rebellious dwell in a parched land. (Ps. 68:5–6)

God himself will be "father of the fatherless." Earthly fathers do nothing more than exercise his fatherhood, and if they will not or cannot fulfill their calling, then God himself will act. Here too is a promise for single mothers. For those who have lost their husbands, God will fulfill their vocation for them. He will be "protector of widows." And he will give those who are lonely and isolated—such as fatherless children, when they grow up—families of their own. "God settles the solitary in a home."

Conclusion

God places enormous responsibility on fathers. And yet, the duties are remarkably simple, straightforward, and ordinary. A father who wants his children to grow up to be happy, successful, Christian adults can start with these few things:

1. Be married to their mother.
2. Do not divorce her.
3. Do not abandon your children.
4. Be involved in your children's lives.
5. Take your children to church.

That would seem to be easy enough. And yet it has become counterintuitive to put our children or spouses first, to sacrifice and place their needs before our wants. Without a thought, many fathers are neglecting these duties. As a result, their children's lives are traumatized, and the very foundations of our culture are being shaken. The path, though, to restoring our children and our culture is clear: be present in your vocation. Obviously there is more to fatherhood than a five-point list. Disciplining and instructing, loving and providing for—these are difficult and personalized tasks. Fathers are called to make sacrifices—not only in money, time, and energy, but in sacrificing their very selves. To put others first, even when they are "only children," can be exhausting. And yet, fathers do not seem to have to do everything right to be effective in their calling. It is precisely in vocation that God works through us even though we never can be, or do, the "best." God occupies fatherhood so completely that his presence in earthly fathers may be efficacious in itself to bring his blessings.

10

The Office of Mother

*On you was I cast from my birth, and from my mother's womb you
have been my God.*

PSALM 22:10

Motherhood is the perfect illustration of vocation. God has empowered
a woman to be a mother, and God works with her to sustain that fragile
child. To understand the breadth of the vocation of mother, we must start
once again with God's work. God created a woman's body in such a way
that it can engender life in the womb. God sustains mother and child and
allows that woman to work with him to sustain and nourish the child he
has given. During pregnancy, a mother shares her body's warmth, nutri-
ents, and even her space with her child! After the child is born, she continues to keep her child alive and to cause the child to develop all the way
into adulthood. The mother's task is profoundly physical—having to do
with her body and with the bodily needs of her child—but her intellect
and soul also serve the child through planning, decision making, and
prayer. God calls her to use the different gifts he has given her to serve
her neighbor, the child.

In a very real sense, a mother is asked to give all she has: time,
energy, intelligence, health, hope, and faith. She teaches, disciplines,
feeds, clothes, washes, and molds. She sets an example of what it means
to live, make choices, explore, and be in relationships. But as much as

the mother is doing, God is present doing even more. God works through her, but he also sustains her as his daughter. God gives meaning to this service, even tying it together with the salvation of the human race. Our Lord works through motherhood so powerfully that, when the time was right, our heavenly Father sent his Son into the womb of a mother to live and die as our Redeemer and Savior. And it is that Christ-child who reveals to us so much about the vocation of mother.

Saved through Childbearing

The vocation of mothers begins at the very beginning. According to Genesis, the office of motherhood entails both creation and redemption. God created the man and then, from his body, the woman. He then gave them a blessing and a commandment: "So God created man in his own image, in the image of God he created him; male and female he created them. And God blessed them. And God said to them, 'Be fruitful and multiply and fill the earth' (Gen. 1:27–28). The distinction between male and female is God's design for how they are to be fruitful and multiply. The man "begets" children, and the woman "conceives and bears" them (see Genesis 4–5, KJV).

As the creation account continues, we learn more about the calling of the mother: "The man called his wife's name Eve, because she was the mother of all living" (Gen. 3:20). Note the word "called." Naming is associated with "calling" and thus with vocation.[1] ("My name is Jessica, but my friends call me Jessie. My daughter calls me Mama, and my students call me Teacher.") The meaning of Eve's name points to the essence of her calling. "Eve" is related to the Hebrew word for *living* and sounds like the word for *life giver*.[2] Eve is "the mother of all living." A mother is a life giver. God has given to women an unimaginably great power: the ability to give life. This is God's power, but he gives it to women; and he exercises his life-giving power through those whom he has called to be mothers.

Eve herself is the mother of us all. Her daughters share in her power and often in her calling. "All living" comes from "living," from the Lifegiver. That is to say, mothers are, through God, the source of life. This is true of conception and birth, and it is also true when a mother's children are older. She continues to be the source of their lives as she cares for them and helps them grow.

Tragically, Satan, in the form of the serpent, tempted Eve and she gave in, as did Adam, to the ruin of "all living." Whereupon her great power and her callings as both mother and wife became crosses for her to bear:

> I will surely multiply your pain in childbearing;
>> in pain you shall bring forth children.
> Your desire shall be for your husband,
>> and he shall rule over you. (Gen. 3:16)

Through the vocation of motherhood, a flesh-and-blood woman is still the source of a child's life, but now the vocation involves difficulty and suffering—and the tribulations of motherhood are not restricted to the delivery room. Her vocation as wife is also complicated and made difficult, as she both desires her husband and endures his rule over her.

But at the same stroke, God redeems motherhood and turns that vocation into the means of bringing redemption. God condemns Satan, the Serpent, through the instrumentality of the mother: "I will put enmity between you and the woman, and between your offspring and her offspring; he shall bruise your head, and you shall bruise his heel" (Gen. 3:15). This is not just saying that women will be afraid of snakes and that their sons will step on them. This is the first prophecy of Christ. As such, it tells us an enormous amount about him—his virgin birth, his crucifixion, and his victory.

The word the ESV renders as "offspring" is literally "seed," as reflected in older translations and in the ESV's footnote to the verse. The "seed" of the woman is not just a way to refer to her collective descendants. It is a "he," who will strike the head of Satan at the same moment that he himself is stricken. The word "seed" in the ancient Hebrew is highly significant.

For most of human history, people did not even realize that a woman had "seed." The assumption was that the man had seed, which was implanted in the woman, who caused it to form and grow. Aristotle believed that embryos grew from eggs that were made by a mixture of the man's semen and the woman's menstrual blood, so that the woman did contribute to the makeup of the baby. Embryology took a step backward from the ancient world with the discovery in 1677, thanks to the microscope, of sperm, which were then thought to contain a miniature but complete embryo. The ovum—the egg produced by a female, her seed—was not discovered until 1827![3]

And yet Genesis specifies that the "seed" of the woman—not the seed of the man, as might be expected—would crush Satan's head. This, of course, is Jesus Christ, who came from the seed of Mary, a daughter of Eve. Mary conceived Jesus by the power of the Holy Spirit, remaining a virgin. But she contributed her DNA—and thus the lineage of Eve, the house of David, and the genetic makeup of the whole human race—to Jesus. Thus, in the words of the Athanasian Creed, "Our Lord Jesus Christ, the Son of God, is God and Man; God of the Substance of the Father, begotten before the worlds; and Man of the substance of His mother, born in the world."[4]

The contusion of the heel is a vivid detail of crucifixion. Satan surely thought he was victorious when Jesus was crucified, the nails in his flesh recalling the bite of a serpent's fangs. And yet with his crucifixion, the Son of Eve through her daughter Mary trampled Satan under his feet (Ps. 91:13). Thus the fall is atoned for and the family of Adam and Eve is redeemed (Rom. 5:17–18).

God's promise of redemption is given to Eve, the first transgressor. God assures this woman, still filled with shame for succumbing to Satan, that he will use her and those who will occupy her office as mother to defeat Satan. Israelite women, remembering God's promise to Eve, knew that someday the Savior would come through a mother. God deemed to use motherhood for his incarnation and his salvation of the world. Not only are mothers interwoven with earthly generations and the ongoing inheritance of the world, but they are joined in a unique way with the very method of salvation.

This is made explicit in a rather puzzling passage in the First Epistle to Timothy. The apostle Paul has just finished explaining why he does not allow women to hold vocations of leadership in the church. Why? Because of Eve. The issue is not whether a woman has strong leadership qualities or an exemplary faith or would make a good pastor. Paul wants us always to be aware of our human complicity in the fall and our collective solidarity with Adam and Eve. "For Adam was formed first, then Eve; and Adam was not deceived, but the woman was deceived and became a transgressor. Yet she will be saved through childbearing—if they continue in faith and love and holiness, with self-control" (1 Tim.

2:13–15). Paul here is conflating Eve and all women. Adam was not deceived because he sinned knowing full well what he was doing, as Milton unforgettably portrays in *Paradise Lost*, which has Adam eating the fruit because he does not want to be parted from Eve. Adam's responsibility is therefore the greater, since he sinned not out of deception but as a deliberate act of rebellion.

But what does it mean to say that "she"—Eve? women in general, with the switch to the plural "they"?—"will be saved through childbearing." Does that mean that God will bring her safely through the ordeal of childbirth? Or that God will save her from her sins if she has children? Surely neither of those interpretations can be valid. In the context, though, the passage is making direct reference to Eve's transgression, followed by a direct reference to her salvation. That is, the passage refers to Genesis 3, which includes both the account of her fall (3:1–7) and the promise of her salvation through her "seed" (3:15). That is, as Paul puts it, "she shall be saved through childbearing." Paul then applies the promise to our mother Eve to all mothers. Eve's childbearing leads to the birth of Christ. All childbearing is thus a sign of the gospel. It must be responded to in "faith and love and holiness" to bring personal salvation, but everyone with the vocation of mother, believer and unbeliever alike, manifests the incarnation of God. Now, every childbirth can remind us of that first Christmas, that holy birth that elevates every other birth.

Thus, the office of motherhood speaks to us of creation and incarnation. It also speaks of the cross—not just prophetically but in what every mother experiences and enacts. A woman's power of bringing new life into the world—through her own suffering—is a sign of the cross. When the Bible refers to the "new life" that comes from being "born again," it is describing the work of Christ in terms of childbearing, which thus becomes a symbol of redemption. A mother in her vocation literally "bears her cross" in giving life to her children.

The Creator of all, who created motherhood itself, found a mother for our Lord in the Israelite maiden Mary. Having the vocation of mother was much the same for Mary as for all mothers. Inside her womb, the incarnate Word grew little ears. Inside her warmth, the Light of the World blinked his eyes. After his miraculous birth, he nursed at her breasts, and later, at her request, he may even have cleaned his room. He certainly changed water into wine for his mother (John 2). And within this great mystery, the incarnation of our living God, this young woman from a small town in Galilee had the opportunity to serve the Savior of the world. Not in flashy or entertaining ways, but in daily, often humble tasks, like those of all mothers.

His Instruments

We have seen the biblical dimension of marriage in which the church is the bride of Christ. Historically, Christians have continued the symbolism, calling the church their mother.[5] That is to say, just as we were born through our earthly mothers who continue to nourish us and take care of us, we are born again through the church which continues to nourish us through the milk of God's Word (1 Pet. 2:2) and takes care of us spiritually throughout our lives.

The church really does function like a mother, bringing forth and caring for Christ's children. By the same token, earthly mothers really do function like the church, bringing new life into this world and, through the Holy Spirit, raising up new citizens for the kingdom of heaven. The ultimate purpose of Christian mothers is to bring up new Christians.

The mother's service to the neighbor of her vocation—that is, her child—is both spiritual and physical, the two being closely related. The services of motherhood begin in pregnancy. The mother nourishes the life within her even before she knows that it is there. How clearly this demonstrates vocation! She is serving her neighbor without even recognizing or choosing to because of how God has chosen to work through her. One of the most beautiful aspects of God's work through vocation is that sometimes we find ourselves serving without even realizing that we are doing so.

From conception, a mother is serving her child. Until the child is born, she cannot help it! Her prenatal service flows from her body without any decision on her part. As hormones shift and the pregnancy progresses, the mother literally is reshaped and restructured into her new and changing roles. The Lord uses the woman physically as his direct form of interaction with the child. God crafts the child, sends nourishment, provides warmth and safety, yet he does so through the mother. The mother receives the gift within her, gives up part of herself to form it, and provides the child with space, nourishment, and protection.

This continues after the child is born. After birth, care must be more intentional as the child is vulnerable and develops in ever-changing ways. The child's needs keep shifting and the mother's service also has to keep shifting. Much of what she does for her child is still almost beyond her conscious understanding. But God continues to care for the child through her.

Luther, in explaining vocation in his *Large Catechism*, uses a nursing mother as one of his examples of how God works through human beings:

> For even though otherwise we experience much good from men, still whatever we receive by His command or arrangement is all received from God. For our parents, and all rulers, and every one besides with respect to his neighbor, have received from God the command that they should do us all manner of good, so that we receive these blessings not from them, but through them, from God. For creatures are only the hands, channels, and means whereby God gives all things, as He gives to the mother breasts and milk to offer to her child, and corn and all manner of produce from the earth for nourishment, none of which blessings could be produced by any creature of itself.[6]

Such is God's providence—how he "provides" for us. The Bible also describes God's love in terms of a mother nursing her baby: "Can a woman forget her nursing child, that she should have no compassion on the son of her womb? Even these may forget, yet I will not forget you" (Isa. 49:15). God's love is described here as *more* than a mother's love. God's care is attentive. He blesses abundantly, not because of how we can repay him—for what can nursing children do to repay their mothers?—but because we are his. The apostle Paul uses the same image in contrasting the way he conducted his ministry of the gospel with those who preach out of greed and a desire for glory: "We were gentle among you, like a nursing mother taking care of her own children" (1 Thess. 2:7). Here Paul is describing the personalized care of his ministry, specifically tying mothers with self-denial and gentleness.

Eating for two, changing diapers, calming tantrums, tending wounds physical and otherwise, ushering children through all of the challenges of growing up, all fall within God's vocation of motherhood. In a wide variety of ways, we see mothers, also in Scripture, doing their best to provide for, protect, and educate their children. As children grow, mothers are bound to shift from stage to stage, parenting according to the changing needs and scenarios of the children. Complicating the tasks is that every child, like every snowflake, is unique. Some children have special needs. Others need varying amounts of company and guidance. Mothers respond according to their own abilities and opportunities and then grow as mothers themselves. For all of the stress and panic and worries of child raising, mothers can rest assured that the burden is not theirs alone. They can have the confidence that God is working through them, even despite themselves sometimes, to form their children for his glory.

Just as fathers have a powerful spiritual influence on their children, it seems mothers have a powerful moral influence. Traditionally, mothers have been credited with teaching moral behavior and developing a conscience in their children. The Victorian era in the nineteenth-century idealized mothers to the point of establishing a so-called "cult of Motherhood." Mothers were seen as the source of all that is fine and ennobling. The moral influence of mothers was hailed in speeches and poems. Men credited the memory of their "sainted mothers" as helping them resist temptation later in life. It was not only conservative traditionalists who idealized, some might say idolized, mothers. So did the early feminists. A major argument for the ultimately successful crusade to give women the vote was to bring the mothers' moral influence into the ballot box and thus into the government.

The Victorian cult of Motherhood, which gave us the holiday of Mother's Day, is not something Christians should completely buy into. Motherhood is a vocation, not a sentimental ideal that is impossible for real women to live up to. A woman who is a mother does not have moral superiority to everyone else, nor does she have to labor under the stress and guilt of not being the archetypal "perfect mother." The doctrine of vocation shifts the burden away from the individual's works and merit, which always fall short, to the work and merit of God, who accomplishes his will regardless of the imperfection of his instruments. This is why the doctrine of vocation is so liberating, as compared to moralistic codes and cultural roles.

And yet the Victorians were not entirely wrong. One reason the Victorians honored mothers so much is that so many of them died in childbirth. Looming behind many of the nineteenth-century panegyrics to Mother is the author's gratitude, sometimes tinged with guilt, that she risked her life—and sometimes gave her life—to bring him into being. "I owe her my life" became a cliché, but it was true.

Also, mothers really are moral influences. This is a common-sense observation, but contemporary research provides the evidence. Nancy Eisenberg, in reviewing research in child psychology and moral development, found that mothers play a major role in their children developing moral faculties such as conscience, guilt, empathy, and sympathy. These grow out of "a secure attachment" between mother and child. They are associated with a "gentle maternal discipline deemphasizing power," presumably in contrast with the more forceful discipline associated with fathers.[7]

Robert Blum and other researchers at the University of Minnesota found that teenagers, both boys and girls, who know that their mothers would "strongly" disapprove of them having sex are less likely to do so. The determining factor, though, according to this study, is whether the teenagers have a close relationship with their mothers. Those who do are more likely to delay sex than those who do not. As we saw with fathers, the influence seems to come not so much from what the parents say to the child, but from the parent's presence in their lives. Blum's study cited the "connectedness" between mother and child as being the key factor in whether a teenager engages in premarital sex. "Connectedness" refers to how close teenagers feel to their mother, how much they feel she cares for them, how loving she is, and how well they communicate with each other.[8]

Again, it appears that the vocation of motherhood itself exerts power and influence over the children. It isn't so much what a mother does or the wise words she finds to say or what philosophy of child raising she adopts. What is most important is that she occupies her office and is fully present for her children. When she is, God is also fully present for her children.

Sacrifice and Motherhood

Labor is marked by pain, and the same could be said of motherhood generally. The physical suffering and even danger of labor soon gives way to the daily drudgery and self-denials that are entailed in raising small children. When the children are older, mothers are still subject to anxieties, stress, and sometimes heartbreak. Yes, motherhood is also full of great joys and satisfactions. But we should not minimize the difficulties. And mothers certainly should not feel guilty when the pains seem to exceed the joys, as if they were bad mothers just because they are not always happy when dealing with their children. Motherhood is a solemn vocation of the greatest importance, and all vocations bring with them their own trials and tribulations. But the sufferings of mothers have another dimension. As was said, motherhood is a sign of the gospel. Motherhood also is an enactment of the gospel; that is, mothers suffer and sacrifice themselves to create and sustain new life.

In pregnancy, life and death are both close at hand. The developing baby is fragile. Miscarriages are frequent. Sometimes, after the nine-month ordeal and despite all hopes and anticipation, the child dies in the delivery room. In the face of such tragedies, the mother can only console herself with the knowledge that she was still a mother to that child, that she still served her child, even when the ways were hidden in the time they had together. Pregnancy also carries risks for the mother. Sometimes the mother dies when giving birth. In that tragedy, she has, literally, sacrificed herself for her child, in what the Bible describes as the ultimate act of love, an emulation of Christ. "By this we know love, that he laid down his life for us, and we ought to lay down our lives for the brothers" (1 John 3:16).

Even in a labor that goes well, the mother—like Christ on the cross—bears in her body the curse of the fall and the penalty for sin. "I will surely multiply your pain in childbearing; in pain you shall bring forth children" (Gen. 3:16). But through the sacrifice of labor, the mother lets the child take its first breath of air.

Afterwards, as the baby grows into childhood, adolescence, and adulthood, the mother still at every stage is denying herself for her child. Even disciplining her child is a kind of self-sacrifice, since she would rather not have to do it, but, nevertheless, she does it against her will for the child's good.

The greatest biblical model for the mother is surely the mother of our Lord, through whom God "brought down the mighty from their thrones and exalted those of humble estate" in remembrance of his mercy (Luke 1:52, 54). Pregnant out of wedlock, she faced social scorn, and even in those days the jeopardy of the death penalty.

Single mothers, too, have Mary as their example. A woman who conceives a baby, whether or not she is married, is thereby called into the vocation of motherhood, with all of the honor and authority that comes with that office. This is true even when the child was conceived in a sinful relationship. What she must not do is abort her baby just because she is unmarried or does not want the baby. Luther commented that childbirth is pleasing to God even if the child is born out of wedlock.[9] The mother will have great difficulties in raising the child without a father, and she might best love and serve her child by the further sacrifice of giving her baby up to be adopted. But, if she is a Christian, she can raise her child in faith, confident that God will help them both, claiming God's promises for both "widows"—women bereft of husbands—and the "fatherless child": "Father of the fatherless and protector of widows is God in his holy habitation" (Ps. 68:5).

Mary was blessed with a just and revelation-believing husband, but her difficulties in bearing the Son of God continued with the travel to Bethlehem at the worst possible time and having to give birth in a stable. But she saw miracles, too, though she did not fully comprehend them at the time. "But Mary treasured up all these things, pondering them in her heart" (Luke 2:19). And then as Jesus grew up, Mary the mother of our Lord—the mother of a perfect child, no less!—felt anxiety and pain as a mother. She had to protect him by fleeing to Egypt; she lost him at Jerusalem; she was confused with his early ministry; she had to watch him be crucified. While her son was on the cross, we see his continued love for his mother as he gave her into John's care. We also see that mothers remain mothers even after their children enter adulthood and continue to suffer when they suffer (John 19:26–27).

The prophet Simeon, as he held the baby Jesus in the temple and predicted his atoning work, had told Mary that she would suffer along with her son: "A sword will pierce through your own soul also" (Luke 2:35). Through it all, she came to faith in her son. She believed that he could turn the water into wine! She saw him raised from the dead! She was with the disciples in the upper room when the Holy Spirit descended (Acts 1:14)!

All mothers, to one extent or another, will have a sword that will pierce through their hearts. But they will also have much to "treasure" and much to ponder in their hearts.

Conclusion

God himself honors mothers and requires that they be honored (Ex. 20:12). The human race would die out if not for the work of mothers.

They also play a critical role in passing on moral and cultural values from one generation to the next, ensuring their survival. So we can hardly praise the vocation of motherhood enough.

And yet, as one mother said after dealing with a particularly messy diaper, "motherhood is gross." For all that we often try to spiritualize motherhood, there is hardly anything so physical as what a mother is called to do. Having a baby is a function of her body. And caring for a baby has to do with the baby's body—feeding (including nursing with her own body), handling excretions, tending to sicknesses, monitoring the baby's physical growth, carrying and cradling the baby's little—and not-so-little—body. And as the child grows, much of the work is still physical—making sure everyone is fed, worrying about nutrition and health, administering first aid and taking to the doctor, driving the kids from place to place. Motherhood is a rebuke to everything gnostic, the heresy that says only spiritual things are worthwhile.

Motherhood is undoubtedly draining. Though the sacrifices of a mother may go so far as to demand her very life, the normal ways she denies herself to love and serve the child who is her neighbor are much more mundane. These services may be the most difficult cross for her to bear. The tedium, the nonstop demands, the sense that it never ends can wear a mother down. "I went to college for this?" "Can't I have a life any-more apart from my kids?" Still, even while these thoughts are running through their minds, mothers can know on the deepest level that this is all worthwhile, feeling an overwhelming love for their children. And if they know about vocation, they can realize that this love is a participa-tion in God's love—for her child, but also for her.

Luther, teaching about the vocation of mothers, shows how even the dirty jobs of motherhood are suffused by the love of God. Paul Althaus quotes and summarizes Luther:

> The services that a mother performs for her children are for the most part small and coarse and hardly noble. However, Christian faith "opens its eyes, looks upon all these insignificant, distasteful, and despised duties in the Spirit, and is aware that they are all adorned with divine approval as with the costli-est gold and jewels." For they are the means whereby God "graciously cares for us like a kind and loving mother." Faith recognizes that what seems to natural man to be nothing but trouble and a burdensome limitation is instead a unique calling to serve God's gracious will and to express our faith and love.

If we recognize that, we "will find delight, love, and joy without end" in the midst of the "bitterness, drudgery, and anguish."[10]

A mother will indeed experience "bitterness, drudgery, and anguish." But faith allows her to see that God, who "graciously cares for us like a kind and loving mother," is working through her.

11

Raising Children

Come and see what God has done: he is awesome in his deeds toward the children of man.

PSALM 66:5

We were on a radio show talking about vocation when a listener called in. She said that she had been a member of a Bible study group in which everyone resolved to make God the first priority in their lives. The members covenanted together that they would each wake up early in the morning to read the Bible and pray as the very first activity of their day.

The woman said that she took up the discipline with eagerness. But every time she would open her Bible, after dragging herself out of bed half an hour earlier than usual, the baby would start crying! She wanted to build up her relationship with God, but the baby kept interrupting. When she was trying to pray, the baby would demand to be fed. When she was trying to read the Bible, the baby would demand to be changed. It was hard to be in a meditative state of mind with a squirming baby on her lap.

She began to resent her baby. He was interfering with her spiritual life. She wanted to serve God, to make him the first priority of her life. But this squealing baby was preventing her from being the good Christian she wanted to be.

But then, she told us on the radio show, she had an insight. When the baby cried, he was calling to her. And through her baby's voice, God was calling to her. What God wanted her to do to serve him, right then and there, was to take care of her baby. When she did, she was honoring God. She realized that the spiritual discipline of waking up early, reading the Bible, and praying for a fixed amount of time, while valuable, was not what God wanted of her at that particular moment. Attending to her baby was also a spiritual discipline. She could love and serve God by loving and serving her baby.

This woman understood vocation. To be sure, a mother with a young child could benefit from having time for Bible reading and prayer. She could use a "quiet time," not just in the sense of personal devotions, but also in the sense of ordinary peace and quiet! Here her husband could exercise his vocation as both a husband and a father to give her some relief! But she understood that the spiritual activities we choose for ourselves, however worthy they may be, especially those "works" we offer to God as a way to get closer to him, are not necessarily what he asks of us.

What he does ask of us is to serve him by serving our neighbors in the vocations to which he has appointed us and to which he has called us. "Only let each person lead the life that the Lord has assigned to him, and to which God has called him. . . . There let him remain with God" (1 Cor. 7:17, 24).

Again, every vocation has its proper work, the particular tasks and duties that the calling entails and authorizes. The work of parents, obviously, is raising children. To "raise" something means to lift it up. Even within perfection, God the Father—without detracting from himself at all—elevated God the Son. The goal of parenthood is to discipline, educate, and provide for children so that they grow into adults. The goal of Christian parents is additionally to equip their children for eternal life. This is to say, the work of the parents' calling is to prepare their children for their callings—as family members, as productive members of society, and as Christians.

What God Does in Parenting

Parenting has become a contentious subject. In the "mommy wars," articles, blogs, books, and personal conversations set women against each other over the best way to raise children, leaving both sides feeling guilty and defensive. Shall I go easy on my child or be a "tiger mother"? Which of the Christian parenting manuals should I follow? The different theories tend to reduce parenting to following rules, which then assume the status of laws. Just as fallen human beings cannot fully satisfy God's law, parents find they cannot fully satisfy whatever law of child raising they embrace. Thus parenting gives rise to pressure, shame, and fear of failure. So much time and effort is spent micromanaging and second-guessing parenthood—our own and that of others—that we may give little thought to what God is doing in parenthood.

It is tempting for parents to be very self-conscious about how they are raising their children. And it can be exceedingly easy to become self-critical, whether or not that is justified. But isn't it ironic that so many of us overemphasize where we could go wrong with our children while also underemphasizing where God can go right? With all of the varied library of parenting material these days, we can forget a very simple fact: with or without parents, children grow up. Children raised under different parenting philosophies grow up, and most of them do fine. *God* is the one who ultimately grants them growth and opportunities for life. And while God has made young children dependent upon their parents, from the first month of life children are already peering away from their parents and toward the rest of the world. The doctrine of vocation allows parents to relax, somewhat, confident that God is the main actor in child raising.

So while it is good, right, and healthy for us as parents to try our best and be as prepared as possible for the sake of our children, we can give thanks every day that our children are in the hands of our gracious God. The same God who knit our children together in their mother's womb now remains active in their lives for all their days. As Scripture says, "In [God's] book were written, every one of them, *the days that were formed for [them]*" (Ps. 139:16).

Of course parents have much to do and figure out. They may adopt one theory of child raising or another. But through it all, they have the privilege of collaborating with God himself in bringing up their child. God is the origin of family, and God is the first and ultimate parent, first of his only-begotten Son and now of all whom he adopts into his family, the church. So what does God do as a parent? And how can we recognize his work hidden behind his servants, earthly parents?

Scripture is full of depictions of God in his deeds on our behalf, but one place where Christ addresses God as *our Father*—that is, as a parent—is in the Lord's Prayer. In the words Jesus told us to pray, we hear and enact the relationship between father and child:

> Our Father, who art in heaven, hallowed be Thy name. Thy kingdom come. Thy will be done on earth as it is in heaven. Give us this day our daily bread, and forgive us our trespasses, as we forgive those who trespass against us, and lead us not into temptation, but deliver us from evil.

These words, addressing our Father, are from the lips of his children. And from this we see that God calls us to approach him, *as our Father,* recognizing him and holding our relationship with him with confidence. We do not approach our Father as we would a stranger but as his loved ones. And since God is our heavenly Father, this prayer points us also to what earthly parents do for their children: hear them, give them their daily bread, forgive them their trespasses, deliver them from evil.

In this prayer, our heavenly Father hears us ask for our daily bread, forgiveness, accountability, guidance, and protection. We give no reasons for him to grant our requests beyond that he is now our Father (thanks be to Christ!). As a parent, he gives us these things, with his attention sweeping over large and small concerns alike. When we pray the Lord's Prayer, we not only ask but we also *expect* our daily bread from our Lord. The nature of our relationship to him as his children gives us that confidence, and that confidence—that faith—seems to be intrinsic to the initial parent-child relationship. Parents give to their children. And, in response, children have faith in their parents.

The prayer begins with a confession of God's holiness, his sovereignty, and his authority. Though to a far lesser degree, parents have authority over their children, and it is often through that authority that they are able to express God's loving care. In the Lord's Prayer, we are *thankful* that our heavenly Father bears authority, and in their daily lives, parents can strive to use their authority so that their children can ultimately be thankful as well. Praying the Lord's Prayer makes us conscious, for all of our claims of independence, that we are actually dependent on God for our physical and spiritual needs. Children truly are dependent upon their parents, and they have the advantage of knowing it.

To pray "Thy will be done" trusts that our Father's will is best and joins our will to his. Children need to obey their parents, but in order to do so on the deepest level, they need to agree with their parents—to trust them.

We ask God for our daily bread, which, as Luther explains in the *Small Catechism*, includes all that we need for this bodily life: "Daily bread includes everything that has to do with the support and needs of the body, such as food, drink, clothing, shoes, house, home, land, animals, money, goods, a devout husband or wife, devout children, devout workers, devout and faithful rulers, good government, good weather, peace, health, self-control, good reputation, good friends, faithful neighbors, and the like."[1] God gives children their daily bread—also their home, clothing, shoes, meals and snacks, pets, allowance, etc.—by means of parents who work hard to provide and prepare what they need.

Whoever prays the Lord's Prayer asks the heavenly Father for forgiveness and promises to forgive others. When we receive God's forgiveness and renewed life through Christ, it motivates ongoing love on earth, as we see our neighbors and their needs in light of God's free, unfettered generosity. By the same token, families are to be places of forgiveness. Husbands and wives are willing to forgive each other. Parents are always forgiving their children, and children are to learn to forgive their parents.

We also ask God that he would not lead us into temptation and that he would deliver us from evil. That is, as his children we ask him to protect us, both from overt evils that might befall us and from the evils that we ourselves might be tempted to commit. Parents, too, must protect their children. This means guarding them against dangers and delivering them from evil of every kind. This includes keeping them safe from accidents—preventing them from wandering into the street or poking electrical outlets—and from people who might harm them. ("Don't talk to strangers!") Parents must also protect their children from temptation. This includes sheltering them from bad moral influences, such as gruesomely violent or sexually explicit movies and music, bad company, and compromising situations. More deeply, this means training children morally, in the pursuit of wisdom, so that when the parents are not around enforcing their rules, they will, of their own free will, with God's grace, do what is right.

The Discipline and Instruction of the Lord

The Bible speaks about the importance of discipline for children. Here again, what parents are to do is connected to what God does:

> And have you forgotten the exhortation that addresses you as sons? "My son, do not regard lightly the discipline of the Lord, nor be weary when reproved by him. For the Lord disciplines the one he loves, and chastises every son whom he receives." It is for discipline that you have to endure. God is treating you as sons. For what son is there whom his father does not discipline? If you are left without discipline, in which all have participated, then you are illegitimate children and not sons. Besides this, we have had earthly fathers who disciplined us and we respected them. Shall we not much more be subject to the Father of spirits and live? For they disciplined us for a short time as it seemed best to them, but he disciplines us for our good, that we may share his holiness. For the moment all discipline seems painful rather than pleasant, but later it yields the peaceful fruit of righteousness to those who have been trained by it. (Heb. 12:5–11)

Discipline is not pleasant, but it is an expression of love. And parents are to make that love clear, even as they discipline their children. "Fathers, do not provoke your children to anger, but bring them up in the discipline and instruction of the Lord" (Eph. 6:4), says the apostle Paul; and "Fathers, do not provoke your children, lest they become discouraged" (Col. 3:21). This is not an impersonal discipline, then, but discipline precisely to serve the child.

Discipline means much more than punishment. The English term "discipline" comes from the same root as "disciple." Both refer to instruction given to a student. To discipline a child means to disciple the child. Certainly the Bible refers to applying the "rod," but even this is described not as punishment but as discipline, growing out of love: "Whoever spares the rod hates his son, but he who loves him is diligent to discipline him" (Prov. 13:24).

Little children are adorable, but they are uncivilized. They need instruction and training. They cannot control themselves physically, emotionally, or morally. As they grow older, they develop more and more self-control. But parents have to teach them what to do. Thus the work of potty training, insisting on "please" and "thank you," shushing them in church, and teaching them "how to behave."

Children, though they seem innocent, bear the fallen human nature.

They are self-centered, willful, indulging every impulse. Parents have to teach them right from wrong. "Don't push your sister down!" "Give back your brother's toy." "Share."

Moral formation has to go beyond rules, punishments, and external controls. When Muslim young men leave home to study in American or European universities, they often experience a moral crisis. Islam imposes a strict system of external controls. The goal is to make it physically impossible to transgress. Thus, women are shrouded from head to toe to protect men from feelings of lust; alcohol is not allowed in Islamic territory; and "non-Islamic" music, movies, and books are nowhere to be found. But when the external controls are no longer present, the sinful nature breaks out. When a Muslim lad leaves Saudi Arabia to study in the West—where young women are dressed very differently than what he was used to and where temptations abound—he sometimes plunges into pornography, substance abuse, and other forbidden fruit (which additionally can cause him to hate the society that has corrupted him and to seek redemption through jihadist martyrdom).[2]

The point is, moral principles, if they are to mean anything when a child grows up and leaves home, must be internalized. The young man does what he should, not because his parents are forcing him to, but because he personally agrees with the principles they taught him. He does what is right not because of external constraints or threats of punishment, but freely, of his own volition. The child must not just be controlled; he must develop self-control.

Christianity, unlike Islam, internalizes the moral law. The gospel transforms a person from the inside. Faith in Christ is active in love, bearing fruit in good works and love of neighbor. "Not by the way of eye-service, as people-pleasers, but as servants of Christ, doing the will of God from the heart, rendering service with a good will as to the Lord and not to man" (Eph. 6:6–7). Moral instruction is no longer just a matter of forcing children to comply with arbitrary-seeming rules; it becomes cultivating in them an internally motivated response to God's grace. This means teaching children to love and serve their neighbors. This involves cultivating empathy, encouraging children to "rejoice with those who rejoice, weep with those who weep" (Rom. 12:15). It involves teaching children to consider the impact of their actions in terms of the Golden Rule. "So whatever you wish that others would do to you, do also to them"

(Matt. 7:12). Thus children develop a conscience. They will still transgress sometimes, but they will also know the true Christian discipline of repenting and finding forgiveness, from their parents and whomever they offended, and from God.

Christian parents can bring the gospel into their child raising. Just as children can have faith in their father, they can have faith in their heavenly Father. Parents can take them to church, see them baptized, and talk to them about Jesus on every occasion. In the context of the gospel, parents can approach their children as fellow Christians. They can bring the law to bear on their children's faults in such a way that they repent, whereupon parents, like God, extend to them forgiveness.

Education

When Luther taught about the duties of parenthood, in the course of explaining the doctrine of vocation in the *Large Catechism*, he put a strong emphasis on the importance of parents giving their children an education: "Therefore let all people know that it is their chief duty—at the risk of losing divine grace—first to bring up their children in the fear and knowledge of God, and, then, if they are so gifted, also to have them engage in formal study and learn so that they may be of service wherever they are needed."[3]

These are strong words. It is the parents' "chief duty" to educate their children. If they do not, they risk "losing divine grace." Above all, parents must educate their children to fear and know God. But they should also educate their children academically, if the children are so gifted. Notice the vocation language here. Academic "gifts" are from God, who bestows talents and abilities to individuals to equip them for his callings. And the purpose of this "formal study" is not just so that the young people can make a living when they are grown up. Rather, the purpose of education is that of all vocations: "so that they may be of service wherever they are needed."

Certainly, according to Scripture, all parents must educate their children in God's Word. A key passage of the Old Testament, which sets forth the essential confession of faith and the summary of the law for the children of Israel, gives the mandate for education: "Hear, O Israel: The LORD our God, the LORD is one. You shall love the LORD your God with all your heart and with all your soul and with all your might. And these words that I command you today shall be on your heart. You shall teach them diligently to your children, and shall talk of them when you sit in your house, and when you walk by the way, and when you lie down, and when you rise" (Deut. 6:4–9).

Parents are told to teach the words of God "diligently to your children." God's words should also be a major topic of conversation in the household and in the course of everyday life, from morning to night. Luther, you will recall, wanted the Bible to be central in the lives of every Christian. He translated the Scriptures into the language of the people. But most people could not read. So Luther opened schools to teach all people—peasants as well as the prosperous, girls as well as boys—how to read the Bible. But Luther did not just open Bible-reading schools. Because of his doctrine of vocation, he wanted children also to have access to all kinds of learning, equipping them for all kinds of service in the world. Luther's schools followed a classical liberal arts curriculum, which gave students a wide-ranging education designed to cultivate all of their God-given powers. Thus, for Luther, spiritual and earthly education went together.

Notice that the education of children is the responsibility of their parents. Parents may undertake this work directly, as homeschoolers are doing. Under the doctrine of vocation, parents may also make use of others who have the specific vocation of being a teacher. But even if they send their children to school, parents remain the critical educators for their children.

Luther insisted that the family is the center for some of the most important of earthly works, going so far as to say parents are *priests* to their children. Priests, as we have said before, sacrifice, and Luther argued that parents fulfill their priestly task by *teaching their children.*[4] Parents sacrifice to educate their children. They spend their money on books, curriculum, and music teachers. They spend their time driving their children to music lessons and soccer practice. They struggle to communicate on the same level as their child and take upon themselves the burden of being understood. They exert every effort to take their children to church, teach them the Scriptures, and build up their faith in Christ.

Education takes place both formally and informally. Play can be highly and surprisingly educational. Play can draw children out of themselves and into interaction with the larger world. When that infant girl reaches her tiny fingers toward her mobile, she is doing what she can to explore God's gifts to her—gifts given through her parents. A young boy playing with his friends is learning how to get along with other human beings. A teenager playing sports is learning priceless lessons about working together with others. Play can teach love and service to the neighbor.

Part of the educational task of parenting is to pass down the elements of their heritage that are worth keeping to the next generation. This is another extension of family: handing down the legacy of parents, grandparents, great-grandparents, and on into the distant past. The customs and values of the culture, national principles and ideals, and the legacy of the civilization that has built up over centuries could all be lost if they are not transmitted. This will call for a good formal education, whether at school or—since many schools today ignore this dimension of education—at home. It also can happen informally, as children learn to follow family traditions, hear about their extended family and their ancestors, and embrace the cultural lore their parents teach them.

Parents also will want to educate their children so that they will turn into productive adults. Parents certainly have an interest in their children growing up and making a living for themselves. Again, an awareness of vocation will be helpful. Parents are sometimes tempted to push a child in a certain vocational direction. But vocation is a calling from God, not from parents. A father may want his son to be an accountant, but if the son is unorganized, bored with details, and no good at math, this will probably not be his calling. Parents should attend to the child's inclinations, abilities, and interests, understanding them as gifts from God for their child. Then parents should provide opportunities—lessons, activities, training, and above all encouragement—for these gifts to blossom. But adulthood is about much more than making a living. Parents need also to prepare their children to have families of their own, to have good marriages, and to be good parents. This they will learn primarily from observation.

Conclusion

Children's life in the family prepares them for having families of their own. Disciplines from toilet training to studying American history equip them for living in society and for the calling of citizenship. Education can also prepare them for vocations in the workplace. And bringing them up in God's Word will enable them to hear that Word as a calling into the Christian faith.

Throughout, children must be taught to love and serve their neighbors. The family is a perfect laboratory for this, with children learning to love and serve their parents and their siblings. Then, as they go outside the family, they will have different occasions for the discipline of love and service: with their friends, their church, the community, and the workplace. Do you see the pattern? The vocational work of parents in child raising is primarily to usher children into their own vocations.

12

The Crosses of Parenthood

*"O my son Absalom, my son, my son Absalom! Would I had died
instead of you, O Absalom, my son, my son!"*

2 SAMUEL 18:33

Parenting after the fall is not easy. Eve is promised pain when she brings
forth the seed of their bodies, and Adam is promised pain when he tries
to raise other kinds of seed. Raising children also has its thorns, its this-
tles, and its sweat.

Parents feel an overwhelming love for their children. They want the
best for them. They want them to be perfect and to have a perfect life.
Parents are subject both to the pain of their children, which they also feel
because of their love, and to the pain their children cause them.

Although God gives parents authority and influence over their children, their power over them is limited. They might force a child to comply with their wishes, but they cannot force a child to obey from the
heart. Nor do parents have the power to protect their children from the
trials, tribulations, and temptations that they will face on their own.

A child is a separate person from the parents, having a distinct will,
moral agency, and spiritual identity. The child is "other" than the parent.
Though parents want the child to be like them, this will not always happen. In fact, attempts to make the child conform in every way—against
the child's own personality—can provoke rebellion. Then again, rebellion

can happen even when parents do everything right. Some of the best and strongest Christian families often include a "problem child," someone whose behavior and attitudes are maddeningly out of sync with the rest of the family.

Some assume that the right parenting philosophy can cure any "problem child," that the right kind of discipline, if we could only find it, can altogether transform a child. Some parents assume that showering enough love on their children can keep them from having any problems, sparing them pain and misfortune and thus giving them an easy and happy life. Realistically, though, parts of a child's life are beyond the parents' control, to their great anguish.

But the child's life is not beyond God's control. In the Christian life, we must walk by faith and not by sight (2 Cor. 5:7). By the same token, in vocation, we must parent by faith. Parents must bear their crosses; that is, they will have to sacrifice themselves for their children, even, to a degree, for the sins of their children. But both the parents and their children are themselves borne up in the cross of Jesus Christ.

Tribulations in Parenting

Most of the trials and tribulations of parenthood are small and, in the vast scheme of things, minor. But there is just so much to worry about when you have children, and at the time you don't know if the anxiety is for something minor or major. Is she safe? Will she go into the street? Will she hurt herself on that slide? What time will he come home? Can he get into college? Will he get a job? Will he ever get married? These chronic concerns are tribulations of a sort.

But parents also have more acute concerns, as their children have more acute needs. Few things tear at a parent's heart more than when a child is hurting, physically or emotionally. Trips to the emergency room, tending a sick child, holding a crying teenager are wrenching.

Many children have serious problems—autism, Down syndrome, debilitating diseases—and parents devote themselves, night and day, to giving them the care they need. Many parents do not just juggle band and soccer practice; they juggle doctors, specialists, and therapists. In addition to trying to teach love and forgiveness along with academics, they manage medical bills, constant stress, and their own nightmares.

Perhaps the worst experience human beings can endure is the death of one's child. Whether the child is an infant or a toddler or an adolescent or an adult, taken by disease or accident or crime or war, there is hardly any consolation for parents bereft of their child. The Bible describes this anguish through the prophet Jeremiah:

> Thus says the LORD:
> "A voice is heard in Ramah,
>   lamentation and bitter weeping.
> Rachel is weeping for her children;
>   she refuses to be comforted for her children,
>   because they are no more." (Jer. 31:15)

Rachel, wife of Jacob, is the mother by blood or office of all Israelites, and her crying echoes through the centuries. Jeremiah is also, by prophecy, hearing the mothers of Bethlehem whose infants were slain by Herod (Matt. 2:18). In the context of Jeremiah's prophecy, though, he is looking ahead to a time when God will turn "mourning into joy" (31:13).

The very next verse after the description of Rachel weeping gives a promise that all bereaved parents can seize upon:

> Thus says the LORD:
> "Keep your voice from weeping,
>   and your eyes from tears,
> for there is a reward for your work,
>   declares the LORD,
>   and they shall come back from the land of the enemy.
> There is hope for your future,
>   declares the LORD,
> and your children shall come back to their own country. (Jer. 31:16–17)

At the resurrection of the dead, the very children Rachel, the Bethlehem mothers, and all other bereaved parents to this day have been mourning "shall come back to their own country," and they will be reunited. In the words of Rev. Charles Lehmann, "Rachel's daughters' tears have been wiped away . . . [by] Jesus, son of David, son of Judah, son of Leah."[1]

These heartbreaking tribulations that some parents are called to—the sickness of a child, the death of a child—are indeed crosses to bear. Parents sacrifice themselves to help their stricken child and they would be glad to make even greater sacrifices if they would bring their child back to health. Grief, too, when a child dies, is a sacrifice. These kinds of tribulations have one mercy: the love between parents and their children is very, very strong. In fact, the parents' natural love for their child is augmented with compassion, another kind of love, so that the love they feel may well be deeper and more intense than it would have been otherwise. That love, which is reciprocated by the sick or dying child, can be healing, even in its way, redemptive.

Some tribulations, though, strike precisely at love. They violate or damage or repudiate the love that is supposed to exist between parents and children. These are ultimately even more crushing, when children reject their parents or parents reject their children.

Prodigal Sons and Prodigal Daughters

We know a fine Christian family, devout and loving and conscientious. One of their sons, though raised in the faith, when he became a teenager, starting selling drugs. Despite interventions, counseling, suspended sentences, he kept going back to that trade. Finally, a judge, who had tried to be lenient with him before, sentenced him to hard time in the penitentiary. It is rare, as our earlier chapter said, for a convict to come from an intact and functional family, but it happened this time.

We know some parents who are faithful Christians, zealous for the Lord and devoted to God's Word. They homeschooled their children, giving them a first-class education, which included a strong dose of apologetics, worldview analysis, and spiritual discipleship. These parents are loving to their children and wise in their discipline and their guidance. One of their children, upon graduating from college, renounced Christianity and has become a militant agnostic.

Sometimes Christian parents are so harsh and so controlling in their child raising that they inadvertently turn their children into rebels. Their version of Christianity is typically legalistic—as if Christianity were just about laws, "Do not handle, Do not taste, Do not touch" (Col. 2:21)—with little flavor of the gospel of Christ or the freedom that he brings. Naturally, their children cannot wait to leave home and leave those restrictions and that belief system behind them. We have known parents like that, also.

If you read the biographies of atheists or talk to them, you will often find that this is the kind of family life and the kind of Christianity that they knew as children and that they are reacting against now. Christian parents must be very careful lest they inadvertently create an environment that turns their children into moral rebels and haters of God. We have seen families that seem sure to be atheist factories. This is a failure of faith—turning Christianity into something more closely resembling Islam—and a failure of vocation, a case of having Christ and the freedom that he brings through the gospel insufficiently manifested in the home (Gal. 5:1). This is also, very likely, an example of "provoking" children to anger (Eph. 6:4) and to discouragement (Col. 3:21). Nevertheless, the anguish these parents feel, made worse by guilt and by their godly intentions, is heartbreaking.

But these particular families we are thinking about here—of the drug dealer and the militant agnostic—were not like that. These parents did everything right in raising their children. We know that because their other children turned out so well. And yet, these parents had prodigal sons.

This, in fact, is common among Christian families. A son or a daughter, as in Christ's parable, goes away, literally or figuratively, to engage in "reckless living" (Luke 15:13). We have known staunchly moral parents who find out their child is gay. We have known quite a few staunchly moral parents whose sons and daughters live with someone they are not married to. The list goes on.

One reaction that we have seen in some Christian parents is to have nothing more to do with their children who transgress. "She is never to come into my house again, as long as she is living with that boy." "If he's gay, I have nothing to say to him." "I refuse to be in the same room with that atheist." "If he's selling drugs, I'm never seeing him again and he can just rot in jail forever."

This is a natural impulse. By rejecting what the parents stand for, the child has rejected the parents. The emotional response is to reject the child in turn. But this is exactly the wrong thing to do. Disinheriting or casting a child out of the household rends the one flesh union that is the family, just as divorce does; although since parents and children literally share the same blood, it is probably even more traumatic for both sides. It is saying no to the cross of parenthood. It is saying no to vocation.

It is critically important when a child has "fallen away" that the parents continue to be there. The child is still a part of the family, no matter what. Continue to invite the erring child to family gatherings and activities. Demonstrate to the child that the sin—which of course the parents disapprove of—does not cancel out their love. The child may reject the parents (and may, for a while, refuse to come back to the family), but the parents do not reject the child, instead continuing to call and invite and help. Showing the offending child this radical love is manifesting God's grace to the child. This is an act of cross bearing at its most profound. The parents suffer, to be sure, but they are also reaching out to the child in love, which is, in vocation, God's love.

After all, who is the Father whose children have most rebelled against him? We are those rebellious children, and yet God brought us back into his family. We should not be surprised, then, that those who have the vocation of parenthood should also have to deal with their children's rebellion. The connection between a father's grace and our heavenly Father's grace is, of course, the message of the Prodigal Son. He was prodigal—that is, extravagantly reckless—in his sins, but his father was prodigal in his forgiveness. God is like this father, and fathers should be like this God.

Another point about the Prodigal Son: he came back. Sometimes, eventually, the constant demonstrable love of the parents can reach the prodigal's heart. Sometimes God reaches him in other ways. For generations, parents have clung to Proverbs 22:6: "Train up a child in the way he should go: and when he is old, he will not depart from it" (KJV).[2] When he is old! When he is young, he might wander away from the path that he was taught, but when he is old he will come back to stay! To be sure, this often happens. Young people who leave the church as soon as they leave home often come back, especially when they have children of their own. Such is the power of vocation.

The parents of the militant agnostic did not abandon their child. The mother says she will pray for him and keep praying for him no matter what. She recalls Monica, the mother of St. Augustine, who prayed for the conversion of her son through all of his heresies and sexual sins, until in the very last year of her life, he did indeed become a Christian, going on to become one of the greatest theologians of the early church! The agnostic's mother said that she would be like Monica. In the meantime, both the mother and the father are staying close to their son, getting together as much as they can.

The parents of the drug dealer did not abandon their son either. They visited him in prison. They wrote to him and called him. After he served his sentence, they welcomed him back home. They helped him get back on his feet. He started his own business—a tattoo parlor, which was not what they would have picked, but they encouraged him. His mother went so far as to get a tasteful little tattoo on her ankle! He is making a success of it. He says he has learned his lesson. He visits his parents on holidays, and sometimes they spend the holidays at his place. We don't know where he is spiritually now, but he painted a picture of Jesus in an elaborate tattoo style and gave it to our church.

Conclusion

The Bible is filled with dysfunctional families. Even the great saints and patriarchs of Scripture had trouble with their children. One of the most poignant and tragic stories in Scripture has to do with David and his son Absalom (2 Samuel 13–20). King David was the man after God's own heart (1 Sam. 13:14), the type and forefather of Jesus Christ himself. David's son Absalom was "rebellious" in the most literal way, staging a rebellion that, for a while, drove his father from his throne.

Children must bear their own responsibility for what they do. When they rebel or go the way of the Prodigal Son, it is not always the parents' fault. Sometimes parents can look back and wonder if they could have done anything differently that might have kept the child on the right path. Usually this is a futile exercise. One can always find fault with one's parenting. The doctrine of vocation encourages parents to consider that they have followed their calling the best they could and to leave the outcome in God's hands.

But sometimes parents did do something wrong that triggered their child's rejection. Sometimes parents are the prodigals, needing forgiveness from their child. More often they both need to forgive each other. At any rate, in his dealings with Absalom and his other children, David certainly failed in his vocations, not only as father but as king.

David had many wives, and the ancient practice of polygamy stretches the one-flesh union that marriage is supposed to be to the breaking point. Each wife had her children, and typically she schemed for their advantage, with the half-brothers and half-sisters being rivals to each other. All of this violated the family unity that God desires. Such enmities plagued David's family, but this case also involved sexual depravity. One of David's sons, Amnon, began lusting after one of David's daughters, Tamar. This incestuous passion for his half-sister was bad enough, but then he brutally raped her!

King David, we are told, "was very angry" (2 Sam. 13:21). But as a father he did not protect or give justice to his daughter. And as a king he did not enforce the law by punishing Amnon. David was a good king to his subjects, but his fault, as the prophet Nathan had previously showed him, is that he did not always apply his laws to himself or to his family. Doubtless, David was torn between his vocation as a father, with the love he still felt for his son, and his vocation as the king, which would require putting his son to death. Ordering one's son to be stoned to death would of course be horrible for any father, but Amnon's offense was so extreme that justice demanded nothing less. And since the crime was against his own family, his own daughter, David's fatherhood should have demanded the death penalty, even against his evil son. But David, neglecting his callings, did nothing.

Tamar, however, had a brother, Absalom. He was resolved to avenge his sister. Biding his time and putting on a façade of friendliness, Absalom invited all of David's sons to a party. And while his half-brother Amnon was "merry with wine" (13:28), Absalom, with the help of his servants, murdered him.

Again, King David did nothing about it. Incest, rape, and now murder. Absalom fled. But David, with feelings that all parents can relate to, was overwhelmed with sorrow, pining after both the son who was dead and the son who killed him. "And the spirit of the king longed to go out to Absalom" (13:39).

Nevertheless, in a sort of punishment that was far less than the death penalty murderers could normally expect in David's kingdom, Absalom was banished. Thus, David was responding in a way that we recommended parents with prodigal children not do. He had no dealings with his son. Even after three years when Absalom was allowed to come back, David said, "He is not to come into my presence" (14:24). David might have talked with Absalom. If he was not going to punish him for his act of fratricide, he might have made him an "avenger," an agent of justice for Tamar, and worked some kind of reconciliation. But in cutting off all contact with his son, David rejected him. And as happens today also, this provoked in Absalom a hurt and bitterness that destroyed their relationship. Absalom's justified anger against Amnon metastasized into anger against his whole family, and especially his father. Two years later, the king finally met with him, but by then it was too late.

Absalom was conspiring to take his father's throne for himself. He would overthrow his father, kill him, and make himself king. Absalom presented himself to the people as someone who would do a better job of administering justice than the king, stirred up the old factions that had backed King Saul, and positioned himself as the leader of everyone discontented with David. "So Absalom stole the hearts of the men of Israel" (15:6). He raised a military force, staged an uprising, and actually drove David and his followers out of Jerusalem. Then, in a grotesque replay of Amnon's sexual depravity, he forced himself on David's ten concubines.

King David may have been an overindulgent father, but he was a formidable adversary. He placed a spy in Absalom's entourage who thwarted his plan to kill his father. Then David gathered his forces in the wilderness, as he had once before under Saul, and attacked the army of his rebellious son. And yet David gave express instructions to his warriors to "deal gently for my sake with the young man Absalom" (18:5). In the battle, Absalom's forces were routed, but at the cost of twenty thousand lives. Absalom, fleeing on his mule, rode under an oak tree, and his head got caught in the branches. He was left hanging from the tree, alive. David's no-nonsense general Joab threw three javelins into his heart.

When David heard about the death of his son, his grief knew no bounds. He wept because his child was dead and also because his child had rejected him and had rejected God for a life of hatred, sin, and rebellion. In some of the most plaintive words in the Bible, David poured out his heart for all parents who have lost children, either to sin or to death. "O my son Absalom, my son, my son Absalom! Would I had died instead of you, O Absalom, my son, my son!" (2 Sam. 18:33).

Would that I could have died in your place! Would that I could have become your substitute! I would gladly hang in that tree in your place. I would gladly be pierced with those spears if only you could be saved.

Parents today often have this exact feeling. They wish that they could have been in that accident instead of their child. In the hospital room, they pray, "Take me instead!"

"She is too young to have to go through chemotherapy. If only I could go through that for her!"

This is to bear the cross at the deepest level: To yearn to die for the one you love. To desire, desperately, to take the place of your child, to suffer instead of your child, so that somehow the child could go free.

David, as much as he wanted to, could not die for Absalom. But his Son who was also his Lord did.[3] Another Son of David, Jesus Christ, hung on a tree, was pierced, and died as the substitute for Absalom, for prodigal children through the centuries, and for all of us. He atoned for the sins of bad parenting—David's and ours—and for the sins of the Absaloms and Amnons, no matter how monstrous, and for all our derelictions of vocation.

This is the love of God, to whom we are all Absaloms and prodigal children. This is the love of Christ's which is channeled in and through the vocation of fathers and mothers.

Part 3

The Vocations of Childhood

13

Childhood

Truly, I say to you, whoever does not receive the kingdom of God like a child shall not enter it.

LUKE 18:17

It probably seems strange to think of being a child as a vocation. What does a child have to *do*? Everyone used to be a child, but then we grow up and enter into our various callings. How could a stage of life so universal and so transient be a vocation? Besides, young children do not have to work for a living, have few responsibilities, and spend much of their time playing. How can that be a vocation?

And yet, Luther and other theologians of vocation made it quite clear that being a child is a calling from God: a sphere of love and service in which God himself is at work. Not only do children complete the substance of parenthood, but also every family contains children, whether the household contains parents. Why? Because we are all children to our parents, even when we grow up. Also, we are all children to God. We have that status by virtue of God's child, his only-begotten Son. We have already asked, "What *is* marriage?" "What *is* a father?" Now it is time to ask, "What *is* a child?" What is this status that we hold through the Son of God?

Children and the Kingdom of God

In the Old Testament, over and over again we hear about God's protection and provision for children. In the New Testament, this is taken further, to the point of lifting up young children as the model for Christian faith: "Jesus called them to him, saying, 'Let the children come to me, and do not hinder them, for to such belongs the kingdom of God. Truly, I say to you, whoever does not receive the kingdom of God like a child shall not enter it'" (Luke 18:16–17). So what is it about children that makes them such exemplary citizens of the kingdom of God?

Notice how children get so much attention in the Bible without being able to even ask for it, let alone earn it! Children receive from their parents. Their mothers and fathers give them everything they need for their very lives—food, shelter, clothing, health care, discipline, education—and whether they deserve it never enters their parents' minds. Children exist in a state of utter dependence on their parents. Christians, too, are utterly dependent on their heavenly Father and trust him to provide everything they need for their lives, both physical and spiritual. This is faith.

The child's vocation of receiving reminds us also that sometimes it matters more who *we are* than *what we do*. The Prodigal Son was welcomed back, not because of his well-planned speech of repentance that he never had the chance to give, but rather because his father recognized him from afar as his child. All the wrongs the son had done did not change that he was his father's *son*. What we do certainly matters and has serious ramifications—if the son continued to flee his father's help, for example, to continue wallowing with the pigs—and yet the relationship of parent and child is permanent. Even after a parent's death, the child remains an heir, a recipient of the parent's legacy. Their relationship is also objective. Children do not choose their parents. And their membership in the family is not contingent upon good behavior, personal commitment, or the paying of dues.

The same holds true for a Christian's status in the kingdom of God. A baptized, born-again Christian can say with confidence, "I am a child of God!" As God's child, the Christian can be certain of the heavenly Father's love. This is possible because Jesus Christ, God's only-begotten Son, shares his inheritance with all of us, the inheritance given by his Father who sees us clothed with his perfect Son (Gal. 3:27). "The Spirit himself bears witness with our spirit that we are children of God, and if children, then heirs—heirs of God and fellow heirs with Christ, provided we suffer with him in order that we may also be glorified with him" (Rom. 8:16–17).

The Son of God

According to the doctrine of vocation, God himself is present in the ordinary callings of everyday life. We have seen this in the vocation of marriage, which is a manifestation of Christ and the church. We have seen this in the vocation of parenthood, which is an expression of God the Father. The vocation of children manifests God the Son.

God is a unity consisting of three persons: Father, Son, and Holy Spirit. Families too consist of distinct persons who comprise a unity. The Trinity, of course, is much more than a family. To help us navigate the mysteries of who God reveals himself to be in Scripture, the early church in the sixth century formulated the Athanasian Creed, one of the so-called "ecumenical creeds" to which all Christians could agree. The text carefully voices the Christian understanding of the Trinity and of the Son as both God and Man.

As the Athanasian Creed explains, in the Godhead, the Father and the Son are equals, but the Son is *begotten*:

> The Father is made of none: neither created nor begotten. The Son is of the Father alone; not made, nor created, but begotten. The Holy Ghost is of the Father and of the Son: neither made, nor created, nor begotten, but proceeding. . . . And in this Trinity none is before or after other; none is greater or less than another; But the whole three Persons are coeternal together, and coequal: so that in all things, as is aforesaid, the Unity in Trinity and the Trinity in Unity is to be worshiped.[1]

Again, a person "creates" something other than himself. He "begets" something that is like himself, though distinct—another person. Thus a man with the vocation of an artist "creates" a work of art. The work is an expression of himself; he may love what he has made, and the work may have great value. But when the artist in his other vocation as a father "begets" a child, he has brought into existence another human being who also, like him, has life, consciousness, and talents.

When we confess that Jesus is begotten of God, we confess a mystery of the Trinity: that God begat God, yet there is only one God. Jesus is true God and Jesus is the Son of God. And, as the son of Mary, Jesus is also fully man:

> We believe and confess that our Lord Jesus Christ, the Son of God, is God and Man; God of the Substance of the Father, begotten before the worlds; and

Man of the substance of His mother, born in the world; Perfect God and perfect Man, of a reasonable soul and human flesh subsisting. Equal to the Father
as touching His Godhead, and inferior to the Father as touching His manhood;
Who, although He be God and Man, yet He is not two, but one Christ: One,
not by conversion of the Godhead into flesh, but by taking the manhood into
God.[2]

The Son of God always existed, having been begotten by the eternal
Father, of one substance with him, but at his incarnation he also became
the Son of Man. His mother was a human being, Mary, who gave him her
"substance" and "human flesh."[3] And in some of the most remarkable
words in Christian theology, we learn that the incarnation was not a matter of the Godhead converting into flesh; but rather, the reverse: "taking
the manhood into God"! Thus, in the Trinity, the Son of God is still incarnate; our human nature, our human substance, and even our human
flesh can be found within the Trinity itself! No wonder our human vocations are tied so closely into the very being of God. The Trinity, though, is
not modeled after human family. The Holy Spirit is not the mother of the
Son of God. Mary is his mother. She conceived him "by the Holy Spirit" as
the Apostles' Creed says (Matt. 1:18–20), but motherhood itself is profoundly human. And because the Son of God in the Trinity remains the
Son of Mary, in a way motherhood, too, is part of that humanity that is
"taken into God." Again we see vocation as the point at which God and
human beings come together.

The relationships within the Trinity are beyond our understanding—
"incomprehensible," as the Athanasian Creed puts it—but obviously it
is a significant thing to *be a child* in a relational sense. Being a child is
not merely a description of age or the waiting room for adulthood, but
a position, one held eternally by the Son of God. And, in our case, we
are children in the early years of our lives, but we retain that position as
adults and into eternity. Significantly, being a child is the one vocation
God has given to all human beings.

The Son of God was a fetus, a baby, a toddler, a youngster, a teenager,
an adult. The fullness of God was conceived in the womb of his mother.
The Son of God served his eternal Father—and all of us—by entering into
the earthly vocation of child. Jesus was no less God when he became a
human embryo and he was no less God when he took his first stumbling
steps. He perfectly fulfilled the will of God at every age in every moment.

In Christ, we see a child who need not put away "childish ways" (1 Cor.13:11). We see the validity and blessedness of being someone's child—being a child instead of merely passing through a child's youthful phases. But Jesus even as a young child still had a vocation to fulfill, as we learn from an episode from Jesus's youth, a family road trip no less:

> Now his parents went to Jerusalem every year at the Feast of the Passover. And when he was twelve years old, they went up according to custom. And when the feast was ended, as they were returning, the boy Jesus stayed behind in Jerusalem. His parents did not know it, but supposing him to be in the group they went a day's journey, but then they began to search for him among their relatives and acquaintances, and when they did not find him, they returned to Jerusalem, searching for him. After three days they found him in the temple, sitting among the teachers, listening to them and asking them questions. And all who heard him were amazed at his understanding and his answers. And when his parents saw him, they were astonished. And his mother said to him, "Son, why have you treated us so? Behold, your father and I have been searching for you in great distress." And he said to them, "Why were you looking for me? Did you not know that I must be in my Father's house?" And they did not understand the saying that he spoke to them. And he went down with them and came to Nazareth and was submissive to them. And his mother treasured up all these things in her heart.
> And Jesus increased in wisdom and in stature and in favor with God and man. (Luke 2:41–52)

Parents may automatically sympathize with Mary and Joseph. Why didn't young Jesus tell them what he was going to do? Why didn't he communicate more? One thing we can learn from this passage is that characteristically childish behavior—even that which annoys and distresses parents—is not necessarily a sin. We know that Jesus was sinless, and yet, like all other children, he did things that worried his parents and got caught up in his own preoccupations. When he was a baby—despite Augustine and the line in "Away in the Manger"—Jesus no doubt cried. Later, he may have broken his share of pottery and had to be reminded to clean up the carpentry shop. A child, by definition, is going to act childishly; but immaturity is no sin, something parents of regular children need to remember.

But turning to the main point of the text, see how seriously twelve-year-old Jesus took his vocations. As soon as Jesus's parents went back to the temple, they saw him listening and talking with the religious teachers. Not playing with other children, forgetful of his obligations, but discussing God and his Word. He was very much mindful of what he should be doing as the Son of God and was already preparing for his vocation as the Savior of the world. Yet Jesus then went back with his parents and lived in Nazareth. This passage goes so far as to say he *was submissive to them"* (Luke 2:51). The Son of God was called to submit to his parents as the human child he had become. He honored his father and his mother, obeying God's commandment as all children should and fulfilling the law on the behalf of children at every stage of childhood.

In this passage, we glimpse the vocation of child when the child is not a sinner. Like Jesus who performed this good work for them, children are called to increase in wisdom, in stature, and in favor with God and man. That is, to learn, to grow, to know God's grace, and to love and serve their neighbors.

Born Again

Our Savior came into the world through the womb of a maiden. Then what does he do? He bears us up, redeems us from our debt and slavery to sin, and he *causes our rebirth*. He makes us children again.

With two births, we have two childhoods and thus two interrelated lives. We are born again not from our mothers' wombs but as children of God. We are called to increase in wisdom, in stature, and in favor with God and man, not only as we grow up with our parents, but now also as children of God. As Christians too, we are to grow spiritually, which includes becoming wiser, stronger, more receptive to the grace of God, and more loving to our neighbors. This growth happens similarly to the way we grew at home: We submitted to our parents, and now we submit to God. Our parents disciplined us, and now we accept discipline from God. In both levels of our lives, God, working also through our parents, frees us to do what we were meant to do: have faith in him and love toward one another. God through our parents helped us to learn, grow, interact, and ultimately enter our adult vocations. That also includes entering into our inheritance in the kingdom of God.

The Bible speaks of our spiritual growth in terms of our physical growth. Christians are to "grow up" in their faith, to move from being a baby Christian or a childish Christian to being an adult Christian. The apostle Paul chastises the Corinthians for their spiritual immaturity, as demonstrated by the rivalries and conflicts within their church: "But I, brothers, could not address you as spiritual people, but as people of the flesh, as infants in Christ. I fed you with milk, not solid food, for you were not ready for it. And even now you are not yet ready, for you are still of the flesh. For while there is jealousy and strife among you, are you not of the flesh and behaving only in a human way?" (1 Cor. 3:1–3). Infants are almost comically self-centered and demanding, wanting their own way no matter what and wailing indignantly when they do not get it. Many Christians are like that. Christians from past centuries, who faced much greater difficulties than we do with much greater spiritual toughness, often seem more "adult" than Christians today, though that is surely an overgeneralization. Christian immaturity has always been a problem in the church, even in the days of the Bible.

The author of the book of Hebrews uses the imagery of parents trying to transition their babies from milk to solids:

> For though by this time you ought to be teachers, you need someone to teach you again the basic principles of the oracles of God. You need milk, not solid food, for everyone who lives on milk is unskilled in the word of righteousness, since he is a child. But solid food is for the mature, for those who have their powers of discernment trained by constant practice to distinguish good from evil. Therefore let us leave the elementary doctrine of Christ and go on to maturity, not laying again a foundation of repentance from dead works and of faith toward God, and of instruction about washings, the laying on of hands, the resurrection of the dead, and eternal judgment. (Hebrews 5:12–6:2)

This is sometimes taken to mean that Christians do not need to keep hearing the gospel anymore, that they should learn to go beyond that to the real "meat" of Christianity, which is usually presented as some kind of good works. But notice how this apostle switches the metaphor from "milk" to "foundation." The "deadness" of works and the necessity of faith, the teachings about baptism, ordination, the resurrection, and the judgment of eternity are not something to be left behind; rather, they are foundational. This faith needs to be lived out, but the power to do so comes precisely from these foundations. As the apostle Peter puts it, "Like newborn infants, long for the pure spiritual milk, that by it you may grow up into salvation" (1 Pet. 2:2).

Even after we have grown, we remain children—children of our parents, when they are old and even after they have died—and children of

Abraham, as Scripture sometimes says ("Know then that it is those of faith who are the sons of Abraham" [Gal. 3:7]). We are also, with Christ, children of God throughout eternity! "Child" becomes our everlasting office, long after our parents have died, long even after we die, as we live forever as God's heirs in his household.

Conclusion

As an adult, Jesus often chose to use the title "Son of Man" for himself, and he continued to call his Father "father," because *he did not outgrow these relationships*. He remains the Son of Man! He remains Son of the Father! And he saved us "so that being justified by his grace we might become heirs according to the hope of eternal life" (Titus 3:7).

This is an important privilege of a child: to be an heir. The whole family legacy with all of its property and titles is given to the child. This is not something the child has earned, though the inheritance might go to one child instead of another. It is contingent only on one thing: the owner of the legacy must die. Through our heavenly Father and the death of his only-begotten Son, we inherit a salvation that is "imperishable, undefiled, and unfading, kept in heaven for you" (1 Pet. 1:4).

We are not merely servants, not even "merely children," but honored heirs! The apostle Paul describes the practice of young children having a guardian until they are old enough to inherit the estate. The guardian he describes as the law, but through Christ we have the independent status of sons and heirs. (Christian women, too, have the status of "sons"; that is, in terms of the day, prime inheritors, so that there is "neither male nor female" in Christ.) Here baptism is the mark of being adopted into God's family, a family of faith that started with Abraham, so that all of God's promises to him and his descendants apply to every Christian: "But now that faith has come, we are no longer under a guardian, for in Christ Jesus you are all sons of God, through faith. For as many of you as were baptized into Christ have put on Christ. There is neither Jew nor Greek, there is neither slave nor free, there is no male and female, for you are all one in Christ Jesus. And if you are Christ's, then you are Abraham's offspring, heirs according to promise" (Gal. 3:25–29). The earthly vocations are temporal and temporary; they are swallowed up in the eternal vocation of being God's child.

14

Growing

For you [Lord] formed my inward parts; you knitted me together in my mother's womb. I praise you, for I am fearfully and wonderfully made. Wonderful are your works; my soul knows it very well. My frame was not hidden from you, when I was being made in secret, intricately woven in the depths of the earth. Your eyes saw my unformed substance; in your book were written, every one of them, the days that were formed for me, when as yet there was none of them.

PSALM 139:13–16.

Children grow. This is what children do, transforming from infant to teenager to adult before their parents' wondering eyes. It has been said that *Peter Pan*, about a boy who doesn't want to grow up, is a fantasy for adults. Actual children can't wait to grow up.[1] And this is what parenting entails—all of the teaching, disciplining, educating, civilizing—helping their children grow to the next level, until they are finally adults themselves.

And, as children of God, we too are growing. We are to "grow in the grace and knowledge of our Lord and Savior Jesus Christ" (2 Pet. 3:18). Our adulthood is when we die and enter into our everlasting life.

We are children, of course, even after we are adults. "Growing up" involves entering other vocations—as citizens, in the workplace, in the church, acquiring other family vocations such as marriage and parenthood—though holding the office of child to one's parents remains. So there is also growth for adults, and not only spiritual growth. Adults continue to enter into other vocations and change and mature throughout their lives.

One misconception about vocations is that they are permanent. Sometimes the doctrine of vocation has been used to keep people in one occupation or station in life. But to the vocation of the child may be added eventually the vocation of marriage and the vocation of parenthood. Similarly, to support the household, a person may be called first to one kind of employment and then to another and possibly another. As the adult changes and grows, new skills may develop and new opportunities arise. New callings may also emerge in the exercise of citizenship and in the church.

The vocation of the child is a model for all vocations. As children grow and no matter how old they get, they also have specific duties: to honor and obey their fathers and their mothers and to love and serve their neighbors in the way appropriate at every stage of their lives.

Honor Your Father and Your Mother

Every vocation has its particular neighbor to love and serve. The child's defining neighbors are the parents. The work God assigns to children—of every age—is of such importance and moral significance that it is enshrined in the Ten Commandments: "Honor your father and your mother, that your days may be long in the land that the LORD your God is giving you" (Ex. 20:12). This commandment is repeated in Scripture verbatim eight times (Ex. 20:12; Deut. 5:16; Matt. 15:4; 19:19; Mark 7:10; 10:19; Luke 18:20; Eph. 6:2). The other nine commandments are prohibitions, saying what must *not* be done. This commandment alone is a positive exhortation. Not only that, as the apostle Paul notes, "This is the first commandment with a promise" (Eph. 6:2).

It sounds as if the promise is long life, but since that does not always seem to bear out, the emphasis must be on remaining in the land—that is, avoiding the sins that led the children of Israel to exile. Indeed, if they had honored their forefather Israel and followed his teachings and remained in his covenant, they would not have fallen away. The more general promise is given the second time Moses was given the Ten

Commandments: "That it may go well with you" (Deut. 5:16). In this even secularist psychologists agree: if you have had good relationships with your parents, you will tend to do well in the world.

So what does it mean to "honor your father and your mother"? In his *Large Catechism*, which authoritatively develops and teaches the doctrine of vocation, Luther speaks at length about this commandment, elaborating on both the high distinction of parenthood and the holy work assigned to children:

> To this estate of fatherhood and motherhood God has given the special distinction above all estates that are beneath it that He not simply commands us to love our parents, but to honor them. For with respect to brothers, sisters, and our neighbors in general He commands nothing higher than that we love them, so that He separates and distinguishes father and mother above all other persons upon earth, and places them at His side. For it is a far higher thing to honor than to love one, inasmuch as it comprehends not only love, but also modesty, humility, and deference as to a majesty there hidden, and requires not only that they be addressed kindly and with reverence, but, most of all, that both in heart and with the body we so act as to show that we esteem them very highly, and that, next to God, we regard them as the very highest. For one whom we are to honor from the heart we must truly regard as high and great.[2]

Such a high command, and God gives it to children! They are to regard parents as "high and great." They are to pay "deference as to a majesty there hidden." The majesty is God's. Thus, honoring parents involves recognizing that in them and in their vocation God himself is hidden. Looming behind an earthly father and working through him is the heavenly Father.

Reading Luther is more enjoyable than reading most theologians because in the midst of some serious discourse he will put in something that makes the reader smile, if not laugh out loud. We learn that parents were embarrassing their children not just today but way back in the sixteenth century! "We must, therefore, impress it upon the young that they should regard their parents as in God's stead, and remember that however lowly, poor, frail, and queer they may be, nevertheless they are father and mother given them by God. They are not to be deprived of their honor because of their conduct or their failings. Therefore we are not to regard their persons, how they may be, but the will of God who has thus created and ordained."[3] If God is hidden in parents, some of them make very good disguises! Another translation reads, no matter how "strange their parents might be."[4] The point is, what gives parents their right to the highest honor is not their personality, virtues, or parental skills. Rather, it is the office they hold.

The distinction between the person and the office is of critical importance in the doctrine of vocation, and it goes back to the church's rejection of the Donatist heresy, which taught that the validity of the sacraments depends on the good character and faithfulness of the clergyman who administered them. But you do not have to get baptized again or remarried just because the preacher who presided got caught embezzling money from the church. Similarly, a judge may have personal quirks and shortcomings, but still has the authority to sentence a lawbreaker to prison. You still have to do what your boss says at the workplace, even though the boss is not always right, simply because he or she is the boss. All of this is "by virtue of the office," not the person. The same holds true for the office of parenthood. The individuals who hold that office may not deserve honor in themselves, but they deserve honor from their children for the office they hold. They may have actually been bad parents—neglectful, selfish, unloving, even abusive. (We'll talk about the hard cases in the next chapter.) But they brought you into this world. You owe them for that, at least. If you cannot honor them, honor the office. Honor God in the office, who, despite your parents' sin, used them to bring you into existence and to sustain your life.

Parents are in "God's stead." That is, parents are the face of God to the young child, doing what God does, giving life, nourishing, protecting, disciplining, forgiving, teaching, causing to grow. Actually, God is the one doing those things, using parents as his instrument, but God commands that they share his honor. Luther describes, in vivid and poignant detail, what that looks like throughout the whole course of life:

> Learn, therefore, first, what is the honor towards parents required by this commandment, to wit, that they be held in distinction and esteem above all things, as the most precious treasure on earth. Furthermore, that also in our words we observe modesty toward them, do not accost them roughly, haughtily, and defiantly, but yield to them and be silent, even though they go too far. Thirdly, that we show them such honor also by works, that is, with our body and possessions, that we serve them, help them, and provide for them when they are old, sick, infirm, or poor, and all that not only gladly, but with humility and reverence, as doing it before God. For he who knows how to regard

> them in his heart will not allow them to suffer want or hunger, but will place them above him and at his side, and will share with them whatever he has and possesses.[5]

A child, young or grown up, should consider parents the "most precious treasure on earth." The child's words to them should always be respectful and deferential, even when the parents "go too far." And when the roles are reversed, when the child is grown and the parents are the ones who need to be taken care of, the child honors them by gladly and humbly providing for their needs.

This kind of honor stems from gratitude. The more you are thankful for your parents and what they have done for you, the more honor you will show them. Again, Luther is characteristically insightful, learned, and humorously earthy:

> God knows very well this perverseness of the world; therefore He admonishes and urges by commandments that every one consider what his parents have done for him, and he will find that he has from them body and life, moreover, that he has been fed and reared when otherwise he would have perished a hundred times in his own filth. Therefore it is a true and good saying of old and wise men: *Deo, parentibus et magistris non potest satis gratiae rependi*, that is, To God, to parents, and to teachers we can never render sufficient gratitude and compensation. He that regards and considers this will indeed without compulsion do all honor to his parents, and bear them up on his hands as those through whom God has done him all good.[6]

Your parents changed your diapers! If not for them, you would have "perished a hundred times in [your] own filth"! You owe them! Be grateful and honor them for that. They also gave you life, fed you, and reared you. You really would have died if they had not taken care of you. They deserve your gratitude and your honor. Your father and your mother are "those through whom God has done [you] all good."

To "honor your father and your mother" is a good work. It is one of God's Ten Commandments, no less. In Luther's day, many people were saying that "good works" are necessary in order to merit salvation. But by "good works" they meant becoming a monk or a nun, saying the daily offices, going on pilgrimages, reciting devotions—none of which God has commanded. Luther points out that the good works that truly please God the most and that he actually commands are not extraordinary feats of self-denial or dramatic commitments or ascetic mortifications.

Rather, they are the simple, everyday works of vocation, done not to get in better with God but out of love for the neighbor. Thus, Luther says,

> Notice how great, good, and holy a work is here assigned children. . . . Thus there would have been no need of inventing monasticism nor spiritual orders, but every child would have abided by this commandment, and could have directed his conscience to God and said: "If I am to do good and holy works, I know of none better than to render all honor and obedience to my parents, because God has Himself commanded it. . . ."
>
> For every child that knows and does this has, in the first place, this great consolation in his heart, that he can joyfully say and boast (in spite of and against all who are occupied with works of their own choice): "Behold, this work is well pleasing to my God in heaven, that I know for certain." Let them all come together with their many great, distressing, and difficult works and make their boast; we will see whether they can show one that is greater and nobler than obedience to father and mother, to whom God has appointed and commanded obedience next to His own majesty. . . .
>
> Oh, what a high price would all Carthusians, monks, and nuns pay, if in all their religious doings they could bring into God's presence a single work done by virtue of His commandment, and be able before His face to say with joyful heart: "Now I know that this work is well pleasing to Thee." Where will these poor wretched persons hide when in the sight of God and all the world they shall blush with shame before a young child who has lived according to this commandment, and shall have to confess that with their whole life they are not worthy to give it a drink of water?[7]

So a little boy who honors his parents—being grateful to them, doing his chores, showing them respect—is performing a greater work than the heroic exercises of monks and nuns, including those of the Carthusians, the order of hermits, with their vows of silence, their solitary isolation, and their refusal to interact with any "neighbors." Recognizing God's gifts and being thankful for them is an expression of faith—faith embodied as love and lived in this life as service to the neighbor.

Honoring parents is not an action, as such. It is a response to a person. When we pray the Lord's Prayer we are honoring our heavenly Father in a way that his Son taught us. In it we acknowledge him and defer to his judgment and power. We also receive his gifts. Although receiving is passive, it is what the giver wants. It is the opposite of rejection. Thus, honoring God partakes of faith.

Honoring parents, though, is usually expressed in action. It has been said that the impulse to throw out the past in favor of whatever is new is a violation of the commandment to honor one's father and mother.[8] Honoring parents has other senses: not bringing shame upon one's family, bringing credit to the family name, living up to one's parents' values, and, of course, doing what they say.

Obeying Parents

The survey of vocations in Ephesians 5–6 has this to say to children, quoting the commandment and drawing out an important corollary: "Children, obey your parents in the Lord, for this is right. 'Honor your father and mother' (this is the first command with a promise), 'that it may go well with you and that you may live long in the land' (Eph. 6:1–3). The child's work is to obey the parents, just as the wife's work is to submit to her husband, and the husband's work is to give himself up for his wife.

Again, the pattern is one of sacrificing the self and the will for the neighbor.

Even children are called to put their sinful and selfish ways behind them and to serve others. Children are to obey their parents "in the Lord," just as wives are to submit to their husbands "as to the Lord." In the vocations of marriage and parenthood, the Lord is hidden, and both submission and obedience are ultimately to him. Children obey not because the parents deserve obedience in themselves, but because God is at work in those parents too.

Does this mean that children must obey—or wives must submit—in *everything*? What if they are told to do something wrong? That their obedience is to be "in the Lord" (or, in the case of wives, "as to the Lord") means that God's righteousness is the limiting factor. As Luther explains, the obedience of children to parents "is subordinated to obedience toward God and is not opposed to the preceding commandments."[9]

Obedience, like submission, grows out of the one-flesh unity of the family—to freely give your will to someone else is a way of loving your neighbor as yourself (Matt. 22:39) and of being one with your neighbor. Of course, our obedience to our parents, like our obedience to God, is imperfect. Children and parents alike are sinners. Parents know how futile it is to simply demand, "Do what I say!" A child might comply when forced to, but inner obedience, from the heart, a free sacrifice of the will out of love—this is hard to come by, and threats and punishments cannot produce it. Ultimately, obedience comes from mutual love.

And the most important obedience and service is that of the Son of God to his heavenly Father on our behalf: "For as by the one man's disobedience the many were made sinners, so by the one man's obedience the many will be made righteous" (Rom. 5:19). When we are in Christ, his obedience counts as ours. His service changes everything. And this is good news for both parents and their children.

The Good Works of Children

The most spiritually significant good works are not those that we might take on to get in better with God, nor are they those that are forced out of us in the name of external compliance. Rather, truly good works flow naturally—even unconsciously—from an inner disposition and from a right relationship. These are the works most prized in vocation, the everyday acts of love and service.

To be sure, young children are sinners. Augustine famously analyzed himself as a crying baby for evidence of that:

> So I threw my limbs about and uttered sounds, signs resembling my wishes, the small number of signs of which I was capable but such signs as lay in my power to use: for there was no real resemblance. When I did not get my way, either because I was not understood or lest it be harmful to me, I used to be indignant with my seniors for their disobedience, and with free people who were not slaves to my interests; and I would revenge myself upon them by weeping. . . . So the feebleness of infant limbs is innocent, not the infant's mind. I have personally watched and studied a jealous baby. He could not yet speak and, pale with jealousy and bitterness, glared at his brother sharing his mother's milk. . . . It can hardly be innocence, when the source of milk is flowing richly and abundantly, not to endure a share going to one's blood-brother, who is in profound need, dependent for life exclusively on that one food. "[10]

And little kids will torture insects and adolescents will form cliques and mercilessly torment each other.

Children must grow not only in stature but in favor with God and man (Luke 2:52); that is, they must grow spiritually and morally. It is futile, of course, to berate a crying baby—though I have heard parents try ("Stop crying! You have to give me a break!")—and the impulse to punish a crying baby has led to child abuse. It is the effort of an entire childhood to develop self-control, concern for others, and a discerning conscience (things many adults still struggle with). Parents trying to instill these disciplines in their children must exercise patience, empathy, and self-sacrificial love. Children pick up these qualities not so much by learning precepts as by emulating what they see in their parents and the rest of their household. Because parents are the face of God to their children, it is vital that the parents show both righteousness and forgiveness, so as to help their children know their heavenly Father, who does not simply punish but offers grace.

Infants primarily do three things: cry out, receive, and respond. That is also a good description of the Christian faith. Infants are crafted to cry out to express their needs. They receive their milk and care from their parents. They respond in various measures to their parents and their environment. Faith instills in us that repentant cry, "Lord, have mercy!" Faith receives God's gifts of mercy and forgiveness. Faith responds with love.

At first a child can only see far enough to see the parents' faces. In time the child can see toys swinging on mobiles above the crib and eventually will reach out to touch them, to play, and to explore the world around. A lot of people wouldn't think of that child, that infant in arms, as having a vocation. But the child brings happiness, and that is a good work. The child needs around-the-clock care. The parents, typically, have been living mostly for themselves, but now they must undergo a tremendous amount of discipline to live also for their child. This is hard and exhausting work for parents, but usually on at least some level they are glad to serve their child, who provokes love in them.

So God is accomplishing good things *through* the baby. But what could God be calling the baby to do *right now*? Is this screaming baby really serving the parents *right now*? We probably should not assume that all the cries of babies and toddlers are righteous cries for mercy, clearly expressing a need. No doubt many of them are Augustinian cries. Still, God works through those cries to create compassion in the parents and to call them to serve. Yes, those cries at 3:00 a.m. might create annoyance rather than compassion, and the call to serve through sleepless nights can be a torment. Nevertheless, the baby is summoning the parents to sacrificial works of love and service. That is to say, the baby's good work is to stir up good works in the parents. Crying babies are doing what God has given them to do. The infant child, an icon of vulnerability, is able to bear the cross of vulnerability for others.

The child, even while growing older, serves as the very real and persistent instrument for the parents' daily discipline and continues to school them in love and service. And for the most part, the love parents feel for their child and the services they render are deeply joyful and satisfying. Through the toddler with persistent questions, God can bring about an ongoing catechesis about the world, as parents answer the child's questions and explain what the child sees. Parents get to delight in creation as they experience it again through their child's eyes.

Children exercise the patience of their parents, and this is good for parents. But children can also provide them an escape. Through them God reminds parents—sometimes forcefully—that there is much more to life than materialistic preoccupations. It's common to ask, "What are good influences for children?" but less so, "How are children good influences on me?" Yet having children is often the impetus for parents to give up bad habits, such as smoking and using bad language. Parents who experimented with drugs and sexual promiscuity when they were younger typically do not want their children to do what they did! Children bring moral clarity. And having children is often what brings their parents back to church. God works through even the youngest as agents of his love and care.

Growing Up

Since children grow, they keep changing. They are so different from year to year, and yet they are nevertheless the same person, even as the child passes into adulthood. "The child is father of the man," wrote Wordsworth, meaning that our childhood helps to make us, for better and for worse, the adult that we grow up to be.[11] But our identity is constant through all of the changes.

The growth of a child is like the growth of a plant. When a seed is planted, it takes a while for it to rise up out of the ground. Flower and fruit come later. Likewise, the child as human seed grows, blossoms, and only bears fruit when the time comes. As children receive love under the forms of nourishment, affection, education, and safety, they also receive more and more ways to express love themselves. They "sprout." They begin to speak, to reach out and touch, to share affection, to ask questions. They enter into the fluctuating realm of vocation, where changing abilities are paired with the neighbor's changing needs.

Throughout the years at home being raised by its parents, the child is learning. This is another major work of the vocation of the child. Just as an important duty of parents is to educate their children, an important duty of the children is to learn. This happens at school or home school. It also happens informally, in the everyday conversations and the parental commentary on what the child is experiencing. Even just playing is a way of fulfilling this vocation, as the young boy uses his imagination, makes up stories with his cars and trains and action figures, and experiments with reality when putting together his Legos. Such exploration becomes preparation for his dominion over creation. His interactions with friends and family members become foundational for wisdom. His life with his parents and his siblings helps prepare him for a family of his own.

The goal of childhood is adulthood. Throughout a child's life, he is growing into an adult. He is also being prepared for adult vocations—to be a husband and father in a family of his own; to develop his talents for the workplace; to be a good citizen; to be a faithful member of Christ's church.

But when the child reaches adulthood, leaves home, and enters into his own callings, including perhaps a family of his own, he is still a child to his parents. He still must honor them as long as they live. Eventually, a strange reversal takes place. The parents have taken care of the child. And then the child takes care of the parents.

That children have an obligation to care for their aging parents is utterly alien to our culture today, though it has been taken for granted in virtually every other culture at every other period in history. And it is clearly and forcefully commanded in Scripture. In the context of discussing how the church should provide for widows, the apostle Paul places the major responsibility on their families: "But if anyone does not provide for his relatives, and especially for members of his household, he has denied the faith and is worse than an unbeliever" (1 Tim. 5:8). To not take care of one's mother when she is old is to deny Christ! It is worse than being an atheist! Those are strong and unsettling words, in our era of warehousing the elderly in nursing homes and forgetting about them, without so much as an occasional visit or phone call.

Paul specifically puts the responsibility upon the elderly mother's children and also grandchildren: "If a widow has children or grandchildren, let them first learn to show godliness to their own household and to make some return to their parents, for this is pleasing in the sight of God" (1 Tim. 5:4). Many aging parents today say, "I don't want to be a burden on my children! I'd rather they just let me die than be dependent on them." But here Scripture tells grown children to "make some return to their parents"! You children were a burden to your parents. You were dependent on them. They changed your diapers. They fed you when you couldn't feed yourself. They took you to the doctor when you were sick. They supported you financially when you could not support yourselves. Now, when your parents are approaching the end of their lives, you can express your gratitude by loving and serving them as they loved and served you. Dependence is not a dirty word, and a child is in the right position to remind the elderly parent that dependence is not humiliating in the hands of our faithful God, that dependence on God is intrinsic to the life of faith, and that God ministers to all of us through the vocations of others, including our children. These transitions are all part of the continuing call in ever-changing circumstances to love and serve the neighbor.

Conclusion

In Psalm 139, quoted as the headnote of this chapter, David describes how the Lord "knitted me together in my mother's womb" (v. 13). God was creating him by means of his mother even before he was born. But not only is he "fearfully and wonderfully made" (Ps. 139:14) at the inception of his life, but God also shapes him as a baby and he continues to do so all his days. God forms those days for him. "In your book were written, every one of them, the days that were formed for me, when as yet there was none of them" (Ps. 139:16).

The days have been formed for children that they may receive life, even eternal life. That means that a child's being and growth are in the hands of God. And since we have all been infants and still have the status of being someone's child, on earth and in heaven, this applies to everyone. Children can be confident that God himself is directing their work of growing—physically, intellectually, emotionally, socially, spiritually—working through parents and the other influences God brings into their lives, and continuing to do so even when they are adults, all the days of their lives.

15

The Crosses of Childhood

Though they plan evil against you, though they devise mischief,
they will not succeed.

PSALM 21:11

Adults sentimentalize childhood. Ah, those days of carefree innocence.
No responsibilities. Childlike wonder. Playing all the time. If only I could
be a child again!

Those sentimental adults, though, would change their tune if they
would remember what their own childhood was actually like: confusion,
fears, humiliations, being constantly under someone else's control, getting bullied, getting snubbed, peer pressure, shame, crying and wanting
to cry. And that would be a normal and relatively happy childhood. Some
children also go through unspeakable agonies—their parents getting a
divorce; their parents abusing them; having to endure disabilities and
diseases; being victims of crime; engaging in acts of self-destruction.

Anyone who thinks the young don't have real problems is sadly mis-
taken. A teacher from a Christian school told us that in her classroom
of thirteen children, there is one boy whose mother is dead; one girl
who lives with an aunt and uncle because her mother left her father and
doesn't want the children; one girl whose biological mother died so she
was adopted by a single woman when she was a baby; and about half the
rest live with one parent due to divorce. One of the children has a brother

who has been in jail. Broken family relationships mean great suffering for children, as do the damaging cycles and inexplicable guilt that often haunts them their entire lives.

If being a child is a vocation, then children, too, must have crosses they have to bear. But not all suffering is a cross. Children are vulnerable, are literally at the mercy of adults, and much of their suffering is due to adults failing to live out their vocations. Such problems should be addressed and not dismissed as inconsequential or unchangeable.

Children and Sacrifice

All vocations—not just in the family but in the workplace, the church, the culture—involve loving and serving one's neighbors, which entails bearing a cross of self-denial for them. Again, wives deny themselves by submitting to their husbands, and husbands deny themselves by giving themselves up for their wives. Parents sacrifice for their children in the routines of taking care of them and making a living, and so carry their cross "daily."

As children grow up, from birth to leaving the nest, they are engaged in a long process of learning to deny themselves. Augustine's self-centered baby has to learn to say no to himself in order to control his impulses, to achieve the right relationship with his parents, and to function in the society that he is growing into. He has to learn how to control his excretory functions, his eating, and his other appetites. He has to learn how to deny his personal desires both to take his sister's toy and to refuse to let her play with his. He has to learn to control his passions and not cry every time he is thwarted. As he grows up, the lessons and the practice in self-denial continue. Education requires self-denial, when he would rather be outside playing than studying his books. Playing sports requires submission to rules. Driving requires submission to the law, both the laws of nature and the laws of the state.

Discipline, in general, involves subjecting and training the will. The goal of discipline is not simply arbitrary control, but developing the virtue of self-control. This means, paradoxically, the voluntary, or willful, rejection of the will, the self-motivated denial of the self. A young athlete may desire to stop running, but he wills himself to run nonetheless, against his will. A young musician may be sick of practicing and yet he practices.

Such self-discipline is difficult, and it is the work of a lifetime. Even adults have to cultivate discipline—craving dessert but not eating it; being angry but holding one's tongue; being tempted but not giving in— and adults, like children, often surrender to their appetites and egos. So discipline has to do with denying the self. And yet, as we have been using the term, cross bearing is not simply suffering. It is suffering for someone. It is not simply self-denial. It is self-denial for one's neighbor.

Discipline is practice in self-denial; but to put self-denial into action and to turn it into a cross, it must serve a neighbor. Doing what Mom and Dad say is denying one's own will to follow theirs. Obeying the teacher is loving and serving the teacher. Sharing toys and repressing the impulse to fight can be ways to bear a cross for brothers and sisters. Clearing the table, picking up the toys in the living room, and other everyday chores are a child's sacrifices for the entire family. Doing these things may require compulsory discipline at first, imposed by the parents, but after a while they can be done voluntarily, out of love, whereupon they become an offering.

Child Sacrifice

Children do deny themselves. They also can deny themselves for others. So they do bear their crosses. And yet, the child's calling, as we discussed earlier, is primarily to receive. Children do not normally have to work to make a living; rather, parents provide for them. "Children are not obligated to save up for their parents," says the apostle Paul, "but parents for their children" (2 Cor. 12:14). Childhood is a time to learn the disciplines that children will need as adults, but they are normally not called to the extremities of self-sacrifice until they reach adulthood. Children may have their small acts of self-sacrifice for others. But children may not *be sacrificed*. The vocation of parents is to sacrifice themselves for their young children. But parents have no calling and no authority to sacrifice their children for themselves.

The Bible devotes considerable space to exhorting parents not to sacrifice their children to idols (Lev. 18:21, 20:2–5; Deut. 18:10). One might assume that parents would not want to kill their children. Perhaps the cruel deities of the false religions might demand that as an extreme test of the parents' devotion. Perhaps parents under the bondage of pagan societies might be forced to do so by murderous priests and kings.

Surely, because of their natural affections, parents would only give their child up to death unwillingly and weeping. And yet, *God's own people*—of their own free will, despite the law's prohibitions and the prophets' repeated threats—insisted on slaughtering their children on pagan altars (2 Kings 16:3; 2 Kings 17:17, 31; 21:6; Jer. 32:35; Ezek. 23:39).

Perhaps they believed the forbidden god Molech might give them prosperity or happiness if they gave him such a precious sacrifice. The God of their fathers, Abraham and Isaac, they knew, is not to be bargained with and refuses to be manipulated. He demands obedience and will not himself obey human beings. Molech, though, is more malleable. He can be placated and put in their debt. He exacts a high price, but to have a god in your service can be worth it. Maybe this was the mind-set of the Israelites who burned their children as an offering to Molech.

To our knowledge today no one practices Molech worship, as such. And yet some people still sacrifice their children to advance their own agendas. A woman who gets an abortion because having a baby would interfere with her career is, arguably, sacrificing her infant's life to promote her worldly success, whether or not she seeks that success from Molech. And not all sacrifices involve the shedding of blood. A father who spends only five minutes per day with his children because he is spending so much time at work may also be sacrificing his children for his job. Turning a child into a fashion accessory, a status symbol, or a trophy at the expense of what the child needs may involve sacrificing the child for the parents' vanity.

There was a time when quarreling husbands and wives would commonly say that they decided not to get a divorce; rather, they would stay together "for the sake of the children." Today, many marriage counselors do not consider that a good reason for keeping a marriage together. And yet, in light of vocation, not getting a divorce "for the sake of the children" is an excellent reason, a sacrifice of the parents' personal happiness for the children they are both called to love and also to serve.

Today, many parents are willing to sacrifice their children's well-being for the sake of their own personal happiness. This kind of child sacrifice violates the vocation of parenthood. "But surely it is better for us to divorce than for our children to see us fighting all the time!" Well, then don't fight, "for the sake of the children." Reconcile, solve the problems in the marriage, "for the sake of the children."

Abraham was willing to sacrifice his son Isaac to the true God, no less, who gave him that horrible command. In taking his long-promised son Isaac to the mountain of Moriah, building an altar, and putting his knife to the boy's throat, Abraham was not demonstrating his faith. He was only demonstrating his obedience. Abraham's faith was evident in his words to his son:

> And Abraham took the wood of the burnt offering and laid it on Isaac his son. And he took in his hand the fire and the knife. So they went both of them together. And Isaac said to his father Abraham, "My father!" And he said, "Here am I, my son." He said, "Behold, the fire and the wood, but where is the lamb for a burnt offering?" Abraham said, "God will provide for himself the lamb for a burnt offering, my son." So they went both of them together. (Gen. 22:6–8)

Abraham's faith was that "God will provide for himself the lamb." Abraham was trusting, despite his own current experience, that God would supply his own offering. That is, even as Abraham was laboring up that mountain under the harshness of the law, he believed the gospel. According to the book of Hebrews, Abraham "considered that God was able even to raise him from the dead, from which, figuratively speaking, he did receive him back" (Heb. 11:19). That is, Abraham believed that even if he did have to kill his son, that God would raise him from the dead.

And, indeed, God intervened. His angel stopped Abraham's hand, told him not to harm the boy, and provided a ram caught in a thicket. "Abraham went and took the ram and offered it up as a burnt offering instead of his son. So Abraham called the name of that place, 'The LORD will provide'; as it is said to this day, 'On the mount of the LORD it shall be provided'" (Gen. 22:13–14).

Abraham's faith, as he told Isaac, was that "God will provide" the lamb, and he did! Abraham names the mountain accordingly. God provided a substitute sacrifice so that Isaac would not have to die. This same location, Mount Moriah, where Abraham was about to sacrifice his son but found "the LORD will provide," would be the site of Solomon's Temple (2 Chron. 3:1). Here priests would make sacrifices to the Lord, but not human sacrifices—that practice of the surrounding nations was decisively repudiated. But on Abraham's mountain worshipers seeking atonement for their sins would lay hands on an animal, like the ram in the thicket, so that it would become their substitute. And what happened on Mount Moriah, both with the ram in the thicket and in Solomon's Temple, signifies Christ, "the Lamb of God, who takes away the sin of the world" (John 1:29).

God did not permit Abraham to sacrifice his only son; instead, God sacrificed his only Son. Jesus Christ, crowned with thorns, is the ram in the thicket, the lamb on the altar, the sacrificed child. He offers himself as our substitute, to take the punishment for our sins and in return to give us his glory. He is thus the hope of the suffering child. And he is the hope of the sinner who caused the child to suffer.

Child Abuse

Probably all parents have lapses in their love and service of their children—the hurtful word that slips out, the bad mood that breaks out in unnecessary harshness, the wrong decision—and thus nearly all children have suffered unjustly at the hands of their parents. This often results in parental remorse, with the children being quick to forgive and forget. But it is also true that some parents sometimes subject their children to cruel and devastating abuse.

Vincent Iannelli, a pediatrician, has pulled together the following statistics about child abuse in the United States:

- More than 1.25 million, or 1 in every 58 children in the United States, were abused in 2006.
- More than half (61 percent) of the children (771,700 children) were victims of neglect, meaning a parent or guardian failed to provide for the child's basic needs. Forms of neglect include educational neglect (360,500 children), physical neglect (295,300 children), and emotional neglect (193,400).
- Another 44 percent were victims of abuse (553,300 children), including physical abuse (325,000 children), sexual abuse (135,000 children), and emotional abuse (148,500 children).[1]

Some of these categories might be questionable. What, one might wonder, constitutes educational neglect? Is that a pretext for going after homeschoolers? Some people consider any use of spanking to be physical abuse. Emotional neglect and emotional abuse may well, in part, be in the eye of the beholder. It has been said that much of the relatively stern discipline practiced by our forebears would be defined as child abuse today. Sometimes charges of child abuse are unjustly levied by the state to usurp the rights of loving parents. Nevertheless, we dare not minimize the reality of child abuse. Though parents are called to love and serve their children, sometimes parents instead are hateful and cruel to their children. Every day in America, an average of four children are abused so badly that they die.[2]

So why would parents harm their own children? It may involve a specific breakdown of vocation. Gustaf Wingren has said that sin in vocation often involves wanting to be served rather than to serve.[3] Instead of loving and serving the neighbor, we demand that the neighbor love and serve *us*. Instead of denying ourselves for our neighbor, we exalt ourselves at the expense of our neighbor.

Parents do have authority over their children and the obligation to discipline them. But even when the neighbor has a vocation that owes us service—as an employee, a wife, a husband, a child—we are to receive that as a response to our own service.

There is hardly anything more futile or more pathetic than trying to browbeat someone into servile submission, especially apart from any kind of positive mutual relationship. "Respect me!" "Do what I say!" "Did you hear me?" When these one-sided demands get nowhere, the impulse is to strike out.

To be sure, in the case of parenting, children must be disciplined and sometimes punished. But, again, discipline in the Bible is always associated with love (e.g., Prov. 13:24). That is, the discipline is for the good of the child. But when the child does not perceive that love and when it seems to the child that the discipline is for the good of the parent, rebellion sets in—which can make the parent's heart harden toward the child. The frustrated parent responds with anger that builds to rage. In a lapse of self-control, the parent, as we say, loses his or her temper and lashes out at the child, verbally or with violence. The child gets hurt, physically because of being so much smaller and also emotionally, even spiritually, because of not being loved.

Even good parents sometimes have confrontations with their children like this, confrontations that end badly. But this kind of behavior can become chronic. Eventually, for all practical purposes, the love between the parents and the child really does die, though it usually still exists deep down, manifesting itself in the parent's guilt and the child's yearning. On the surface, though, there is no more love or service, only bruises, lacerations, and cigarette burns.

Everyone in vocations of authority, especially parents, needs to realize that God calls no one to sin. Nor does he ever authorize, by vocation, anyone to sin. Yes, your office may call for respect and obedience, but you, in your person, remain subject to God and have no authority to harm those whom God has placed under your care.

The best environment for raising and disciplining children in love is in marriage. According to a US Department of Health & Human Services report, the rate of abuse in single-parent households is nearly twice as high as in married households (27.3 children per 1,000 vs. 15.5).[4] Raising children is a difficult, two-person job, and single parents, of course, are under incredible stress. Sometimes they snap under the pressure. The most dangerous living situation for a child is the combination of single parenthood and cohabitation out of wedlock. Dr. Iannelli found that "living with a single parent and a live-in partner increased the risk of abuse and neglect to more than eight times that of other children."[5] Dr. Iannelli concludes that "living with their married biological parents places kids at the lowest risk for child abuse and neglect."[6]

For all of the stereotypes about the nurturing mother and the brutal father, according to another report from the US Department of Health & Human Services, "mothers are almost twice as likely to be directly involved in child maltreatment as fathers."[7] This holds true for abuse both in marriage and outside of marriage. This might be accounted for because mothers tend to spend more time with their children than the fathers do. Nevertheless, the study found many strains of evidence that point to the same conclusion: "A father in the home can be a strong protective factor for children."[8] Even if the father is outside the home, due to divorce, if he maintains a presence in the child's life, he is a protective factor. If the child has a strong, positive relationship with the father, research shows that even if he does not live with the mother and the children, the risk of child abuse decreases.[9] Again we see the uncanny power inherent in the father's vocation.

An especially heinous kind of mistreatment of children is sexual abuse. The statistics are beyond comprehension. According to a government report, as many as one out of four girls and one out of six boys have been or will be sexually abused by the time they are eighteen.[10] That is, used sexually—whether by intercourse, fondling, indecent exposure, or other sexually related activity—by an adult. One out of four girls! One out of six boys![11]

The report goes on to say that some 60 percent of the abusers are known to the child but are not family. These would include teachers, caregivers, and—notoriously—ministers. Only 10 percent of the abusers are strangers. That leaves 30 percent of the abusers who are members of the child's immediate or extended family.[12]

The sexual abuse of children is monstrous, and that it has become so commonplace is surely a sign of a wickedness that strikes at the heart of the entire culture. Sex, which is designed for marriage to engender children and create families, is turned inside out when children themselves are turned into objects of sexual desire. Families are designed to care for children, not rape them. When pastors, teachers, and family members make use of their high callings to sexually abuse children, vocation itself is desecrated. Why anyone would do this to children is a mystery of iniquity, a depravity that can be resolved only in hell.

Experiencing such things at a young age, when they are supposed to be experiencing love and security, can haunt children for their whole lives. Child abuse victims often turn to alcohol or drugs to dull their pain. (They are two and one-half times more likely to abuse alcohol and nearly four times more likely to develop drug addictions.)[13] Increased rates of depression, eating disorders, and crime are also associated with having been abused as a child, especially sexual abuse. Having been abused sexually is also connected to a whole range of sexual confusions and disorders, including promiscuity.[14] And sexual abuse by someone of the same sex is strongly correlated with homosexuality. A study published in the *Archives of Sexual Behavior* found that 46 percent of homosexual men and 22 percent of homosexual women had been the victims of homosexual molestation as children.[15]

So how is a child who has been mistreated physically, emotionally, or sexually to live? How can a child be expected to "honor" a father or a mother who has abused them? Some Christians immediately exhort abused children and adults still scarred by childhood abuse to forgive their abusers. This is, indeed, the highest spiritual achievement, the one way to erase the horrors of their past and to achieve reconciliation even with their tormenters. But forgiveness cannot be a moral mandate. The forgiveness of a child—or of a wife or of anyone who has been abused or victimized—like God's forgiveness, is not a requirement, something owed to the sinner; rather, forgiveness must always be a free gift issuing from grace. On the moral level, victims who are sinned against need and crave justice.[16] They need the assurance that those who harmed them will be punished, that they will pay for what they did. They may find their solace in the God who rights wrongs, who damns evildoers to hell—God the avenger.

Yes, we are told to forgive those who trespass against us, but being able to do that in the case of some trespasses requires great spiritual maturity in the gospel. Sometimes it may not happen until the abused daughter pities her abusive father on his deathbed. But God does avenge the abuse of children, whether in hell or, in the case of abusive parents who turn to Christ, in pouring out his wrath for their depravity onto his own Son as their substitute.

In the meantime, how can a Christian child, young or grown up, follow the commandment to "honor your father and your mother" if one or both of them did not live out their vocation as parents? If parenthood is a calling, it is more than just a biological fact. Some people who have a baby, for one reason or another, do not want the vocation of parenthood. Instead, they give up their baby for adoption to someone who does want that vocation. This is an act of love and service from both parties. Can it be that those who repudiate that calling through extreme mistreatment or neglect of their children have also vacated their office? In extreme cases, their children might consider that they have no parents to take care of them. They can go directly to God for their parenthood, the Father of the fatherless (Ps. 68:5).

Short of that, the problem remains. How can a person "honor" someone who deserves little or no respect? If the commandment said "obey," that could be done as an external action apart from any personal feelings. But "honor" requires a personal feeling. How can that attitude be conjured up for someone whose behavior has been dishonorable? Perhaps the child can honor the office, if not the person who holds the office. Perhaps the child can feel gratitude for simple existence, if nothing else, and honor the parent for that. At some point, though, the child might receive from God the grace to honor the abusing parents despite themselves. This is the unmerited honor that God gives to sinners through his Son.

The Hebrew word for "honor" used in the commandment has the additional sense of "weight."[17] To honor God or the king or parents is to "give weight" to them. But the word in this context also has the connotation of being weighed down, carrying something heavy, as in bearing a cross.

Sometimes—and not just in the extreme cases of abuse—the cross that the child must bear is the child's own parents. Just as the Son of Man carried the sins of man, earthly sons and daughters must sometimes carry the sins of their parents. They also, like Christ, suffer for those sins. The difference is that Christ atoned for the sins of the world, and regular sons and daughters cannot atone for the sins of their parents, as such. But they can, in a sense, offer their suffering so that it is "for" someone.

One of the horrific consequences of child abuse is that it can create a cycle that continues for generations. Some 30 percent of child abuse victims grow up to abuse their own children.[18] But that means 70 percent of child abuse victims do *not* abuse their own children. These are the ones who remember how they were treated and resolve not to treat their own children that way. They break the cycle of abuse for the next generation. It ends with them.

Some liberal and postmodernist theologians, with jaw-dropping spiritual shallowness, are dismissing the doctrine of the atonement as "cosmic child abuse."[19] God punishing his Son for what other people did is just not fair, they say. In causing Jesus to be crucified, they say, God was abusing his Son. Surely God is not like that, they reason, so the atonement cannot be true. These theologians understand nothing of the Trinity, that the Father and the Son together with the Holy Spirit are One God. They understand nothing of the gospel, and their alternative Christianities are little more than politicized moralisms that leave us in our sins. And yet, it may be that an abused child can see himself in Jesus, forsaken by his Father. If so, the abused child may experience how his cross is taken up into the cross of Jesus, who bears not just our transgressions and iniquities—including those of the abusive parents—but also our griefs and sorrow (Isa. 53:4–5).

Conclusion

The very last verse of the Old Testament describes the work of the prophet who will herald the new age. It also describes what is at stake, the consequences if the prophet's words are ignored: "And he will turn the hearts of fathers to their children and the hearts of children to their fathers, lest I come and strike the land with a decree of utter destruction" (Mal. 4:6). This segues perfectly into the New Testament, where we learn that the prophet is John the Baptist, with the angel Gabriel saying of him that he will "turn many of the children of Israel to the Lord their God, and he will go before him in the spirit and power of Elijah, to turn the hearts of the fathers to the children, and the disobedient to the wisdom of the just, to make ready for the Lord a people prepared" (Luke 1:16–17). Thus the reconciliation of fathers and their children and their mutual love for one another is a sign of Christ's kingdom.

Children, in their vocations, are given a great power. They are so easy to love. This is God's gift and a sign of Christ. Even husbands and wives who are at each other's throats tend to love their children passionately. This may manifest itself either in fighting over them in the divorce court or in reconciling for their sake. Children pull love out of their parents and even out of strangers. Because children provoke such love, the spectacle of their suffering is more than many adults can bear. And those who cause their suffering are especially loathsome, even to themselves.

But children are also given another power. They tend to have great faith. To them belongs the kingdom of heaven (Matt. 19:14; Mark 10:15).

So children do have crosses to bear. In addition to the trials and tribulations we discussed in detail in this chapter, they have many more—peer pressure, bullying, temptations, broken homes, disabilities, sicknesses. These can devastate children. At the same time, though, children going through these tribulations often demonstrate heroic spiritual strength.

When you visit a child who is lying in a hospital bed, the sacrifice, the love, and the service is palpable—not only the child's, but also the parents' and that of the medical staff. And if you have spent much time in hospitals, you may have noticed something counterintuitive: patients are often calmer than visitors. The little girl with her pink bandana may be coloring a banana after chemotherapy while her grandmother sobs in the waiting room down the hall. The little boy on the transplant list tells his mother he'll be all right when he goes with Jesus. A hospital chaplain friend of ours said 90 percent of her ministry is taken up comforting not the patient but the family.

Christ takes little children into his arms and blesses them (Mark 10:16). Jesus pronounces himself the advocate and avenger of children: "Whoever causes one of these little ones who believe in me to sin, it would be better for him to have a great millstone fastened around his neck and to be drowned in the depth of the sea"(Matt. 18:6). "See that you do not despise one of these little ones. For I tell you that in heaven their angels always see the face of my Father who is in heaven" (Matt. 18:10). More than that, Jesus says, "Whoever receives one such child in my name receives me" (Matt. 18:5). That means Christ is hidden in children, so that the way we treat a child is the way we treat Christ, and their crosses are his cross.

16

The Rest of the Family

Who has performed and done this, calling the generations from the beginning? I, the LORD, the first, and with the last; I am he.
ISAIAH 41:4

Families grow. Families *extend*. A husband and a wife become a father and a mother. These parents have a child, then more children. Another relationship, another calling, comes into play: brothers and sisters. After a while, those children grow up. They become husbands and wives, fathers and mothers. The brothers and sisters become aunts and uncles to each other's children. The various children become cousins to each other. The parents are transformed into grandparents.

In a family, the number of relationships rises in what mathematicians call a triangular function. A husband and wife have one relationship between them. Add a child, and now the family has three relationships (father and mother; father and child; mother and child). Add a sister and the four member family now has six relationships (father and mother; father and first child; mother and first child; father and second child; mother and second child; first child and second child). Add a third child, and the family of five will have ten relationships. And so on. A family of twelve children would have one hundred five relationships for the parents to have to supervise! Think of all of the potential squabbles—and also the potential close family bonds![1]

The same phenomenon, of course, applies to any group of people. When our whole extended family, including spouses but not including great-uncles and their progeny, gets together over the holidays, we have seventeen people, which comes to one hundred fifty-three relationships. That is quite a network—a lot of people to love and serve.

When we do get together, we enact family traditions. At Christmastime, we have certain foods and drinks that we enjoy every year—casseroles that we don't particularly like but that we eat out of principle; a mysterious "holiday brew"; a delicious cornbread dressing that has been passed down from antiquity. On Christmas morning, we all line up in the hallway; the eldest patriarch present goes into the family room to plug in the Christmas tree lights and puts on the record player, then stereo, then tape deck, then CD player, then MP3 device, Julie Andrews singing "Joy to the World." After the excruciatingly long instrumental fanfare, as soon as we hear the first words of the song, we all run madly to the presents. Now we have four generations doing that.

We are all united by flesh. Many of us look alike. Some came in by marriage, but that is a one-flesh union that connects to the rest of us, just as adoption is also an incorporation into the family. We are united by our common history. We have similar senses of humor. We like the same foods and enjoy the same games. We may argue politics and now belong to several different churches, but we get along and take pleasure in each other's company. We are a family, all seventeen of us, all one hundred fifty-three relationships. And each of us has multiple vocations in this mass of relations, including those we have discussed earlier, but also grandparents and grandchildren, brothers and sisters, uncles, aunts, and cousins.

Some people claim they have no vocation because they are unemployed or unmarried, perhaps retired or widowed. But all of these family relationships constitute vocations that are enough to keep anyone—single or married—busy for a lifetime.

The Household

The family in the biblical days was far more than our "nuclear family" of parents and children. First, all members of the nation of Israel considered themselves to be related to each other, since they were all descendants of Abraham. The family identity of every ancient Hebrew was found next in his tribe, that is his descent from one of the twelve sons of Jacob, aka, Israel (Judah, Benjamin, Levi, etc.).[2] The tribe was then subdivided into clans, which consisted of many related extended families descended from one of the sons of the twelve patriarchs.

The smallest family unit was the "house" or "household," which consisted of the oldest living male relative and all of his descendants. This could mean several generations all living under one roof or in close proximity. The "head of the house" might be the grandfather, and his house would include his sons, their wives and children, and *their* wives and children.[3] This means cousins would live together as part of one family unit. When the grandfather died, his oldest son would assume the mantle of "head of the house." Those fathers of fathers would be remembered throughout the family line. Jesus was a member of the tribe of Judah, but he was of the "house" of David.[4]

Tribal societies all over the world—in Africa, New Guinea, Australia—and all through history (think of the Germanic tribes, the Scottish clans, the Native American tribes) have this basic family structure.[5] In our modern world, we have narrowed family considerably with our emphasis on the isolated nuclear family. In other times and cultures, family was not just a nucleus but, to continue the analogy, many nuclei joined together into molecules, which in turn came together in cells and organisms.

Notice that nuclear families, by their nature, do not last: the parents grow old and eventually die, while the children grow up and start nuclear families of their own. The extended family, however—the lines of descent and the multiplying web of kinship—is permanent, existing in the past, the present, and the future. Perhaps a serious rebuilding of the family in our times would involve recovering these broader networks of a common flesh and blood.

At any rate, knowing about how families in the ancient world lived in extended family "households" extends the scope of certain passages of Scripture. Consider the passage we have already discussed as it relates to elderly parents: "But if anyone does not provide for his relatives, and especially for members of his household, he has denied the faith and is worse than an unbeliever" (1 Tim. 5:8). For the apostle Paul and Timothy, this would probably have referred not just to parents and children but to grandparents, uncles, aunts, and cousins as well. Also, in the early days of apostolic evangelism, we learn of whole households being baptized

(Acts 16:15, 31–35; 1 Corinthians 1:16). This also extends the scope of the estate of the household, as the Reformers understood it, with its many different family vocations.

Grandparents

With the birth of a child to their child, God calls men and women to be grandparents. Their vocation as parents thus expands into service to the next generation. Today, with our nuclear view of the family, this is usually treated as a vocation with all benefits and no responsibilities. As grandparents are always saying, "We get to spoil the kids and then give them back to their parents." But under the "household" family structure that the Bible assumes and that many cultures preserve to this day, the grandfather had a genuine authority. His office of "father" was still binding on his sons, even when they themselves became fathers, and he was the head of the extended family.

The continuing authority of the grandparents over their children did not mean, however, that grandparents were in charge of their *grandchildren*, whose own parents exercised authority over them. Still, grandparents and the aged in general were venerated. The Mosaic law connected honoring and showing respect to an elderly man with the fear of God, who is hidden in his office: "You shall stand up before the gray head and honor the face of an old man, and you shall fear your God: I am the LORD" (Lev. 19:32). The New Testament urges the same kind of deference, even outside a specific family bond: "Do not rebuke an older man but encourage him as you would a father" (1 Tim. 5:1). This contrasts sharply with the general treatment of the aged in our contemporary culture, which tends to mock or condescend to the elderly, who, no longer working or exercising a determined role in the nuclearized family, are often treated as if they have no vocation.

The Bible, though, makes it clear that grandparents are morally and spiritually influential and that their lives literally haunt the lives of their children and grandchildren. This influence is for bad as well as good. The Bible teaches the hard truth that the sins of the grandparents reverberate in the lives of their children, their grandchildren, and even their great-grandchildren: "The LORD passed before [Moses on Mount Sinai] and proclaimed, 'The LORD, the LORD, a God merciful and gracious, slow to anger, and abounding in steadfast love and faithfulness, keeping steadfast love for thousands, forgiving iniquity and transgression and sin, but who will by no means clear the guilty, visiting the iniquity of the fathers on the children and the children's children, to the third and the fourth generation' (Ex. 34:6–7). This terrible revelation about the consequences of sin seems to be especially related to idolatry, since the words are specifically attached to the prohibition of idolatry in the Ten Commandments: "You shall not make for yourself a carved image, or any likeness of anything that is in heaven above, or that is in the earth beneath, or that is in the water under the earth. You shall not bow down to them or serve them, for I the LORD your God am a jealous God, visiting the iniquity of the fathers on the children to the third and the fourth generation of those who hate me, but showing steadfast love to thousands of those who love me and keep my commandments" (Ex. 20:4–6).

In what sense are the iniquities of a father "visited" upon his children, grandchildren, and great-grandchildren? It is not that children and grandchildren will be punished for their grandfather's sin, as Ezekiel 18 explains. Nevertheless, the sin itself is often passed down from generation to generation like a cursed heirloom. Parents who abuse their children often had been abused themselves by their parents, who in turn had been abused by *their* parents. Nicholas H. Wolfinger has documented "the divorce cycle" and has shown that when parents get a divorce, their children are twice as likely to get a divorce themselves, compared to children from intact families—a phenomenon that can continue for generations.[6] Drug addiction and alcohol abuse can also be multigenerational.[7]

In terms of the commandment against idolatry, a person's embrace of a false religion will certainly affect the children who are raised in it, as well as their children. This holds true for converts to Islam or Buddhism or Unitarianism, as well as membership in cults or heterodox churches. Having no religion at all can be passed down through the generations. Online atheism forums feature testimonies from "second-generation" and "third-generation" atheists. Just the habit of not attending church out of apathy rather than conviction can be passed down to one's grandchildren. And yet, these cycles can be broken at any point by the grace of God.

Indeed, righteousness and the love of God can also be passed on from generation to generation. "The steadfast love of the LORD is from everlasting to everlasting on those who fear him, and his righteousness to children's children" (Ps. 103:17). Strong families beget strong families. Loving families beget loving families. Christian families beget Christian families. Parents who decide to join a good church that teaches God's Word and that proclaims the gospel of Christ will shape their children spiritually, who, in turn, will shape their children. The apostle Paul saw the multigenerational transmission of faith in the work of a grandmother named Lois, who transmitted the love and righteousness of God through her daughter and eventually to a young man named Timothy: "I am reminded of your sincere faith, a faith that dwelt first in your grandmother Lois and your mother Eunice and now, I am sure, dwells in you as well" (2 Tim. 1:5).

To be a grandparent is described in Scripture as a great blessing. "The LORD bless you from Zion!" says the psalmist; "May you see your children's children!" (Ps. 128:5–6). To have grandchildren is the culmination of life, a crown of honor. So says Solomon, who adds that, from the point of view of the children, having fathers and grandfathers is a "glory." "Grandchildren are the crown of the aged, and the glory of children is their fathers" (Prov. 17:6).

Grandparents can revel in their vocation and in their grandchildren. By remaining in their vocations as parents and grandparents, they continue to model and influence as long as they live—even after they die, in memory. They might also do what they can, if only to repent and pray, to mitigate the effects of their own sin on their children and grandchildren. And that will involve becoming a child once more, a child of God, dependent on the forgiveness and mercy of Christ for themselves and their progeny. In this way, they will convey the steadfast love of the Lord to their children's children.

Brothers and Sisters

After the relationship between parent and children, the closest blood kin are brothers and sisters. Despite the closeness of the relationship between siblings, sometimes they have trouble getting along. This is certainly the case in the Bible. The very first child born to Adam and Eve, Cain, murdered his younger brother Abel (Genesis 4). Jacob swindled his twin brother Esau out of his birthright, that is the right to inherit from their father Isaac the headship of the house (Genesis 25, 27). The sons of

Jacob who were the progenitors of the twelve tribes of Israel hated their brother Joseph and sold him into slavery (Genesis 37).

Brothers and sisters can compete with each other for the affection of their parents. This can begin at a young age, when a new baby enters the household and takes away the attention from the older brother. (Remember the baby in St. Augustine's story that glared with jealousy at the other nursing baby.) That hostility usually passes, but sometimes older and grown-up siblings can be rivals. Who can win the most approval from their parents—whether from financial success, or having children, or climbing the social ladder—can be a family-destroying game. The winners can be prideful and unloving, while the losers can become bitter and hostile, often to the whole family. ("It's not fair! You always get your way." "Mom always loved you best!" "I can never be good enough to please Dad.") Brothers and sisters can fight over property, from the big brother taking away his little sister's toy and pushing her down, to adults squabbling over who gets what in their father's will.

These are more or less the same conflicts that are in the biblical accounts of antagonistic brothers. Parents must remember not to show favoritism to one sibling over the others. If you give one of them a coat of many colors, give the rest something just as good.

So if being a brother or a sister is a vocation, what is its proper work? The biblical answer may be given in the tragic account of Cain and Abel. Here the two were competing not for favor with their parents but for favor with God. Cain worked hard tilling the ground, under the curse placed on his father, and with the sweat of his brow he grew grain. Cain offered God the fruits of his labor. His brother Abel, though, a shepherd, offered God the blood of a lamb. This episode, like all of the Old Testament, points ahead to Christ. The fruit of our labor, our good works, are not sufficient to make us right with God. We have fallen too far. We need a blood sacrifice. "Without the shedding of blood there is no forgiveness of sins" (Heb. 9:22). The wages of our sin is death, and only an innocent victim dying in our place as our substitute can reconcile us to God. Actually, the only victim who can truly die for us is the Son of God, who as John the Baptizer recognized, he is "the Lamb of God, who takes away the sin of the world!" (John 1:29). All other sacrificial lambs in the Old Testament proclaim him.

At any rate, God accepted Abel's offering and rejected Cain's. With his supreme sense of his own righteousness, Cain believed that was not fair. And as sometimes happens in a horrible irony, self-righteousness can turn to hatred. Cain killed his brother. "Then the LORD said to Cain, 'Where is Abel your brother?' He said, 'I do not know; am I my brother's keeper?'" (Gen. 4:9). The correct answer is yes. And that may be the best expression of the proper work of siblings. Brothers and sisters are to "keep" each other.

The other family vocations involve neighbor relationships between people of different callings. Husbands and wives are not the same, nor is a parent the same as the child in the work they do for each other. But brothers and sisters are equal to their other brothers and sisters. They have the same calling as child and exist on the same level in the family. The brother's neighbor, in his vocation of brotherhood, is the person to whom he is a brother, that is to his brothers and sisters. To be a "keeper" to one's brother means to watch over, to guard, to protect. Brothers, as we say, "have each other's backs." More than that, "keeping" means helping, holding onto, maintaining the relationship and the family at almost any cost. To be a "keeper" requires forgiveness, keeping the brotherly bond, despite any wrongs that might have been done. After all, siblings are each other's "flesh and blood," and so they are to serve the greater good of the family (the one flesh) and the greater good of each member. Actually, the warring brothers in the Bible sometimes came to a happy reconciliation. After many long years, Jacob expected Esau to avenge the wrongs that he had done to him. "But Esau ran to meet him and embraced him and fell on his neck and kissed him, and they wept" (Gen. 33:4). Esau kept his brother. Joseph remained his brothers' keeper, though they did not keep him, having sold him into slavery. Joseph preserved their lives, forgave them, and gave them a new home (Genesis 45).

One set of brothers who did not reconcile is recounted precisely as a rejection of forgiveness, not only on the personal level, but as a rejection of the principle of the gospel. The parable of the prodigal son describes how the father forgave his sinful child, as we discussed, but it goes on to show how the older brother repudiated that forgiveness:

> Now his older son was in the field, and as he came and drew near to the house, he heard music and dancing. And he called one of the servants and asked what these things meant. And he said to him, "Your brother has come, and your father has killed the fattened calf, because he has received him back safe and sound." But he was angry and refused to go in. His father came out

and entreated him, but he answered his father, "Look, these many years I have served you, and I never disobeyed your command, yet you never gave me a young goat, that I might celebrate with my friends. But when this son of yours came, who has devoured your property with prostitutes, you killed the fattened calf for him!" And he said to him, "Son, you are always with me, and all that is mine is yours. It was fitting to celebrate and be glad, for this your brother was dead, and is alive; he was lost, and is found." (Luke 15:25–32)

The older son is like Cain, insisting on his righteousness—"I never disobeyed your command"—a self-righteousness that is twisted into anger, jealousy, and hatred for his brother. The older son resists his brother's restoration, standing on the grounds of justice, believing that his wastrel brother does not deserve their father's grace. The older brother refuses to come into the feast. But the father is prodigal with grace for this son, too, giving him his presence and all his possessions.

Where is God in brotherhood? Christ, says the apostle Paul, is "the firstborn among many brothers" (Rom. 8:29). Jesus is our brother. He is God's Son, and so are we. He is the only-begotten Son of God, and we are adopted sons, but we both have the same heavenly Father. Jesus, as our brother, is also our keeper. And we keep him by faith.

That Jesus is in brotherhood means that he is the source of forgiveness for our brothers. Jesus in his earthly ministry underscored the importance of forgiving our brothers: "Then Peter came up and said to him, 'Lord, how often will my brother sin against me, and I forgive him? As many as seven times?' Jesus said to him, 'I do not say to you seven times, but up to seventy times seven'" (Matt. 18:21–22).

Though siblings are often in conflict with each other in the Bible, the Scriptures also cite the strong bond between brothers when they are keeping each other.

> Behold, how good and pleasant it is
>   when brothers dwell in unity!
> It is like the precious oil on the head,
>   running down on the beard,
> on the beard of Aaron,
>   running down on the collar of his robes!
> It is like the dew of Hermon,
>   which falls on the mountains of Zion!
> For there the LORD has commanded the blessing,
>   life forevermore. (Ps. 133:1–3)

It is not only good but also pleasant when brothers live in unity with each other. It is like the oil that anoints the priest, the dew on the temple mount. It is like God's blessing, like eternal life.

The Household of Faith

The Bible also describes the church as a "household" and the relationship between Christians as that of brothers and sisters. "For through [Christ] we both have access in one Spirit to the Father. So then you are no longer strangers and aliens, but you are fellow citizens with the saints and members of the household of God" (Eph. 2:18–19). "So then, as we have opportunity, let us do good to everyone, and especially to those who are of the household of faith" (Gal. 6:10).

Thus, Christians are members of the same family. Indeed, from the earliest days of the church to this day, Christians have referred to each other as brothers and sisters. In the Epistles, which record this usage frequently (e.g., Rom. 16:1; 1 Cor. 7:15; James 2:15), we see that referring to one's fellow Christians with the language of the household was not a matter of mere titles but a description of how fellow Christians were to treat each other: "Do not rebuke an older man but encourage him as you would a father, younger men as brothers, older women as mothers, younger women as sisters, in all purity" (1 Tim. 5:1–2).

That the church is a household means that Christians are united with each other. God calls us, as members of the brotherhood, to "bear one another's burdens" and "if anyone is caught in any transgression, you who are spiritual should restore him in a spirit of gentleness" (Gal. 6:1–2). Fellow Christians are to "love one another with brotherly affection" and "outdo one another in showing honor" (Rom. 12:10). The unity of Christians extends beyond the local congregation to embrace brothers and sisters one has never met. The apostle Peter describes Christians' conflict with the Devil and the fellowship of common suffering that binds the household together: "Your adversary the devil prowls around like a roaring lion, seeking someone to devour. Resist him, firm in your faith, knowing that the same kinds of suffering are being experienced by your brotherhood throughout the world" (1 Pet. 5:8–9).

The basis for our unity with fellow Christians is our unity with Christ. In his redeeming work, his crucifixion and resurrection, he calls us "brothers" (Heb. 2:10–12). Jesus also refers to the hungry, the thirsty, the stranger, the naked, the sick, the imprisoned as "my brothers" (Matt. 25:40), showing his presence in our neighbors whom we are to love and serve. But fellow believers are our flesh and blood, that is we are united in Christ's flesh and blood.

Conclusion

Just as the relationship between Christ and the church underlies marriage and just as the person of the heavenly Father underlies parenthood, the household of faith underlies all human households. Jesus said as much of his own earthly family: "While he was still speaking to the people, behold, his mother and his brothers stood outside, asking to speak to him. But he replied to the man who told him, 'Who is my mother, and who are my brothers?' And stretching out his hand toward his disciples, he said, 'Here are my mother and my brothers! For whoever does the will of my Father in heaven is my brother and sister and mother'" (Matt. 12:46–50).

Those who obey the heavenly Father are his brother and sister and mother, even more so than the members of his own earthly household. The same is true for those who follow Jesus, which may explain the disturbing passages about his followers having to leave or even "hate" their families (Matt. 19:28–30; Luke 14:25–27).

Certainly in the earliest days of Christianity, those who came to faith in Christ nearly always would have had to defy their families, including the head of the household, who was the guardian of the extended family's religious life. Like Christian converts in Islamic families today, they would likely have been ostracized and cast out of the house for following this new Messiah rather than the traditions of the fathers. Thus in the New Testament era, believers really did need to count the cost of discipleship and be willing to repudiate their own families in order to follow Jesus. Even today, becoming a Christian sometimes creates family conflicts. Jesus is saying here that "family values" must not trump a person's relationship with him. But those who give up their families for the kingdom of heaven will receive another family: "Jesus said, 'Truly, I say to you, there is no one who has left house or brothers or sisters or mother or father or children or lands, for my sake and for the gospel, who will not receive a hundredfold now in this time, houses and brothers and sisters and mothers and children and lands, with persecutions, and in the age to come eternal life'" (Mark 10:29–30).

This should be a comfort to Christians who have left or lost their families. The church will be your family. Just as your heavenly Father is more of a father than your biological father and Christ is more of a husband than a woman's earthly husband, the church is more of a family than your biological family. But happy are those households whose members are also members of the household of faith, whose grandparents, parents, brothers, and sisters are also brothers and sisters in Christ.

17

CONCLUSION

Restoring the Family

The children of your servants shall dwell secure; their offspring shall be established before you.

PSALM 102:28

The family is under attack, we keep saying. We must fight the culture war. Antifamily forces are out to destroy marriage. Churches must defend "family values."

To be sure, sin is wreaking havoc in families. Marriages are breaking up, parents are aborting or neglecting their children, sex has become a destructive force instead of a creative force. This is deadly serious business. Yet what we face is not so much a war, with two sides contending against each other, but a vast confusion on all sides. Christians and non-Christians alike have problems with their marriages and with their children, and they are the same problems.

Our culture today has no common framework for addressing some very basic and urgent questions: Why should anyone wait to get married before having sex? Why should you get married before having children? Why should we stay together if we don't love each other anymore? Why shouldn't gays get married to each other? Why can't everyone seek their own fulfillment however they see fit? Lacking a foundation of understanding—or even a way to speak about these things—even more families drift and break apart.

Since the family is the basic unit of the culture, family dysfunctions will mean cultural dysfunctions. Our culture is having problems socializing its children and transmitting its values, not knowing exactly what those values are anymore. We need to relearn what family is.

Christians are in a position to set the family right again, to recover what marriage means and what parenting entails and how to raise children. But they cannot do that simply by means of imposing laws and following rules, figuring out who has to obey whom, and conforming to an ideal of family perfection. Christians should know from the New Testament the futility of that sort of thing. Rather, what is needed is inner transformation. This comes from faith in the gospel of Jesus Christ. And vocation teaches how that faith can be lived out in love and service to the neighbor, including the neighbors in one's family.

But Christians must take care not to idolize the family. Christianity does not consist of just family values. In fact, parts of the New Testament could be described as undermining family values. Jesus said, "Do you think that I have come to give peace on earth? No, I tell you, but rather division. For from now on in one house there will be five divided, three against two and two against three. They will be divided, father against son and son against father, mother against daughter and daughter against mother, mother-in-law against her daughter-in-law and daughter-in-law against mother-in-law" (Luke 12:51–53). Christianity must always be about Christ and the gospel of the forgiveness of sins through his atoning death and resurrection. But faith in this gospel not only transforms lives, but it also transfigures families, as the eyes of faith see Christ in marriage, the heavenly Father in parenthood, and the Son of God in childhood.

Family is not merely a cultural phenomenon. It encompasses far more than the exercise of power. Frankly, the pursuit of personal fulfillment is at odds with the corporate nature of marriage and parenthood. Those who above everything else want self-fulfillment would do well to skip getting married and forget about having children. All of those idealistic expectations about how fulfilling marriage and parenthood are supposed to be can yield frustration, conflict, and disappointment when flesh-and-blood people share a home and live together day after day. Those vocations require self-denial and self-sacrifice to work. They do yield the deepest satisfaction and happiness, but this can only be known to those willing to deny themselves for the sake of their spouses (the wife submitting to her husband; the husband giving himself up for his wife) and children (parents sacrificing for their children; children obeying their parents).

Family is not a human construct; rather, it is a construct, a gift, and a tool from our God. As such, God is the one who calls human beings into families. And he will defend those families with his power and his presence. Families, throughout history and throughout constant cultural change, have always had their problems. Still, they have been preserved. Through all of the changes and in the face of every challenge to the institution of the family, the doctrine of vocation has always held true. And at key points in history, the doctrine of vocation, as expressed in the New Testament teachings about marriage and parenthood, has brought new life—God's life—into the family.

The Premodern Family Wars

As we have said, the family in the ancient and Biblical world was more extended than we are used to today in our nuclear families, which are often separated by vast geographical distance from grandparents, uncles, and cousins. Family involved tribe, clan, and, finally, the house, led by a father, grandfather, or other patriarch. His job was not just spoiling the grandkids. Rather, he had real authority over all of his descendants and was venerated by each generation. Of course, when his sons became fathers, they too had authority over their children, and someday they would become patriarchs of their households.

These families generally worked together, with the men, women, and children all doing their part to farm the land, which would have been handed down from one generation to the next from time immemorial, to tend the sheep, and to do whatever was needed for the family to survive and thrive. Some houses were of merchants or craftsmen. That Joseph was a carpenter meant that young Jesus undoubtedly worked with him in his trade. Thus, the vocation of worker was closely tied to the vocations of family.

The houses of Israel were very similar in their family organization to those of the Greeks and the Romans.[1] The Roman *pater familias* had absolute power over the members of his family, including the right to have handicapped or otherwise unwanted babies killed, a practice also found in Greek households, but never in Jewish or Christian families. So the original audiences of Paul's epistles, which teach about the family vocations, would have had this high—even excessively high—view of family.

The coming of Christianity did not change the existing family organization externally, but it did change its inner workings and its personal relationships. The French scholar Servais Pinckaers has shown how Christianity—and specifically the apostle Paul's teachings on vocation—revolutionized the sometimes harsh rule of the *pater familias* and "conveyed a transformation in depth" of the ancient family. He notes specifically Paul's teachings about "reciprocal duties" (that is, as we have been discussing, wives submitting, husbands giving themselves up; children obeying, fathers not provoking), which were "nonexistent in the Roman family," which knew only absolute rule.[2]

By the time of the Middle Ages, family had been "Christianized," with weddings and marriages brought under the authority of the church, rather than the state or the culture. Patterns of descent and kinship were still extremely important for the medieval family, especially in the aristocracy, but the multigenerational households seem to have given way to just the nuclear family of parents and children living together. And yet, spinning around this nucleus were *nonrelated* people—servants, retainers, orphans taken in, foster children, warriors, apprentices, employees—who lived with the family and were also considered part of the household.[3] This was the family-and-living structure during the time of the Reformers, who wrote about vocation in terms of the "estate of the household," which included the callings of both family and work.

In the Middle Ages, the church held complete sway over marriage and thus the family. Recognizing that Christ is in marriage, the church taught that marriage is a sacrament, despite the fact that non-Christians, too, can get married. But there were few people outside the church in Europe during the Middle Ages. The church's canon law regulated marriage, settled family-related disputes, and forbade divorce. But the medieval family was undermined by two major problems: vows of celibacy and the cult of romantic love.

We have discussed how the church in the Middle Ages considered the married life to be a lesser spiritual state than that of the clergy, who followed the "counsels of perfection" in renouncing the world to devote themselves full time to God's service. Priests, monks, and nuns took vows of celibacy, as well as vows of poverty and obedience to the church. The Reformation doctrine of vocation, as has been said, would challenge that, insisting that marriage, parenthood, the workplace, and living in the world are true callings from God and spheres of Christian service.

In the medieval family, as well as the households of the ancient world and in many other cultures today, marriages were usually arranged. Marriage was thought to be too important to leave to the whims of the young. After all, when a young man from one family marries a young woman from another family, their two families are brought together. Therefore, who marries whom was a family decision. Additionally, the medieval economy was based largely on landholdings and hereditary property. Marriage often functioned something like a business merger: The groom's father would typically settle upon his son a share of the family's holdings, and the bride's father would give his daughter a dowry of land. The couple would thus start their new family with landed wealth of their own. And their child might well inherit the accumulated wealth of both families.

If the families involved were of the nobility or of royal blood, the stakes were even higher. Alliances by marriage could have important political and military implications. Two nations that were at war with each other often made peace by having the prince of one of the countries marry the princess of the other. And their son might well become the king of both lands, uniting the two smaller realms into a larger, richer, and more powerful kingdom.

But what about love? What if the prince and princess didn't love each other? Or what if they didn't like each other? Very often, in the case of royal marriages, the bride and groom never laid eyes on each other until their wedding day. To be sure, the church's canon law for the sacrament of matrimony required that both parties "consent" to the union before there could be a valid marriage. Both the man and the woman had this right, so that a bride could always, at the last minute, refuse to go through with the marriage to a man she found repulsive. Still, the bride and groom would both be schooled in the customs of their time, and it would probably never have occurred to either of them that they should "be in love" with the person they were marrying. Love did indeed grow in medieval marriages, but it was the fruit of a long life together, not a prerequisite for getting married in the first place.

And yet, for reasons no one quite understands, during the Middle Ages arose a different kind of love, with new models of behavior, and new issues and challenges for the vocation of marriage: romantic love. The name comes from the "romances," the tales of knights and fair ladies that spread this new intoxication. It is also called "courtly love," since it flourished in the fashionable royal courts. But from this medieval sensibility came the feelings and expectations that remain with us today. A man and woman "fall in love"—often, at first sight. In some versions, the man falls in love with the lady from afar, though she does not even know he exists. In other versions, she scorns him. But his love remains true. He pines for his beloved night and day. He serves her. In some versions, especially the literary versions, he does great deeds for her. Perhaps there are great obstacles to their love. Often, he has to win her. But eventually, after many trials, tribulations, and misunderstandings, she returns his love. Eventually, they can be together. And they live happily ever after.

Romantic love has inspired countless books and movies, love poems and love songs. And of course it is not just a literary phenomenon. A man and a woman may indeed experience mad infatuations for each other. They may indeed live out the passions in the romance novels. Today, men and women often *expect* to feel this kind of love. Some search for it their whole lives. Romantic love is a real experience, and it can be precious in many ways.

But here was the problem in the Middle Ages: romantic love, both in literature and in real life was nearly always extramarital and often *adulterous*. The knight fell in love with the fair lady, but she would already be married—maybe to the king. The knight might be married himself. The obstacles they would have to overcome included the jealousy of their spouses, the difficulties of finding a way to be alone together, and the danger if they would be caught. Romantic love often presented itself as platonic, a higher and nobler feeling than mere physical desire that had nothing to do with the flesh and that could be seen as almost spiritual. And yet, human nature being what it is, romantic love would often turn nonplatonic—shall we say, Aristotelian?—and sexual. The adultery inspired by romantic love profoundly undermined marriage.

Most of us know C. S. Lewis as a great Christian apologist and fantasy author. He was also, in his vocation in the workplace, a brilliant and widely acclaimed literary historian. His first book, *The Allegory of Love*, was about this very subject, the rise of romantic love and its representations in medieval literature. Lewis describes the low state of marriage in the Middle Ages and how it contributed to the allure of adulterous romantic love:

> Marriages had nothing to do with love, and no "nonsense" about marriage was tolerated. All matches were matches of interest, and, worse still, of an interest that was continually changing. When the alliance which had answered would answer no longer, the husband's object was to get rid of the lady as quickly as possible. Marriages were frequently dissolved. The same woman who was the lady and "the dearest dread" of her vassals was often little better than a piece of property to her husband. He was master in his own house. So far from being a natural channel for the new kind of love, marriage was rather the drab background against which that love stood out in all the contrast of its new tenderness and delicacy. The situation is indeed a very simple one, and not peculiar to the Middle Ages. Any idealization of sexual love, in a society where marriage is purely utilitarian, must begin by being an idealization of adultery.[4]

Another factor, according to Lewis, was the view—which we discussed earlier—that sexual desire, even within marriage, is intrinsically sinful:

> The second factor is the medieval theory of marriage—what may be called, by a convenient modern barbarism, the "sexology" of the medieval church. A nineteenth-century Englishman felt that the same passion—romantic love— could be either virtuous or vicious according as it was directed towards marriage or not. But according to the medieval view passionate love itself was wicked, and did not cease to be wicked if the object of it were your wife. If a man had once yielded to this emotion he had no choice between "guilty" and "innocent" love before him: he had only the choice, either of repentance, or else of different forms of guilt.[5]

Lewis cites the medieval theologian Peter Lombard, who taught that "passionate love of a man's own wife is adultery."[6] If a man can commit adultery with his own wife, why not commit adultery with someone he loves?

The Reformation was not just a reformation of religion. It also proved to be, indirectly, a reformation of society.[7] The doctrine of vocation restored the spiritual significance of marriage. It restored the spiritual significance of sexuality. And one of its byproducts was to channel romantic love into marriage.

People in the Middle Ages recognized the problem. That romantic love leading to adultery brings on personal and social tragedy is abundantly illustrated in the popular King Arthur romances, in which the affair of Sir Lancelot and Queen Guinevere leads to the destruction of Camelot. Chaucer's "Franklin's Tale" is a romance with the novelty for the time of depicting a case of romantic love that ends in marriage. The difficulty was that in romantic love, the woman is supposed to rule the man, so that he does whatever she desires. The understanding of marriage was that the husband rules the wife. In Chaucer's story, the lovers actually marry each other and together they agree to form a pact: The husband will be the woman's "Servant in love, and lord in marriage."[8] Insofar as she is the object of his romantic love, he will serve her. But insofar as he is her husband, he will be her lord, and she will serve him. This comes close to the mutual love and service called for in the doctrine of vocation.

But it was the Reformation that emphasized that the highest form of love between a man and a woman is fulfilled in marriage. "Part of Luther's legacy is that he introduced love as an essential element of marriage," observes Justin Taylor, quoting the Reformer and historians. "Luther was at the forefront of advocating marital love and making it the norm for entering into marriage and thriving within marriage."[9]

Lewis credits the Protestant poet Sir Edmund Spenser for doing the imaginative work of associating romantic love with marriage instead of with adultery.[10] Spenser's sonnet sequence *Amoretti* depicts the ups and downs of a young man passionately in love with a young woman. In this it is like untold numbers of other sonnet sequences. But *Amoretti* is about Spenser's courtship of an actual woman, Elizabeth Boyle. After his romantic torments and pleadings, she eventually accepts his proposal of marriage. Then follows one of the greatest poems in the English language, "Epithalamion," about their wedding day. It includes a Christian meditation on their wedding night, which shows also a more biblical perspective on sex: In "the safety of our joy," the newlyweds enjoy "the sweet pleasures of their love's delight" in the hopes of engendering new immortal souls for Heaven, begetting children who will grow up to be "bless'd

Saints."[11] Thereafter, as we see in Shakespeare's comedies, the novels of Jane Austen, cinematic love stories, and the experience of ordinary couples, romantic love leads to marriage, where it continues to reside.

Even though the doctrine of vocation helped to associate romantic love with marriage, it is important to realize that romantic love does not make the marriage or validate the marriage. Today, couples writing their own wedding ceremony sometimes have been known to change the traditional vows about loving and keeping each other in sickness and in health and forsaking all others "as long as we both shall live" to "as long as we both shall love." The assumption is that if the couple stops loving each other, then the marriage is no longer valid. "I don't love you anymore" becomes the justification for divorce. Sometimes, as in the Middle Ages, romantic love becomes an excuse for committing adultery, as in, "I'm in love with someone else." The problem is that romantic love, by its nature, is an unstable passion, ebbing and flowing over time.

The love between a husband and wife in marriage grows and deepens, and becomes much more than the infatuation the two might have felt for each other when they first met. As Luther put it, "The first love is drunken. When the intoxication wears off, then comes the real marriage love."[12] He explains, "It is the highest grace of God, when love continues to flourish in married life. The first love is ardent, is an intoxication love, so that we are blinded and are drawn to marriage. After we have slept off our intoxication, sincere love remains in the married life of the godly; but the ungodly are sorry they ever married."[13] The ungodly would presumably be those who base their marriage on "intoxication love" alone. His biographer Roland Bainton summarizes Luther's teachings about marital love and its connection to the mandate of vocation: "Love indeed there is in Christian marriage, but it is only a heightening of that Christian love which is enjoined toward all. We are told to love our neighbors. The wife is the nearest neighbor. She should therefore be the most beloved."[14]

Building a marriage upon romantic love alone—without a sense of being called to this person no matter what—is to build on a foundation of sand. Experienced lovers in marriage agree with Dietrich Bonhoeffer, the martyred theologian who wrote perceptively about vocation, who said in a wedding sermon written from a Nazi prison, "It is not your love that sustains the marriage, but from now on the marriage that sustains your love."[15]

The Modern Family Wars

The industrial revolution brought new challenges to the family. In the earliest days of industrialism, masses of people moved from their ancestral farms in the country to the burgeoning factories of the big cities, leaving behind both their extended families and the rural culture that sustained them. Those early eighteenth- and nineteenth-century factories wreaked havoc with family life, employing not only men, but also women, and even children as young as six years old. Because of the low wages, everyone in the family often had to work, putting in twelve- to fourteen-hour days with only Sundays off.[16]

In the premodern economy, everyone in the family tended to work—on the farm, in the workshop, making for themselves the necessities of life such as food and clothing—but they worked at home. The household was the workplace. In the modern economy, at first everyone worked, but outside the home. The household and the workplace became separated, pulling family members in different directions.

As working conditions improved, at least for the growing and increasingly affluent middle class, the family began to be seen as a place of refuge from the demands of the workplace and the conflicts of the world in general. In the Victorian ideal, the family, the "home," was a haven of love, warm sentiments, and happiness in an otherwise harsh and unfeeling world. Home is where the heart is. There is no place like home. Presiding over the home was the wife and mother. It was her job, her vocation, to ensure the moral tone and the loving feelings of the home, as she cared for the children and made the home a beautiful space. The husband and father worked outside the home, slaving away and battered by the realities of making a living; but when he came home, he could put all of that behind him, basking in the love of his wife and children.

It is fashionable today to disparage the nineteenth-century ideal of the home as a haven from the cares of the world. Arguably, this model of the family was a great cultural advance. It is good for human beings to be able to get away from work and to escape from "the real world." The Victorian home opened up a space for privacy, intimacy, and personal life. The home as a haven was also a place for spiritual reflection and growth. The Reformation displaced vocation and the spiritual life from the monastery to the home. In the Victorian era, the home became something akin to a monastery.

Of course, not all homes were havens, which led to disillusionment and shattered expectations. And many women chafed at their lack of involvement in the world outside their homes. Already in the nineteenth century, many women in the United States and other democracies yearned for a say in their governments and clamored for the right to vote. The church gave women an outlet for social activism, with many women working in church-related crusades against slavery, alcohol, and poverty. Many women also wanted to work outside the home. By the middle of the twentieth century, having achieved legal and educational parity with men, wives and mothers flooded into the workplace. Today, in the twenty-first century, women comprise 47 percent of the workforce.[17] That includes 72.9 percent of mothers with a child under eighteen.[18]

This is the occasion of much controversy among many Christians today. Should married women work outside the home? Should mothers forego the workplace and stay at home with their families to concentrate on raising their children? Christian women are often torn over this issue. Even women who believe they *should* stay home often, as the statistics would suggest, find themselves in the workplace, to their guilt and angst. Other women, bucking the trends, do stay home, only to face condescension from people who consider being a housewife to be somehow inferior to having a career.

What does the doctrine of vocation have to say about these issues? Again, God's calling is unique and personal, so we have been avoiding giving blanket rules that apply to everyone. But here are some considerations:

First, being a mother *is* a vocation. In fact, being a mother is more important than most other vocations, including those of the workplace. The comedienne Phyllis Diller used to do a schtick about a friend with a career who looked down on her for being a stay-at-home mom. The friend's career? Working the candy counter at a department store. To her, selling candy was more important than raising the next generation of human beings. Clearly, those who devote full-time attention to their

God-given callings as parents to their children—including stay-at-home dads—deserve honor and commendation.

At the same time, the doctrine of vocation includes the possibility that a mother might be called to other positions as well, including vocations in the workplace. God may have prepared her, by education, inclination, and opportunity for service in a job or profession. The doctrine of vocation tends to be leery of monastic isolation from the world, which would include an overly monastic or cloistered family. The woman at the candy counter may be loving and serving her family by helping them make a living. In the past, wives and mothers helped the family economically, and a Christian view of the family should not rule out that task automatically. As the Industrial Revolution gives way to the "information revolution," the new technology holds the potential for decentralizing work and putting it back in the home, as we are already seeing with Internet businesses, online teaching, and telecommuting. But in the meantime, Christian mothers who have a calling to work outside the home do not need to feel guilty about it. There are different ways to serve your family.

Again, Christians have multiple vocations in the family, the workplace, the church, and the culture. It isn't a matter of "balancing them" necessarily, as if they all demanded equal attention. Nor is it a matter of setting rigid priorities (as in, God, first; family, second; job, third). As was said earlier, since all vocations are about loving and serving the neighbor, when vocations conflict, they should be resolved by attending to the neighbor with the greatest need. A woman may find that her newborn baby needs her more than her clients at the office. At another point of her life, she may find that her teenaged children do not need her presence with them quite as much as they used to, though they are going to need money for college, which she could earn by going back to the office.

The things that come up in the course of an ordinary week often involve confronting neighbors with different needs and activating different vocations. A member of the church dies suddenly, and the demands of both children and work may need to be set aside for a while to attend to the grieving family. Sometimes one's spouse is the neighbor who has the greatest need, and children, work, and even church meetings may have to wait. Modernity may have fragmented our lives and our families, but the doctrine of vocation can give modern families and those who inhabit them a way to pull their lives together. And living by vocation brings the Christian faith—repentance, the cross, Christ, self-denying love—into an otherwise meaningless world.

The Postmodern Family Wars

Economic and cultural changes have impacted the family. And so have ideas and shifts in worldview. As modernity progressed, with its age of reason and trust in science, a parallel movement that put its trust instead in emotion and subjectivity tagged along and would later become dominant. As the materialists were reducing the universe, including the family, to evolutionary conflict, the romantics were exalting the self. As progressives were celebrating the inevitable progress of the human race, which involved transcending old ideas and old institutions, Nietzsche was lauding the will to power. Soon after, the Enlightenment insisted that the only kind of objective truth was scientific truth, skeptical philosophers began insisting that there is no objective truth at all.

Both worldviews undermined Christianity and the family, though for different reasons. The imperative to fulfill the self replaced the Christian injunction to deny the self. As a result, countless men and women have abandoned their marriages and their children in a futile quest for self-fulfillment. Others have reasoned that marriage is an old-fashioned institution, based on male oppression and out-moded morality, and that having children damages the environment.

Today we are in the postmodern era, which assumes that truth, morality, and culture—including the family—are all nothing more than "constructions." And what has been constructed can be deconstructed and reconstructed. The contemporary climate is well-known to contemporary readers. We could look at the feminist critique of the family, at the totalitarian impulse for the state to raise children, at the pop culture with its hedonism and its consumerism. We have already looked at what may be the biggest factor in family problems today, the fallout from previous generations of divorce and absent fathers. But let's look at what has happened to sex.

As we said before, one cultural contribution of the modern world was the invention of adolescence.[19] From ancient times through much of the nineteenth century, people passed relatively smoothly from child-hood to adulthood. Once children passed through puberty, they were considered "young men" and "young women" who entered straight into the responsibilities and privileges of adulthood. The teenaged boy would typically go into the workforce and as soon as he earned enough money to support a family, say, at eighteen, he would get married to a girl younger than he was, maybe sixteen.

Today, though, before they can be counted as adults, young people must go through a protracted period of "adolescence," a word and con-cept first noted in 1905.[20] It is a netherworld between childhood and adulthood. Though adolescents are physically adults, they are still con-sidered children, remaining under their parents' control. Though physi-cally mature, they are not allowed to enter the full-time workplace or be treated as adults. Though sexually ready, they are not allowed to get mar-ried. No wonder teenagers today are often tormented and angst ridden, rebelling against their parents' authority and struggling with their iden-tity. No wonder teenagers, filled with raging hormones and stimulated by a hypersexualized pop culture, have problems with chastity.

But then the so-called "youth culture" of the 1960s gave full vent and approval to adolescent rebellion and premarital sex. And what was at first a subculture became the culture. Today, our popular music, mov-ies, television shows, video games, and the entertainment industry as a whole are geared for adolescent tastes. And even aging adults often try to look and act young. Some adults remember their youth so fondly—after all, it was a time of irresponsibility and self-indulgence—that they remain in a state of "perpetual adolescence," at the expense of ever form-ing mature relationships or accepting grown-up responsibilities.

Perhaps in some way the invention of adolescence was a cultural advance, like the home being a haven, an extension of the carefree days of childhood before the burdens of adult responsibilities. But culturally, marriage got pushed to the side and parenthood became something to avoid. Contraceptive and birth-controlling technology with abortion on demand made that possible. Sex apart from marriage and with no ref-erence to parenthood became first technologically possible and then socially acceptable.

Interestingly, though, people still wanted to get married, and some wanted to have children. God's design is not easily thwarted. But since marriage was no longer assumed to be necessary for sex or parenthood, one element remained: romantic love.

Both men and women dreamed of finding that perfect soul mate, falling in love, and getting married. Something remained, too, of the home as a haven. In the chaos of contemporary culture, that was an attractive ideal, minus perhaps the part about the woman staying at home. But couples liked the idea of having an idyllic home—maybe eventually with one or two perfect children.

Today we are contemplating and in some jurisdictions have already enacted the biggest change in the family in the history of the human race, something no other culture has even contemplated—gay marriage—making it so that men can marry men, and women can marry women. And why not? If marriage is based on nothing more than romantic attachment, why shouldn't people who have romantic attachments to individuals of their same sex get married? Surely they too have a right to the same haven that heterosexuals enjoy. And if marriage is merely a social construction, it does not need to be tied to an objective moral code or even to nature. Our society should be able to construct marriage.

What Do We Do?

So how can we protect the family against such powerful cultural tides? The postmodernists, of course, are easy to answer, though the answers tend to have little impact on postmodernists. Christians know that human beings do not construct truth, morality, or the family. God constructed—that is, created—them. God does not call men to marry men and women to marry women. Marriage cannot turn same-sex couples into one flesh. Nor can they have children with each other. Begetting a child, for all of the in vitro technology, still requires a male and a female. Nature itself is on the Christians' side.

Christians are increasingly demonized and marginalized for thinking this way. So what are Christians supposed to do if or when the family gets radically reconstructed, when the culture legalizes gay marriage and abandons traditional marriage in favor of cohabitation and single parenthood? Perhaps Christians should adopt the postmodernist mantra of diversity, taking their own distinct place as one of many cultural alternatives. Christians could just have their own families, in accordance with their beliefs, and let non-Christians have the social arrangements of their choice.

Some conservatives of a libertarian bent, including some Christians, are saying that the government should get out of the marriage business. Marriage is a Christian sacrament or vocation, so let churches deal with that. Liberal churches would be free to conduct gay weddings, and conservative churches would be free to just conduct straight weddings. Individuals could enter into whatever contracts or relationships they want. The government would have nothing to do with it.

Perhaps it may someday come to that, if the government repeals all marriage laws. But marriage is *not* just for Christians. The Reformers worked hard to give the state authority over marriage *rather* than the church.[21] That was because marriage has to do with the temporal, earthly kingdom, which makes it the responsibility of the God-ordained vocations of earthly rulers. The church's business is proclaiming the gospel, not promulgating laws for the society. The church does bless weddings, but the license is issued by the state, which regulates marriage under its laws. The Reformers, remember, were insisting on the spiritual significance of the *secular* vocations—not only the family, but also the state—and, far from creating a theocracy, they wanted the church to have *less* political power and to rule *less* than it already did under the Pope.

So, in terms of the doctrine of vocation, it does matter what laws the state passes about marriage. Of course, the authorities of the state only have the authority that God has given them (Rom. 13:1–7). They do not have the authority or the ability to overturn what God has ordained. They cannot change what marriage is, any more than King Canute's commands could stop the tide from coming in.

And this is the hope for Christians. *God* builds the family. *God* is present in the family. *God* protects the family. Human beings may sin against the family. They may evade it. They may create their own pretend family, like children playing house. But God, like his Word, is living and active. We do not need to defend him. He defends us.

Furthermore, God is the one who calls people into families. "God sets the lonely in families" (Ps. 68:6 NIV). Luther says God drives and compels men and women to get married.[22] So marriage continues, even among those who seemingly have no basis for marriage. What the promiscuous heroines on *Sex in the City* want, it turns out, is to get married.

Those who seemingly have no basis for wanting children still often crave to be parents. And marriage and parenthood change them, turning their orientation away from themselves to a neighbor, if only for a while.

The compulsion to be in a family, the impulses to marry and to have children, is part of the human condition. It springs up of itself by virtue of our creation and through the powerful echoes of God's words: "Be fruitful and multiply."

Many have abandoned the blessings of family. Many others are bereft of the blessings of family against their wills. Even those who appreciate its various relationships may struggle and may not understand all that is going on. But God is still blessing through family. He is giving his gifts—including his presence—not because of our understanding, how good we are as parents or in our marriage, or anything other than because he loves his Son and all who have been adopted through him. He keeps his promises and these promises are for you, for me, for our children and grandchildren until the end of time and beyond.

In the meantime, what do we do? Vocation centers on the ordinary and the mundane. Reviving the family in the culture starts with one's own marriage, one's own parenthood, one's own extended family. Christians can start by viewing the members of their families as gifts of God, indeed, as masks of God. If Christians can live out their faith in love and service to their spouses, children, and parents, then the institutions of marriage, parenthood, and the family itself will be transfigured. Restored Christian families could become a catalyst for the restoration of families throughout the culture.

It will also help to recover the doctrine of vocation—teaching it to children, so that they will understand what will be happening in their lives, and throughout the church, so that Christians will understand how and where to live out their faith. The message is simple, though the task can only be carried out through the cross of Christ: Love and serve your wife. Love and serve your husband. Love and serve your children. Love and serve your parents. Love and serve.

Bibliography

Althaus, Paul. *Ethics of Martin Luther*. Minneapolis, MN: Augsburg Fortress, 1972.

Eschelbach, Michael. *Marriage and the Counsel of God*. Eugene, OR: Wipf & Stock, 2007.

Eyer, Richard. *Marriage Is Like Dancing*. St. Louis, MO: Concordia, 2007.

Karant-Nunn, Susan, and Merry Wiesner. *Luther on Women: A Sourcebook*. New York: Cambridge University Press, 2003.

Kleinig, John. *Leviticus*. Concordia Commentary Series. St. Louis, MO: Concordia, 2003.

_____. "Ordered Community: Order and Subordination in the New Testament." In *Women Pastors? The Ordination of Women in Biblical Lutheran Perspective*. Edited by Matthew Harrison and John Pless. 2nd ed. St. Louis, MO: Concordia, 2009.

Luther, Martin. *The Christian in Society I*. Luther's Works, vol. 44. Edited by James Atkinson and Helmut Lehmann. Philadelphia, PA: Fortress, 1966.

_____. *The Christian in Society II*. Luther's Works, vol. 45. Edited by Helmut Lehmann and James Atkinson. Philadelphia, PA: Fortress, 1962.

_____. "The Freedom of the Christian." In *Three Treatises*. Translated by Charles Jacobs, A. T. W. Steinhauser, and W. A. Lambert. Philadelphia, PA: Fortress, 1970.

_____. *Small Catechism*. St. Louis, MO: Concordia, 1986.

Moore, Russell. *Adopted for Life: The Priority of Adoption for Christian Families and Churches*. Wheaton, IL: Crossway, 2009.

Parsons, Michael, *Reformation Marriage: The Husband and Wife Relationship in the Theology of Luther and Calvin*. Edinburgh: Rutherford, 2005.

Pearcey, Nancy. *Total Truth: Liberating Christianity from Its Cultural Captivity*. Wheaton, IL: Crossway, 2004.

Piper, John, and Justin Taylor, eds. *Sex and the Supremacy of Christ*. Wheaton, IL: Crossway, 2005.

Rosenberg, Jeffrey, and W. Bradford Wilcox. *The Importance of Fathers in the Health Development of Children*, Office on Child Abuse and Neglect. Washington, DC: Department of Health & Human Services, 2006.

Spencer, Aída Besançon., William David Spencer, Steve Tracy, and Celestia Tracy. *Marriage at the Crossroads: Couples in Conversation about Discipleship, Gender Roles, Decision Making and Intimacy*. Downers Grove, IL: InterVarsity, 2009.

Triglot Concordia: The Symbolical Books of the Evangelical Lutheran Church: German-Latin-English. Translated by W. H. T. Dau and F. Bente St. Louis, MO: Concordia, 1921. These texts are in the public domain and may be freely copied. Available online at www.bookofconcord.com. References by book, article, and paragraph.

Veith, Gene Edward. *God at Work: Your Christian Vocation in All of Life.* Wheaton, IL: Crossway, 2002.

Waite, Linda J. and Maggie Gallagher. *The Case for Marriage.* New York: Broadway, 2000.

Wangerin, Walter Jr. *As For Me and My House: Crafting Your Marriage to Last.* Nashville, TN: Thomas Nelson, 2001.

Wingren, Gustaf. *Luther on Vocation.* Translated by Carl C. Rasmussen. Evansville, IN: Ballast, 1999. Translation now available through Wipf & Stock Publishers.

Winner, Lauren. *Real Sex: The Naked Truth about Chastity.* Grand Rapids, MI: Brazos, 2006.

Wolfinger, Nicholas. *Understanding the Divorce Cycle: The Children of Divorce in Their Own Marriages.* New York: Cambridge University Press, 2005.

Wright, Bradley R. E. *Christians Are Hate-Filled Hypocrites . . . and Other Lies You've Been Told: A Sociologist Shatters Myths from the Secular and Christian Media.* Minneapolis, MN: Bethany, 2010.

Yahnke, Beverly, "When God's Good Gifts are Defiled: The Sinned and the Sinned Against." Paper presented at the conference In the Image of God: A Christian Vision for Love and Marriage at Concordia Theological Seminary, Fort Wayne, IN, September 18–20, 2006. Paper available online at www.cranach.org /imageofgod/papers.php.

Notes

Chapter 1: Introduction: Confusing the Family

1. "New Marriage and Divorce Statistics Released," Barna Group, March 31, 2008, http://www.barna.org/barna-update/article/15-familykids/42-new-marriage-and-divorce-statistics-released.

2. Lydia Saad, "Cultural Tolerance for Divorce Grows to 70%," *Gallup*, May 19, 2008, http://www.gallup.com/poll/107380/Cultural-Tolerance-Divorce-Grows-70.aspx.

3. Lydia Saad, "By Age 24, Marriage Wins Out," *Gallup*, August 11, 2008, http://www.gallup.com/poll/109402/Age-24-Marriage-Wins.aspx#1.

4. Saad, "Cultural Tolerance."

5. Ibid.

6. See Stanley Kurtz, "The End of Marriage in Scandinavia," *The Weekly Standard*, February, 2, 2004, 22–26.

7. "America's Children: Key National Indicators Of Well-Being, 2009," Federal Interagency Forum on Child and Family Statistics, http://www.childstats.gov/americaschildren/glance.asp.

8. "New Marriage and Divorce Statistics."

9. Bradley, R. E. Wright, *Christians Are Hate-Filled Hypocrites . . . and Other Lies You've Been Told: A Sociologist Shatters Myths from the Secular and Christian Media* (Minneapolis, MN: Bethany, 2010).

10. "Table of Duties," *Luther's Small Catechism* (St. Louis, MO: Concordia, 1986), 35.

Chapter 2: Vocation in the Nourishing Estate

1. See my book *God at Work: Your Christian Vocation in All of Life* (Wheaton, IL: Crossway, 2002). This summary of Luther's doctrine of vocation also draws on Gustaf Wingren, *Luther on Vocation* (Evansville, IN: Ballast, 1994).

2. See Nancy Pearcey, *Total Truth: Liberating Christianity from Its Cultural Captivity* (Wheaton, IL: Crossway, 2004).

3. See Einar Billing, *Our Calling* (Philadelphia, PA: Fortress, 1964), 30.

4. Johann Gerhard, trans. Elmer Hohle, *Schola Pietatis* (1623), vol. 1 (Malone, TX: Repristination, 2006), 261, 269.

5. Martin Luther, "The Estate of Marriage, 1522," *Luther's Works*, vol. 45, ed. Walther I. Brandt (Philadelphia, PA: Fortress, 1962), 39–41.

6. Paul Althaus, *Ethics of Martin Luther* (Minneapolis, MN: Augsburg Fortress, 1972), xix.

Chapter 3: Marriage

1. Consider what Luther says is involved with being one flesh: "These words are not to be understood to mean that they only physically become one flesh and blood, but they pertain to everything that belongs to outward physical life. The written word *flesh* means everything that belongs to the flesh, that a person has to have: servants, children, money, fields, meadow, property, honor or poverty, shame, illness and health, and so forth—whatever may befall one in life. In other words, *flesh* means one's outward life in the flesh. It should transpire that everything belongs to both of them and that they accept everything together and that each one brings to the other body, goods, honor, shame, poverty, illness, and whatever else there is." (Sermons on Genesis, 1527, [WA XXIV], quoted in Susan C. Karant-Nunn and Merry E. Wiesner, *Luther on Women: A Sourcebook*, [New York: Cambridge University Press, 2003], 18.)

2. Martin Luther, "A Sermon on the Estate of Marriage, 1519," *Luther's Works*, vol. 44, ed. James Atkinson (Philadelphia, PA: Fortress, 1966), 8.

3. The eloquent fourth-century preacher Chrysostom expands on just how mysterious marriage is: "Indeed, of all actions, it is a mystery, a great mystery indeed, that a man should

leave him who gave life to him and brought him up and her who suffered in labor and child-birth. For a man to leave those who have favored him with so many great blessings, those with whom he has been in such close contact, and be united to one whom he has not always known and who often has nothing in common with him, and should honor her more than all others—that is a mystery indeed. Yet parents are not distressed when marriages take place, but when they don't! They are delighted to spend money lavishly on weddings—another great mystery indeed! And one that contains some hidden wisdom: Moses prophetically showed this to be so from the very beginning and Paul proclaims it now, when he compares it to Christ and the Church" (Chrysostom, *On Marriage and Family Life*, [Yonkers, NY: St. Vladimir's Seminary Press, 1986], 52–53).

4. Beverly Yahnke, "When God's Good Gifts are Defiled: The Sinner and the Sinned Against," presented at "In the Image of God: A Christian Vision for Love and Marriage," a conference through the Cranach Institute and Concordia Theological Seminary, Fort Wayne, IN, 2006, available online at http://www.cranach.org/imageofgod/papers/yahnke_when_Gods_good_gifts_are_defiled.pdf.

Chapter 4: The Office of Husband

1. "Just as our neighbor is in need and lacks that in which we abound, so we were in need before God and lacked his mercy. Hence, as our heavenly Father has in Christ freely come to our aid, we also ought freely to help our neighbor through our body and its works, and each one should become as it were a Christ to the other that we may be Christs to one another and Christ may be the same in all, that is, that we may be truly Christians." Martin Luther, "The Freedom of the Christian," *Three Treatises* (Minneapolis, MN: Augsburg Fortress, 1970), 305.

2. Ray LaMontagne, "Trouble," *Absolute Lyrics: The Music Lyrics Database*, accessed on September 14, 2011, www.absolutelyrics.com.

3. Don Cook, Ronnie Dunn, Kix Brooks, "Brand New Man," Absolute Lyrics: The Music Lyrics Database, accessed on September 14, 2011, www.absolutelyrics.com.

4. See John Kleinig, *Leviticus,* Concordia Commentary Series (St. Louis, MO: Concordia, 2003).

5. Here is Luther's understanding of holiness in the context of vocation:
Accordingly, when asked, What is meant by the commandment: Thou shalt sanctify the holy day? answer: To sanctify the holy day is the same as to keep it holy. But what is meant by keeping it holy? Nothing else than to be occupied in holy words, works, and life. For the day needs no sanctification for itself; for in itself it has been created holy [from the beginning of the creation it was sanctified by its Creator]. But God desires it to be holy to you. Therefore it becomes holy or unholy on your account, according as you are occupied on the same with things that are holy or unholy.

How, then, does such sanctification take place? Not in this manner, that [with folded hands] we sit behind the stove and do no rough [external] work, or deck ourselves with a wreath and put on our best clothes, but (as has been said) that we occupy ourselves with God's Word, and exercise ourselves therein.

And, indeed we Christians ought always to keep such a holy day, and be occupied with nothing but holy things, i.e., daily be engaged upon God's Word, and carry it in our hearts and upon our lips. (Luther, "Large Catechism, Ten Commandments, Third Commandment," paragraphs 87–89, *Book of Concord*, accessed on August 24, 2011, http://www.bookofconcord.org/lc-3-tencommandments.php#para88.)

6. Walter Wangerin, Jr., in his book on marriage, *As for Me and My House: Crafting Your Marriage to Last* (Nashville, TN: Thomas Nelson, 2001), develops this idea, that the key to a strong marriage is forgiveness.

7. See, for example, Phillip Melanchthon's "Defense of the Augsburg Confession," Article XXIII, section 28.

8. Aída Bensançon Spencer et al., *Marriage at the Crossroads: Couples in Conversation About Discipleship, Gender Roles, Decision Making and Intimacy* (Downers Grove, IL: InterVarsity, 2009), 37.

9. Richard Eyer, *Marriage Is Like Dancing,* (St. Louis, MO: Concordia, 2007), 52.

10. Spencer et al., *Marriage at the Crossroads,* 63.

11. Ibid., 64.

12. The apostle Paul uses vessel language of both men and women: "Therefore, if anyone cleanses himself from what is dishonorable, he will be a vessel for honorable use, set apart as holy, useful to the master of the house, ready for every good work" (2 Tim. 2:21).

13. *The Epistles of St. Peter and St. Jude Preached and Explained by Martin Luther,* trans. and ed. John Nicholas Lenker (Minneapolis, MN: Lutherans in all Lands, 1904), 139.

Chapter 5: The Office of Wife

1. John W Kleinig, "Ordered Community: Order and Subordination in the New Testament," *Lutheran Theological Journal* 39:2/3 (2005), 196–209.

2. Ibid.

3. See the structure of "The Table of Duties" in Luther's *Small Catechism,* the definitive instruction manual for teaching the doctrine of vocation during and in the aftermath of the Reformation.

Chapter 6: Sex and Vocation

1. Linda J. Waite and Maggie Gallagher, *The Case for Marriage* (New York: Broadway, 2000), 82–89.

2. Lauren Winner, *Real Sex: The Naked Truth about Chastity* (Grand Rapids, MI: Brazos, 2006). Another extremely useful book is John Piper and Justin Taylor, eds., *Sex and the Supremacy of Christ* (Wheaton, IL: Crossway, 2005). The book contains essays by various writers on a wide range of issues regarding a Christian perspective on sex.

3. See Harold Bloom, *The American Religion* (New York: Simon & Schuster, 1993), who argues that America's religion is actually gnosticism. Elaine Pagels is a contemporary theologian who is arguing for a revival of Gnosticism, which she believes accords better with a feminist agenda than orthodox Christianity. See, for example, her book *The Gnostic Gospels* (New York: Vintage, 1979). For a critique of Gnostic elements in contemporary Protestantism, see Philip Lee, *Against the Protestant Gnostics* (New York: Oxford University Press, 1987).

4. As was said in the introduction to this book, in the medieval period marriage and sex in general were treated as a concession to the weakness of the flesh. In the face of the rampant abuses from the religious orders of that day, Martin Luther criticized vows of celibacy in favor of vocation of marriage. Luther agreed with his associate Melanchthon, who penned the following as contained in the *Book of Concord*:

> If continence were possible to all, it would not require a peculiar gift. But Christ shows that it has need of a peculiar gift; therefore it does not belong to all. God wishes the rest to use the common law of nature which He has instituted. For God does not wish His ordinances, His creations to be despised. He wishes men to be chaste in this way, that they use the remedy divinely presented, just as He wishes to nourish our life in this way, that we use food and drink. Gerson also testifies that there have been many good men who endeavored to subdue the body, and yet made little progress. Accordingly, Ambrose is right in saying: Virginity is only a thing that can be recommended, but not commanded; it is a matter of vow rather than of precept. If any one here would raise the objection that Christ praises those which have made themselves eunuchs for the kingdom of heaven's sake, Matt. 19:12, let him also consider this, that He is praising such as have the gift of continence; for on this account He adds: He that is able to receive it, let him receive it. For an impure continence [such as there is in monasteries and cloisters] does not please Christ. We also praise true continence. But now we are disputing concerning the law, and concerning those who do not have the gift of continence. The matter ought to be left free, and snares ought not to be cast upon the weak through this law.

"The Apology of the Augsburg Confession," Article XXIII "Of the Marriage of Priests," paragraphs 19–22 *Triglot Concordia: The Symbolical Books of the Evangelical Lutheran Church: German-Latin-English* (St. Louis, MO: Concordia, 1921).

5. See "The Invention of Adolescence," *Psychology Today,* 1 January 1995, p. 66, and Frank A. Fasick, "On the 'Invention' of Adolescence," *The Journal of Early Adolescence,* (1994) 14:6–23.

6. See J. E. Rosenbaum, "Patient Teenagers: A Comparison of the Sexual Behavior of Virginity Pledgers and Non-Pledgers," *Pediatrics*, (2009), 123:110–21

7. The article "The Case for Early Marriage" was published in *Christianity Today* on July 31, 2009, and is available online at http://www.christianitytoday.com/ct/2009/august/16.22.html.

8. See Augustine, *On Marriage and Concupiscence*, chapter 16, available online at http://www.newadvent.org/fathers/1507.htm.

9. As Luther says directly: "All stations are so oriented that they serve others." Quote taken from Gustaf Wingren, trans. Carl C. Rasmussen, *Luther on Vocation* (Evansville, IN: Ballast, 1999), 5, as translated from Luther's *Complete Works* (WA 15, 625).

Chapter 7: The Crosses of Marriage

1. Gustaf Wingren, trans. Carl C. Rasmussen, *Luther on Vocation* (Evansville, IN: Ballast, 1999). "In one's vocation there is a cross—for prince, husband, father, daughter, for everyone—and on this cross the old human nature is to be crucified" (p. 29). "The cross is not to be chosen by us; it is laid upon us by God, i.e. the cross comes to us uninvoked in our vocation" (p. 53).

2. Ibid., 6.

3. Ibid., 5.

4. Beverly Yahnke, "When God's Good Gifts are Defiled: The Sinner and the Sinned Against," presented at "In the Image of God: A Christian Vision for Love and Marriage," a conference through the Cranach Institute and Concordia Theological Seminary, Fort Wayne, Ind., 2006, available online at http://www.cranach.org/imageofgod/papers/yahnke_when_Gods_good_gifts_are_defiled.pdf.

5. Eschelbach, Michael, *Marriage and the Counsel of God* (Eugene OR: Wipf & Stock, 2007), 53.

6. Althaus, Paul, *Ethics of Martin Luther* (Minneapolis, MN: Augsburg Fortress, 1972), 84.

7. Ibid., 95.

8. Ibid.

9. Ibid., 97.

10. Ibid., 92.

11. Ibid.

12. Ibid., 95.

13. Yahnke, "When God's Good Gifts Are Defiled," 15.

14. Ibid., 13.

Chapter 8: Parenthood

1. James I. Lamb is the Executive Director of Lutherans for Life. Quoted from "Life Quotes: Christ and Adoption," on the *Lutherans For Life* website: http://www.lutheransforlife.org/media/life-quotes/.

2. The word in the original Greek is *monogene*. The KJV renders it, literally, as "only begotten." Modern translations leave the "begotten" out of the verse, referring to God's "one and only Son" (NIV) or "only son" (ESV). But in this case the KJV retains an important sense of the word, one that becomes important in historic Christology. This is reflected in the Nicene Creed, which affirms that the Son of God is "begotten, not made."

3. Russell Moore, *Adopted for Life: The Priority of Adoption for Christian Families and Churches* (Wheaton, IL: Crossway, 2009).

4. Ibid., 106.

5. See, for example, Ex. 22:22; Deut.10:18; Ps. 10:18; 68:5; 146:9; Isa. 1:17; Jer. 22:3; Ezek. 22:7; Zech. 7:10; Mal. 3:5.

6. *The State of the World's Children* (New York: UNICEF, 2008), 159.

7. See Richard Eyer, "An Approach to Bioethics," *Life Library—Bioethics*, The Lutheran Church Missouri Synod, accessed on September 14, 2011, www.lcms.org/page.aspx?pid=7268docid=506.

8. *The Colbert Report*, Comedy Central, 9 April 2009. Quoted and discussed in Rene Black, "The Word Made Fresh: A Theological Exploration of Stephen Colbert," *Concept*, 33 (2001), accessed on September 14, 2011, www.concept.journals.villanova.edu.

9. "Now you tell me, when a father goes ahead and washes diapers or performs some other mean task for his child, and someone ridicules him as an effeminate fool—though that father is acting in the spirit just described and in Christian faith—my dear fellow you tell me, which of the two is most keenly ridiculing the other? God, with all his angels and creatures, is smiling—not because that father is washing diapers, but because he is doing so in Christian faith. Those who sneer at him and see only the task but not the faith are ridiculing God with all his creatures, as the biggest fool on earth. Indeed, they are only ridiculing themselves; with all their cleverness they are nothing but devil's fools." Martin Luther, "Sermon on Marriage," *Luther's Works*, vol. 45, eds. J. J. Pelikan, H. C. Oswald, and H. T. Lehmann (Philadelphia, PA: Fortress, 1999), 40–41.

Chapter 9: The Office of Father

1. Nancy Leigh DeMoss, ed., *Biblical Womanhood in the Home* (Wheaton, IL: Crossway, 2002), 49.

2. Marvin R. Vincent, "Ephesians 3:15," *Vincent's Word Studies in the New Testament* (Peabody, MA: Hendrickson, 1985).

3. "The Lord's Prayer, The Introduction and Meaning," *Luther's Small Catechism with Explanation* (St. Louis, MO: Concordia, 1986), 19.

4. Robbie Low, "The Truth About Men & Church," *Touchstone*, June 2003. The original study is Werner Haug and Phillipe Warner, "The Demographic Characteristics of the Linguistic and Religious Groups in Switzerland," in *The Demographic Characteristics of National Minorities in Certain European States*, vol. 2, eds. Werner Haug, et al. (Strasbourg, France: The Council of Europe Directorate General III, Social Cohesion, 2000).

5. Ibid.

6. "America's Children: Key National Indicators of Well-Being, 2011," Federal Interagency Forum on Child and Family Statistics, http://www.childstats.gov/americaschildren/glance.asp. Accessed 14 November, 2011.

7. Robert Rector, "Out-of-Wedlock Childbearing and Paternal Absence: Trends and Social Effects," *Proceedings of the 14th General Assembly of the Pontifical Council for the Family*, 1999, accessed on September 14, 2011, www.catholicculture.org/culture/library/view.cfm?id=1446&repos=1&subrepos=0&searchid=808177. This study gives a helpful compendium of research into these issues.

8. Ibid.

9. Catherine Edwards, "Divorced Dads," *Insight*, June 18, 2001.

10. Rector, "Out-of-Wedlock Childbearing."

11. Wisconsin Department of Health and Social Services, Division of Youth Services, *Family Status of Delinquents in Juvenile Correctional Facilities in Wisconsin*, April 1994.

12. Douglas Smith and G. Roger Jarjoura, "Social Structure and Criminal Victimization," *Journal of Research in Crime and Delinquency*, February 1988, 27–52.

13. Rector, "Out-of-Wedlock Childbearing."

14. Ibid.

15. See Elijah Anderson, *Streetwise: Race, Class, and Change in an Urban Community* (Chicago: University of Chicago Press, 1990), 112–19.

16. See Melissa McKelvie and Steven R. Gold, "Hyperfemininity: Further Definition of the Construct," *The Journal of Sex Research* (1994), 31:219–28. The article also summarizes research on hypermasculinity.

17. See Focus on the Family (http://www.focusonthefamily.com) or Exodus International (http://exodusinternational.org).

18. Mary Eberstadt, "Eminem is Right," *Policy Review* (2004), 128 .

Chapter 10: The Office of Mother

1. See Os Guinness, *The Call* (Nashville, TN: Word, 1998), 30.

2. See the footnote for this verse in the English Standard Version.

3. Arthur William Meyer, *The Rise of Embryology* (Stanford, CA: Stanford University Press, 1939), 24, 129. The female egg was discovered by Prussian-Estonian embryologist Karl Ernst von Baer.

4. "The Athanasian Creed," in *The Book of Concord*, (St. Louis, MO: Concordia, 1921), 32–33, lines 28–29, accessed August 24, 2011, http://bookofconcord.org/index.php.

5. Cyprian, a bishop in Carthage, born around the year 208, is most famous for saying in his work, *De unitate ecclesiae,* "He can no longer have God for his Father who has not the Church for his mother" (Alexander Roberts and James Donaldson, *The Writings of Cyprian: Ante-Nicene Christian Library Translations of the Writings of the Fathers Down to AD 325 Part Eight* (Whitefish, MT: Kessinger, 2004), 382.

6. "The First Commandment," *Large Catechism,* in *The Book of Concord,* para. 26, accessed August 24, 2011, http://bookofconcord.org/lc-3-tencommandments.php.

7. Nancy Eisenberg, "Emotion, Regulation, and Moral Development," *Annual Review of Psychology* (2000), 51:680–81.

8. Robert Blum, et al., "Mothers' influence on the timing of first sex among 14- and 15-year-olds," *Journal of Adolescent Health* (2002), 31:256–65.

9. Michael Parsons, *Reformation Marriage: The Husband and Wife Relationship in the Theology of Luther and Calvin* (Edinburgh: Rutherford, 2005), 171.

10. Paul Althaus, *Ethics of Martin Luther* (Philadelphia, PA: Fortress, 1972), 97.

Chapter 11: Raising Children

1. Luther's *Small Catechism,* the fourth petition of the Lord's Prayer (St. Louis, MO: Concordia, 1986), 20-21.

2. I have observed this syndrome while working with Muslim college students. See also chapter 3 in my book, *Christianity in an Age of Terrorism* (St. Louis, MO: Concordia, 2002).

3. "The Fourth Commandment," *The Large Catechism,* in Robert Kolb and Timothy J. Wengert, eds., *The Book of Concord: The Confessions of the Evangelical Lutheran Church* (Minneapolis, MN: Augsburg Fortress, 2000), 410.

4. Luther relates the priestly nature of parents educating their children by going so far as to say that the wife at home shares the task of preaching with her husband. See Theo Bell's article "Man is a Microcosmos: Adam and Eve in Luther's *Lectures on Genesis* (1535–1545)," *Concordia Theological Quarterly.* 69:2, April 2005, 172, available online at http://www.ctsfw .edu/library/files/pb/1962.

Chapter 12: The Crosses of Parenthood

1. Charles Lehmann, "Sermon for the second Sunday after Christmas," at Saint John's in the Cove, Accident, Maryland, on December 30, 2010.

2. "And when he is old" is the reading of the King James Version and the New International Version (1984). The ESV and the later versions of the NIV have "even when he is old," somewhat weakening the promise.

3. See James Jacob Prasch, "The Death of Absalom," *Moriel Ministries,* accessed on August 24, 2011, http://www.moriel.org/Teaching/Online/Death_of_Absalom/11_King.html

Chapter 13: Childhood

1. "The Athanasian Creed," in *The Book of Concord,* accessed August 24, 2011, http:// bookofconcord.org/index.php.

2. Ibid.

3. "The tension between Christ's omnipotence, according to His divine nature and His weakness, according to the human nature, is best demonstrated in His birth. On the one hand He rules heaven and earth from His mother's arms, but on the other He is completely dependent upon her for His life and sustenance. All kings do His will, but at His birth He is a subject of Caesar Augustus and His life is endangered by the murderous King Herod." David P. Scaer, "Christology," in *Confessional Lutheran Dogmatics,* Robert Preus, ed. (Northville, SD: The Luther Academy, 1989), 4:61.

Chapter 14: Growing

1. A. S. Neill, *The Free Child* (London: Herbert Jenkins, 1953), 81.

2. "The Fourth Commandment," *The Large Catechism, Triglot Concordia* (St. Louis, MO: Concordia, 1921), section 105–6, www.bookofconcord.org.

3. Ibid., 108.

4. *Concordia: The Lutheran Confessions* (St. Louis, MO: Concordia, 2006), 371.

5. "The Fourth Commandment," sections 109–111.

6. Ibid., sections 129–30.

7. Ibid., sections 112, 115–116, 118.

8. See, for example, this sermon by David W. Adkins, "Honor Thy Father and Mother," www.starlingavenuebc.org/SermonNotes/HonorThyFatherandMother.dsp.

9. "The Fourth Commandment," section 116.

10. Augustine, *Confessions,* trans., Henry Chadwick (New York: Oxford University Press, 1991), I.8.7; I.10.9.

11. William Wordsworth, "My Heart Leaps Up," 1.7. The image is repeated and developed further in "Ode: Intimations of Immortality." Available online at http://www.bartleby.com/145/.

Chapter 15: The Crosses of Childhood

1. Vincent Iannelli, "Child Abuse Statistics," *About.com Guide,* April 21, 2010, http://pediatrics.about.com/od/childabuse/a/05_abuse_stats.htm.

2. Ibid.

3. Gustaf Wingren, *Luther on Vocation* (Evansville, IN: Ballast, 1999), 128–29.

4. J. Goldman et al., *A Coordinated Response to Child Abuse and Neglect: The Foundation for Practice,* Office on Child Abuse and Neglect (Washington, DC: Department of Health & Human Services, 2003), http://www.childwelfare.gov/pubs/usermanuals/foundation /foundatione.cfm.

5. Ianelli, "Child Abuse Statistics."

6. Ibid.

7. Jeffrey Rosenberg and W. Bradford Wilcox, *The Importance of Fathers in the Health Development of Children,* Office on Child Abuse and Neglect (Washington, DC: Department of Health & Human Services, 2006), http://www.childwelfare.gov/pubs/usermanuals /fatherhood/chapterthree.cfm

8. Ibid.

9. Goldman et al., *A Coordinated Response.*

10. Julia Whealin and Erin Barnett, *Child Sexual Abuse,* National Center for PTSD (Washington, DC: Department of Veterans' Affairs, 2010), http://www.ptsd.va.gov /professional/pages/child_sexual_abuse.asp.

11. For a more thorough discussion of these statistics, including an argument that the rate for girls is more like one in five, see also D. Finkelhor, "Current Information on the Scope and Nature of Child Sexual Abuse," *The Future of Children* (1994), 4:31–53, http://www.unh .edu/ccrc/pdf/VS75.pdf.

12. Ibid.

13. National Child Abuse Statistics, *Childhelp,* http://www.childhelp.org/pages /statistics#abuse-criminal.

14. Whealin and Barnett, *Child Sexual Abuse.*

15. Marie E. Tomeo et al., "Comparative Data of Childhood and Adolescence Molestation in Heterosexual and Homosexual Persons," *Archives of Sexual Behavior* (2001), 30:539.

16. See Beverly Yahnke, "When God's Good Gifts are Defiled: The Sinner and the Sinned Against," presented at "In the Image of God: A Christian Vision for Love and Marriage," a conference through the Cranach Institute and Concordia Theological Seminary, Fort Wayne, Ind., 2006, available online at www.cranach.org/imageofgod/papers.php.

17. See, for example, *The International Standard Bible Encyclopedia* (Grand Rapids, MI: Eerdmans, 1982) 2:478.

18. National Child Abuse Statistics, *Childhelp.*

19. For a discussion of the term and various theologians who have used it, see, for example, Paul Dean, "The Cross: 'Cosmic Child Abuse?'" *Crosswalk.com,* May 14, 2007, http://www.crosswalk.com/pastors/11540700/.

Chapter 16: The Rest of the Family

1. We owe the observation to Jackquelyn Veith.

2. All Israelites were also descended from Abraham's son Isaac, and his son Jacob. Both Abraham and Isaac had another son, but the fathers' blessings made these sons the bearers of Abraham's "line."

3. Married daughters would be part of the "house" of their husbands.

4. See Eugene W. Bunkowske, ed., "The Image of God in the Family" in *The Christian Family: Nurture and Outreach*, (Ft. Wayne, IN: The Great Commission Resource Library, 1993), 60–61. See also A. C. Dickett and J. B. Payne, "Household," in *The International Standard Bible Encyclopedia*, ed. Geoffrey W. Bromiley et al. (Grand Rapids, MI: Eerdmans, 1982), 2:773.

5. With variations, of course. The study of "kinship systems" is a staple of the field of anthropology.

6. Nicholas H. Wolfinger, *Understanding the Divorce Cycle: The Children of Divorce in Their Own Marriages* (New York: Cambridge University Press, 2005), 55. The entire book documents related marital problems that are passed down from generation to generation.

7. Kathy Leigh Willis, *A Neurobiological Approach to Multi-Generational Addiction* (Malibu, CA: Malibu Beach Recovery Center).

Chapter 17: Conclusion: Restoring the Family

1. See Sarah B. Pomeroy, *Ancient Greece: A Political, Social, and Cultural History* (New York: Oxford University Press, 1999), 162–63, and J. Paul Sampley, *Paul in the Greco-Roman World* (Harrisburg, PA: Trinity Press International, 2003), 457–68.

2. Servais Pinckaers, *Sources of Christian Ethics* (Washington, DC: Catholic University Press, 1995), 129.

3. Linda Elizabeth Mitchell, *Family Life in the Middle Ages* (Westport, CN: Greenwood, 2007), 33–34.

4. C. S. Lewis, *The Allegory of Love: A Study in Medieval Tradition* (New York: Oxford University Press, 1958), 13.

5. Ibid., 13–14.

6. Ibid., 15.

7. For the bad state of the family in the late Middle Ages and for the impact of the Reformation see Steven Ozment, *When Fathers Ruled: Family Life in Reformation Europe* (Cambridge, MA: Harvard University Press, 1983).

8. Geoffrey Chaucer, "The Franklin's Tale," in *The Canterbury Tales*, line 65.

9. Justin Taylor, "Martin Luther's Reform of Marriage," in *Sex and the Supremacy of Christ*, eds. John Piper and Justin Taylor (Wheaton, IL: Crossway, 2005), 239.

10. See Lewis, *Allegory of Love*, 197–360. Lewis in particular cites what Spenser does in *The Fairie Queene*.

11. Edmund Spenser, "Epithalamion," lines 325, 401, 423.

12. Quoted in Taylor, "Martin Luther's Reforms," 239.

13. Quoted in Ibid., 239–40.

14. Roland Bainton, *What Christianity Says about Love, Sex, and Marriage* (New York: Association Press, 1957), 81, quoted in Ibid., 241.

15. Dietrich Bonhoeffer, "Wedding Sermon from the Prison Cell," *Letters and Papers from Prison, Works* (Minneapolis, MN: Augsburg Fortress, 2010), 8:83–84.

16. See Pat Hudson, *The Industrial Revolution* (New York: Oxford University Press, 1998).

17. "Women in the Labor Force, 2009," *US Department of Labor*, http://www.dol.gov /wb/Qf-laborforce-09.htm.

18. *Working in the 21ˢᵗ Century*, Bureau of Labor Statistics, *US Department of Labor*, http://www.bls.gov/opub/working/page16b.htm.

19. Barbara Finkelstein, "Is Adolescence Here to Stay?: Historical Perspectives on Youth and Education," in *Adolescence and Education*, eds. Tim Urdan and Frank Pajares (Charlotte, NC: Information Age, 2001), 1–32.

20. Ibid., 4–5.

21. See, for example, "The Treatise on the Power and Primacy of the Pope," sections 77–78 in the *Book of Concord*, accessed on September 14, 2011, www.bookofconcord.org /treatise.php.

22. See, Martin Luther, "The Estate of Marriage, 1522," *Luther's Works*, vol. 45, ed. Walther I. Brandt (Philadelphia, PA: Fortress, 1962), 18.

General Index

Scripture Index

DISCOVER YOUR CHRISTIAN VOCATION IN ALL OF LIFE

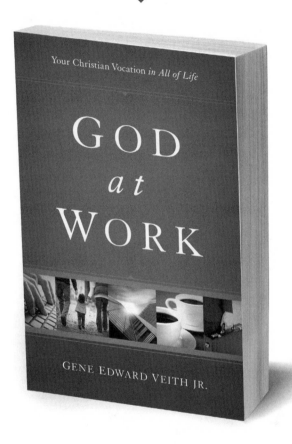

This newly redesigned book unpacks the Bible's teaching about the doctrine of vocation. Gene Veith guides readers in discovering God's purpose and calling in those seemingly ordinary areas of life by providing a spiritual framework for thinking about and acting in each sphere.